CAMBRIDGE SOUTH ASIAN STUDIES

TRADE AND EMPIRE IN WESTERN INDIA

1784–1806

CAMBRIDGE SOUTH ASIAN STUDIES

These monographs are published by the Syndics of Cambridge University Press in association with the Cambridge University Centre for South Asian Studies. The following books have been published in this series:

TRADE AND EMPIRE IN WESTERN INDIA

1784–1806

BY

PAMELA NIGHTINGALE, Ph.D.

CAMBRIDGE

AT THE UNIVERSITY PRESS

1970

Published by the Syndics of the Cambridge University Press
Bentley House, 200 Euston Road, London N.W. 1
American Branch: 32 East 57th Street, New York, N.Y. 10022

© Cambridge University Press 1970

Library of Congress Catalogue Card Number: 76–98698

Standard Book Number: 521 07651 X

Set in 11 on 12-point Monotype Plantin
and printed in Great Britain by
Alden & Mowbray Ltd at the Alden Press, Oxford

It seems to be too much the practice to neglect the western parts of India, and to value nothing but the fertile fields of Bengal, while in point of real riches, I am not sure but we excel them.

—General Stuart to Henry Dundas,
on leaving Bombay, 31 January 1800

CONTENTS

PREFACE

This study examines the influence of commercial interests on the expansion of the British empire in western India in the age of Cornwallis and Wellesley. It questions some of the assumptions which hitherto have been accepted as explanations of British imperialism in that part of India. The chief of these is that the reform of the East India Company's administration in the 1780s brought the policy of the Bombay presidency under the firm control of the governor-general in Bengal and of the Court of Directors and the Board of Control in London. The interpretation which has followed this assumption is that the East India Company extended its possessions along the west coast of India as a defence against the renewed French threat to India. The conclusions reached in this study are that, on the contrary, British policy in western India was still largely independent of the authorities in Bengal and London, and that territorial expansion was a response chiefly to local conditions which were restricting the commercial interests of private British traders.

The chief sources I have used are the records of the East India Company which are kept in the India Office Records in the India Office Library. I have used all the main classes which relate to the Bombay presidency in this period: the Bombay Political, Commercial and Revenue Proceedings; Letters Received from Bombay; Surat and Cambay Factory Records, and Bombay Reports on External Commerce. The Bombay Mayor's Court Proceedings give useful information on the activities of private merchants and the volumes of Personal Records give considerable detail about the careers of many of the Company's servants as well as notes and memoranda. There is a wealth of material in the Home Miscellaneous Series including collections of private letters received by the Board of Control from Walter Ewer, George Smith and Captain John Taylor, while small collections of papers such as the Forbes letters in the European Manuscripts series at the India Office Library, the papers held by the Forbes family, and the Michie papers in the Guildhall Library Muniment Room supplement the official records. I have explored the policy of the Bengal government as it related to Bombay by an extensive use of the

Cornwallis papers at the Public Record Office. This collection is particularly useful for the letters it contains from Charles Malet and Henry Dundas, some of the most important of which are not printed by Ross. I have also gone through the Wellesley papers in the British Museum which relate to Bombay, particularly Jonathan Duncan's correspondence with the governor-general, which is supplemented by that in the Home Miscellaneous Series. Sir John Shore's correspondence with Henry Dundas is printed by H. Furber and many of Shore's papers are also in the Home Miscellaneous Series. The published volumes of *The Poona Residency Correspondence* give a good account of the supreme government's diplomacy with the Marathas. I have studied the policy of the Court of Directors in their Despatches to Bombay, Letters from the Court to the Board, and in *The Correspondence of David Scott*, edited by Professor Philips. For the policy of the Board of Control I have made a thorough study of Henry Dundas's papers in the Home Miscellaneous Series, and the collections at the John Rylands Library, Manchester, and at the National Library of Scotland. I have also used the India Office Library's microfilms of the Melville papers at Harvard and in the Ames Library of South Asia in Minnesota. At the National Library of Scotland in Edinburgh there is an important collection of papers which has been used for the first time for this study. This is the Walker of Bowland deposit which is yet unsorted and uncatalogued. This makes reference to it difficult as there exists only a rough press list of the boxes as they stand on the shelves and the unsorted documents within them are not numbered. When the collection is re-arranged and catalogued the press numbers will be replaced, but there is no alternative at present but to use them.

Parliamentary papers yield considerable information, while Professor Philips's book, *The East India Company, 1784–1834*, and Professor Furber's *John Company at Work* are the essential secondary works for a study of this kind.

In using quotations I have copied the exact spelling and punctuation of the original, but otherwise I have adopted the method of spelling Indian words which is used in *The Imperial Gazetteer*.

I should like to express my gratitude to Dr T. G. P. Spear for his unfailing kindness and support since I first worked under him, to Dr Peter Marshall for his helpful comments, the staff of the India Office Library and Records, the Public Record Office, the

Preface

John Rylands Library, the Bedford and Lincoln County Record Offices, and the National Library of Scotland for their friendliness and help. I owe much to my college, Newnham, and to my teachers there, Miss K. Hughes and Miss B. Behrens. I am grateful to Mr B. H. Farmer of the Cambridge Centre for South Asian Studies for including my book in this series, and to the publishers and printers in their handling of a difficult text. Finally I wish to thank my husband for his advice and work in correcting the proofs. I dedicate this book to him, to my son Giles and to my parents.

2 St Mary's Square,   PAMELA NIGHTINGALE
Aylesbury

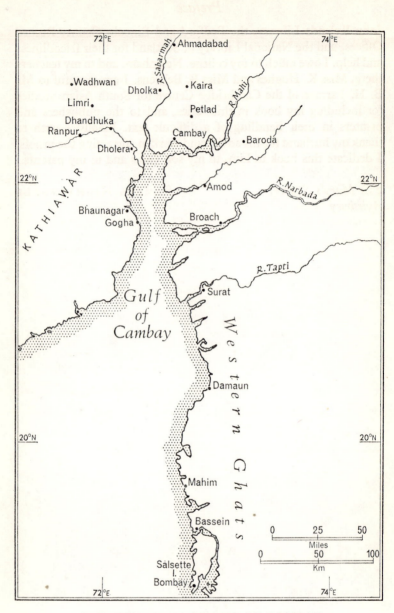

WESTERN INDIA NORTH OF BOMBAY

xii

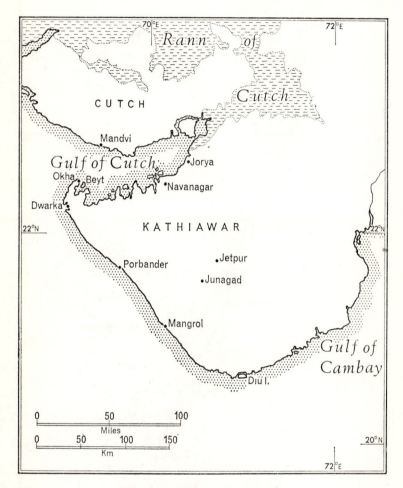

KATHIAWAR AND CUTCH

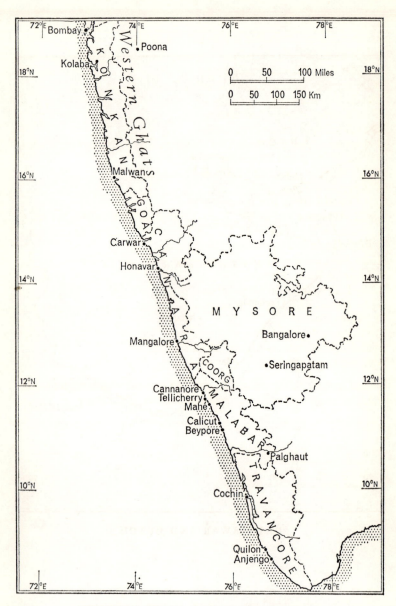

WESTERN INDIA SOUTH OF BOMBAY

ABBREVIATIONS

Add. MSS: Additional Manuscripts
BCP: Bombay Commercial Proceedings
BM: British Museum
BPC: Bombay Public Consultations
BRP: Bombay Revenue Proceedings
Bombay Selections: Selections from the records of the Bombay presidency
BSP: Bombay Secret Proceedings
BSPP: Bombay Secret and Political Proceedings
BT: Board of Trade
CO: Colonial Office
CSCB: Consultations of the Select Committee of Bombay (the early
    volumes in the series of Bombay Secret and Political Proceedings)
HMC: Historical Manuscripts Commission
Home Misc.: Home Miscellaneous Series
IOL: India Office Library
LAO: Lincolnshire Archives Office
NLS: National Library of Scotland
PC: Privy Council
PRO: Public Record Office
Rylands: John Rylands Library, Manchester
WB: Walker of Bowland

Roman capitals in the references give the number of the volume, and
arabic or small roman figures give the number of the page.

CHAPTER I

TRADERS AND GOVERNORS

When the first East India Company vessel sailed up to the city of Surat in 1608 not even the boldest of forecasters would have linked the destinies of the empire of the Moghuls with what Napoleon was later to call the nation of shopkeepers. There was little to suggest from the abject humility with which Captain Hawkins pleaded for permission to trade in Surat that his struggling new company would two hundred years later have in their power the great emperor Akbar's descendant, a pitiable blind old man of eighty-three seated under a small tattered canopy in Delhi. Between these two events the decisions were taken and the battles fought which turned the merchant company into the strongest power of the Indian sub-continent. Another hundred years was to see the company disappear under the weight of empire. Where once ill-paid clerks had laboriously copied profits and losses into morocco-bound ledgers, the officials of the Raj, the gifted products of the Oxford and Cambridge honours schools, were to decide the destinies of India with all the arrogance of a ruling caste. Trade became slightly discreditable, and the Europeans who engaged in it moved in different social circles from those of the official and military elite. The once honourable profession of the East India Company found little place in the imperial splendours of New Delhi.

It was a curious development, on the surface affected by events in Europe, but worked on beneath by strong contrary currents. Before the eighteenth century was out it was remarked that Englishmen who stayed for any time in India either became 'sultanised' or 'Brahminised' and Lord Wellesley was cited as an example of the former.[1] Despite the great changes in nineteenth- and twentieth-century Europe towards democracy, urbanisation and the levelling of social classes, the British Raj remained almost to the last an oligarchic and militaristic caste ruling an agrarian and largely illiterate peasant society. Although Britain might have a socialist prime minister the viceroy of India had to be a peer. At the

[1] See below, p. 137.

B   I

greatest crises of the Second World War when Britain's very survival was in doubt, the viceroy and secretary of state were still obliged to concern themselves personally with the distribution of honours among the various ranks of the civil service. In the last years of the Raj there was still glamour and prestige, idealism and dedication, but when the break came the England of the welfare state had little in common with an India where communal hatreds and mass poverty had proved stronger than the liberal ideas and democratic machinery imported from Europe. Whatever force had bound India and Britain together for two hundred years it seemed in 1947 as irrelevant as the use of elephants in the armies of the nuclear age.

And yet this later estrangement has obscured the fact that there must have been in the beginning a more vital connexion than a love of fighting and national pride. Armies are always costly to raise and maintain, and while the cause of national prestige has led many governments to incautious steps it does not usually lead them to embark on the domination of a sub-continent. Least of all could the British government be tempted in this way when its inglorious defeat by the American colonists in 1783 had shown that the price of maintaining national prestige could be too high. What was it, then, which brought about this strange connexion between Britain and India? Was it an historical accident, the aspirations of ambitious individuals, the effect of European rivalries, the lure of wealth and trade, or even compensation for the loss of the American colonies? All have been put forward as explanations, and if one thing is certain it is that one is not valid to the exclusion of all the others. The territorial expansion of the Indian empire covered more than a century of history in which world powers rose and fell, whole economies changed and the climate of political thought went through a revolution. Such was the effect of these changes that what might be advanced as the reason for maintaining or expanding the empire in 1850 may bear little relation to those put forward eighty or fifty years earlier.

But perhaps the fundamental questions to ask are which are the critical periods when the extension of British territorial power in India became inevitable? Was it then inevitable because there was no real alternative, or because the possibility of retrenchment or severe limitation was swept aside by the more powerful pressure to intervene? Who was responsible for this pressure and can one distinguish the real motives behind it? Was the relationship between Britain and India brought about by strategic, political or mainly economic needs? When the problem is approached on these lines it is apparent that the whole process began in the eighteenth century in two critical periods, the first coinciding with and immediately following the Franco-British conflict of the Seven Years' War which brought Bengal and eastern India under British control, and the second roughly coinciding with the French revolutionary and Napoleonic wars when British power was extended to northern and western India. By the end of Wellesley's governor-generalship in 1805 the East India Company was irrevocably committed to territorial power in India.

The obvious conclusion would seem to be that the conquests in India were undertaken as part of the wider European contest for sea power, overseas territories and trade which in the sixteenth and seventeenth centuries had brought the Portuguese, the Spaniards and the Dutch to the Americas and to Asia. In the eighteenth century it was the turn of the British and the French, newly strengthened at home, to take the major role in this overseas expansion as the financial and naval strength of their rivals decreased. In the economic thinking of the time the amount of the world's wealth and trade was fixed and nations became powerful by wresting from others their share of trade. Since trade was also thought to depend largely on territorial possessions, the contest for European power was extended overseas. The ambitions of the British and French to acquire wealth equal to the gold and spices which the Spaniards and Dutch had won from their overseas enterprise, and the belief that colonies were an important part of commercial and naval power, were largely behind the long-drawn-out struggle which engaged the fleets and armies of France and Britain in America, Canada, Africa and the West Indies, as well as in the east. In India it was the fear of the alliances which the French under Dupleix were making with Indian princes on the Coromandel coast and which threatened to cut off English trade from its hinterland, which first brought the East India Company into open warfare. Even when the French had been decisively defeated in India by 1761 the English still feared that they would attempt to re-establish their power, and after the final naval victory of Trafalgar the protagonists of the expansionist policy continued to justify it in terms of the French menace.

3

But attractive though this explanation is, it leaves important facts out of account. The area where English and French armies actually fought each other in southern India during the Seven Years' War and where the French had their strongest base at Pondicherry, was not the scene of the East India Company's first and greatest territorial acquisitions. The very real menace to English interests which Dupleix and his French force had been, and Madras had actually been in their hands from 1746 to 1748, did not produce any appreciable expansion of English power on the Coromandel coast (apart from the acquisition of the Northern Circars) until the nineteenth century. It was quarrels with Indian rulers over issues of Indian power politics which brought the first harvest of territorial gains, and these were where the dissolution of the Moghul empire had gone furthest.

Far more important than the conflicts between the European powers for the control of India in the eighteenth century was the fate of the Moghul empire. While the empire remained strong the Europeans were insignificant traders dependent for their existence on the privileges which the Moghuls permitted them. The administrative machine which the great sixteenth-century emperor Akbar bequeathed to his successors survived even the break-up of central authority, and it was only the persistent failure of ability in the eighteenth-century emperors which brought about the decline and eventual dissolution of the empire. Towards the end of the seventeenth century the emperor Aurangzeb began the process by reversing some of the policies which had given India a long period of peace and stability. He declared outright but unsuccessful war on the Marathas, a militant Hindu people of the Deccan, and ended the policy of tolerating the Hindus and taking them into partnership in the empire. From the time of his death in 1707 the empire broke up steadily, and under Maratha attacks, succession disputes, a Persian invasion and civil war, power increasingly fell into the hands of provincial governors or adventurers who set up their own succession states.

Despite these disasters India was not a prize to be had for the taking in the eighteenth century by any European soldier of fortune. There remained a nucleus of Moghul power in the important state of Hyderabad which was sufficiently strong to block foreign ambitions in that quarter, while the Carnatic was ruled by a Moghul deputy until 1801. Some of the succession states proved to

4

be strong and stable and were quick to adopt European military techniques. The future Duke of Wellington was to find India a tough training ground for his later campaigns against the French. The north and west were dominated by the Marathas who were feared throughout India for their marauding attacks, while in the second half of the eighteenth century the power of Mysore under Haidar Ali and his son Tipu grew and threatened the south.

Only in the east where the dissolution of Moghul power had gone furthest and government was weakest was an opening given to Europeans. The English were able to take advantage of this because their Dutch and French rivals could not equal them at that time in sea power and commercial strength. Nevertheless the English Company was drawn into Bengal politics first in self-defence. Its trade had been restricted in the 1740s and '50s by the ruling nawab who was strong enough to subdue the foreigners. But it was only when it was threatened with annihilation by his weak but headstrong successor Siraj-ud-daula who attacked the Bengal settlements in 1756 that the English Company made war. Once it was involved, the weakness and chaos of the local political scene made retreat difficult, even if it had been desirable, and by 1760 Bengal and Bihar were virtually under the rule of the Company. The Company's servants used their new power to enrich themselves shamelessly by private trade through avoiding the taxes which were imposed on their Indian competitors. For most of them this was their only means of earning a competence as their official salaries were inadequate. A sufficient number of fortunes were made and flaunted in Bengal to make the establishments of Madras and Bombay wish to copy Bengal's example, and in the 1770s they plunged the Company into disastrous wars with the Marathas and Mysore which brought it to the verge of ruin.

If Clive's intervention in Bengal to avenge Siraj-ud-daula's attack marked the first step on the road to empire, the crisis which confronted the East India Company and the whole imperial strategy of the British nation in the early 1780s was for both the more critical. All at once several chickens came home to roost and the flamboyant successes of the Seven Years' War came to a drab end. The failure of the British to subdue their rebellious American colonies and the ignominy which the treaty of Versailles in 1783 meant to a proud nation could not fail to produce deep heart-searching about the value of overseas territorial possessions. New economic ideas began to circulate which suggested that commercial growth was not necessarily dependent on political control, a theory which was borne out by the great increase of trade between Britain and her former American colonies after they had won their independence. The growing enterprise of navigators and traders in the eastern seas had opened up new opportunities in the inter-Asian trade and in the tea trade with China. Pamphleteers and intelligent observers began to suggest that Britain's real interest lay not in territorial acquisitions but in developing strategic posts on the trade routes which could provide dockyards for her merchant ships and marts where the goods of Asia could be exchanged without the expense and trouble of large-scale political responsibilities. These views were gaining ground in Government circles even before the failures of the American campaign made continental entanglements of dubious appeal.[1]

But even where the loss of the American colonies produced the contrary effect, as Pitt claimed in 1784, of making the Indian possessions seem more valuable,[2] all who were acquainted with the real state of British affairs in India at the end of the American war could not be optimistic about the future. The Court of Directors, the governing body of the East India Company, was concerned at the ever-rising cost of military expenditure. In 1773 they were forced to raise a loan of £1 million from the state to remain solvent and in return had to submit to the Regulating Act which introduced the first measure of Government control. But with the independent attempts of Bombay and Madras to emulate Bengal's success which led to their costly failures in war, the Company's debts rose to an estimated £8 million in 1784.[3]

Moreover, the trading accounts of the Company did not hold out much promise of reducing this vast debt. The long-established trade in woven piece-goods which the Company shipped from India to Europe had ceased to expand and was beginning to be challenged by the machine-made products of Lancashire. The Company had never been very successful in selling British goods in India and there seemed to be no immediate prospect of improving the situation. If it had been forced to rely on its Indian trade the Company could not have escaped bankruptcy. But fortunately for

[1] V. T. Harlow, *The Founding of the Second British Empire, 1763–93*, I.
[2] Cobbett, *Parliamentary History* XXIV, 1085–1100.
[3] Philips, *The East India Company 1784–1834* (1961), 46.

its affairs the fashion for drinking China tea seized eighteenth-century Europe and the Company's trade with Canton boomed. In 1784 this trade took an exceptional turn. Before that date the British government had levied duties of 115 per cent on all imports of tea which had made smuggling highly profitable. As a result foreign ships had competed with the Company's at Canton and shipped the tea to Europe whence it was smuggled into Britain to the Company's loss. But in 1784 Pitt introduced a Commutation Bill which reduced the duty on tea to 12 per cent and so made smuggling unprofitable. The result was spectacular. The Company was able to price its competitors out of the British and most of the European market and its China trade leapt in value. But this brought its own problem, because unless it exported bullion to Canton from Britain or India, a course which was highly un-desirable, the Company had no easy means of paying for the tea as China was no better market for British goods than India. But the new demand served to stimulate the enterprise of British private traders who were based in India, and although forbidden by the Company's monopoly to trade with Europe, they were allowed to export Indian produce to China. They paid the proceeds of their sales into the Company's treasury in Canton and received in return bills of the Company to be drawn in India or Britain.[1] The arrangement suited both the Company and the private mer-chants, and drew Britain, India and China into a close commercial relationship. Nevertheless, even the profits of the tea trade could not outweigh the mounting debts caused by Indian entanglements.

These financial embarrassments brought the Company's affairs more closely to the attention of parliament. The misgovern-ment and blatant corruption which had come near to impoverish-ing Bengal in the fifteen years after Plassey, and the wealth of the returning nabobs, were criticised in parliament in the early 1770s and in the reports of the select committee which preceded the Regulating Act. This revulsion against exploitation and costly military adventures in India came to a head in the House-of-Commons resolution of 1782 demanding the recall of Warren Hastings and the governor of Bombay, and it subsequently led to Hastings's impeachment. The need for some measure of government control over Indian affairs was urgent and in 1784

---

[1] E. H. Pritchard, *The Crucial Years of Early Anglo-Chinese Relations, 1750–1800* (Research Studies of the State College of Washington IV, 1936).

Pitt passed his India Act. In introducing the Bill he maintained that:

The first and principal object would be to take care to prevent the Government from being ambitious and bent on conquest. Propensities of that nature had already involved India in great expenses, and cost much bloodshed. These, therefore, ought most studiously to be avoided. Commerce was our object, and with a view to its extension, a pacific system should prevail, and a system of defence and conciliation. The Government there ought, therefore, in an especial manner to avoid wars, or entering into alliances likely to create wars...[1]

To make sure that this should not be merely a pious resolution, the Act provided that the political power which had hitherto been exercised by the Court of Directors of the East India Company should be supervised by a new government department, the Board of Control. The directors were to retain their powers of patronage but the governor-general was strictly forbidden to make war without the express approval of the Court of Directors unless forced into it by the hostile preparations of an enemy. And to make sure that there should be no repetition of the circumstances in which Bombay and Madras had dragged the Company into wars of their own making, the act forbade them to make treaties or declare war without the assent of the governor-general or Court of Directors unless forced by a dire emergency. The officials of the subordinate presidencies were firmly put under the authority of the governor-general and were ordered to obey him on pain of suspension from their office. The days of buccaneering in India, insofar as legislation could decide, were over.

But it would be a mistake to see the situation created by Pitt's India Act in modern terms as a Whitehall attempt to control a giant corporation in the public interest. Eighteenth-century politics knew no such thing as impartial civil service control or any clear distinction between public and private interest. Rather there were many sectional interests jostling for office and patronage. This was as true of the East India Company as it was of the House of Commons. Individuals collected round themselves men of like concerns and through family connexions, wealth or political alliances, sought to build up a following which might procure them further places and patronage. In the East India Company this

[1] Cobbett, *Parliamentary History* XXIV, 1085–1100.

meant that from the newest recruit to the most powerful director there was little idea of the interest of the shareholders or of the Court of Directors being distinct from their private interest. Every recruit to the Company's service owed his much sought after position to his personal or financial connexion with one of the directors. Not only did he feel bound to support his patron's interests but he relied on him for recommendations in the presidency to which he was sent and for help in winning promotion. To have the patronage of a powerful director was a most valuable asset.

Moreover the directors were not appointed primarily to protect the interests of the shareholders. To qualify for the position a man had to possess £2,000 of East India stock, and although theoretically he had to be elected by the shareholders in practice the directors elected each other virtually for life. Vacancies only occurred on the death or disqualification of a director and if a man aspired to the job it involved him in an expensive contest. But no matter how much money he spent he had little chance of success without the support of one of the great interests of the day. For the Company was not a monolithic structure but a body in which at different times separate and sometimes quite opposing interests fought for control. The real money was made not from dividends on shares but from the commercial and financial possibilities which a position inside the Company afforded. This could be the right to engage in private trade in India and eastern waters which, until the time of Cornwallis, every Company's servant had, or it could be the right of the Company's shipowners, ships' captains and officers to take on board a fixed amount of 'privileged' cargo, free of charge, which they could sell in the east. The Company was honeycombed with a multitude of these private interests and perquisites, the holders of which banded together and sought to protect or extend them by seeking control of the Court of Directors.

At the end of the eighteenth century the Indian interest of returned nabobs with financial stakes still in India competed with the City and shipping interests whose concern was chiefly to retain the Company's monopoly of trade with India. The latter were to be challenged by the private trading interest who fought for its abolition. These interests embraced shareholders and Company servants alike, so that decisions about the Company's policy in India could often be the result of contests at home between the different factions. The practical effect of Pitt's India Act between

9

1788 and 1800 was only to introduce a new factor, the ministerial interest of Henry Dundas, the president of the Board of Control, who sought by the same methods to gain control of the Company's policy. The consistency of the Company's policy in India and the smoothness with which it was carried out depended partially on the extent to which the ministerial and directorial interests worked in harmony. When they came into conflict the repercussions could be felt from Bombay to Canton. That conflict was inevitable appears from a study of East India politics in London. 'It becomes clear that neither Parliament and the Board of Control, nor the directors and shareholders of the Company acted in agreement or pursued any consistent policy, but were each swayed by powerful groups formed for the promotion of special, often antagonistic, interests.'[1]

But India was several months' sailing distance from London, and powerful though the directors and Board of Control were the final decisions about war and peace, treaties and annexations were more often than not made in India under the influence of Indian politics and the Indian interests of the Company's servants. For just as the decisions made in London were the result of sectional conflicts and compromises so the politics of the Company's representatives in India were shot through with private motives. In the first period of conquest before the reforms of Clive and Hastings these motives could be unbridled desire for loot and the wealth which could be made from private trade concessions extorted by terrorising the countryside. With the sudden acquisition of power the respect in which the Company's servants had formerly held both their own masters in London and the local Indian rulers was largely dissipated, and there began a period of feverish acquisitiveness, luxury and corruption. Where the opportunities for exploitation were so great and official remuneration so low it was the very exceptional man who put the Company's interest before his own, even when it was possible to identify it. This was true from the lowest to the highest ranks. Without some private source of income the newly arrived recruit could hardly make a shift to live in the hard-drinking, gambling and extravagant society in which he found himself. In 1762 it was reported from Madras that few private gentlemen spent less than £5,000–£6,000 a year and the governor lived at the rate of £20,000 a year.[2] It was

[1] Philips, *The East India Company*, viii.
[2] T. G. P. Spear, *The Nabobs* (1963), 39.

a cut-and-thrust competitive world of gambling for high stakes, an atmosphere conducive to the bold throw, the daring risk, in which the cautious or scrupulous went to the wall. The men who got on were not made in the mould of nineteenth-century civil servants and it was to take more than an act of parliament to change them.

Nevertheless the period of unbridled exploitation in Bengal was not long-lasting, and Clive in his second governorship struggled to reform some of the worst abuses, not unsuccessfully. Hastings continued the process so that by the time of Pitt's India Act the Company's civil service with its perquisites rather than the path of the adventurer was seen as the road to fortune. But while the Company itself was dominated by sectional groups and while there remained sufficient legal private interests to preoccupy its servants, these interests could not fail to influence the course of policy in India. It remained to be seen how Lord Cornwallis, the first governor-general to be appointed by the Crown under the new India Act, could control the ambitions of his officials and keep the Company out of further entanglements in India. The vanquished general of Yorktown had come through the American war with an untarnished reputation for courage and integrity, but were the facts of the Indian situation, like those of the American, to prove too strong for him? The nation's and the Company's needs combined to dictate economy, retrenchment and avoidance of political and military entanglements for its Indian policy, and in 1784 few people would have foreseen that it was on the brink of another stride into empire. Why and how that stride was taken which brought western India under British domination is the concern of this book.

CHAPTER 2

WESTERN INDIA

If one thing seemed obvious in the crisis which faced the Company's affairs in 1784 it was that western India held no prospects but those of defeat and gloom. The golden opportunities which had been Bengal's since Plassey and which had come to Madras on a smaller scale with the cession of the Northern Circars and the presidency's controlling interest in the Carnatic had done no more than beckon to Bombay and pass her by. For a brief period after Bombay's acquisition as part of the dowry brought by Catherine of Braganza to Charles II, the Company's trade had flourished there and at Surat, and the west coast had prospered under the orderly government of the Moghul empire. But a premature attempt to escape from its narrow confines brought defeat in a war against Aurangzeb, and for most of the eighteenth century Bombay did not recover but remained 'the unhealthiest, the poorest, and the most despised' of all the English settlements.[1]

While the Moghul grip was relaxing throughout India, Bombay was unfortunate in that it was surrounded by the two strongest Indian powers, the Marathas in the north and Mysore in the south. The Maratha armies had harassed India since the middle of the seventeenth century but although they were feared for their devastation their leaders appeared to lack the will or ability to govern. They put loot and extortion before the encouragement of trade or agriculture, and their leadership was constantly dissolving into rival factions. In 1761 they were resoundingly defeated by an invading Afghan army at the battle of Panipat, but since the Afghans showed no inclination to take over the Moghul empire Maratha military power revived over northern India. Despite their divisions they were too strong for the ambitions of the English in Bombay. When the Bombay armies tried to take advantage of a succession dispute in 1775 in order to break out of the Maratha stranglehold and win territory on the continent they were severely defeated, and in 1782 the Company had to submit to the humiliating terms of the treaty of Salbai which reaffirmed the Maratha

[1] Spear, *The Nabobs*, 66.

12

ascendancy. Bombay seemed doomed to another half-century of insignificance.

The presidency could not hope to find compensations in the south, for there its way was blocked by the armies of Mysore. Haidar Ali, the Mysorean ruler, was an upstart adventurer who had displaced the old royal house and with ruthless ability sought to extend his power over southern India. In 1766 he invaded the independent kingdoms of Malabar and put in peril Bombay's trading settlements on the coast. In 1780 he swept through the Carnatic and threatened Madras. Bombay's attempt to strengthen its hold on the Malabar Coast was defeated by Haidar's son, Tipu, who inherited his father's ability and ambitions. In 1784 Bombay was forced to sign the Treaty of Mangalore which confined the Company to its small and practically defenceless trading posts in Malabar, mere islands in the sea of Mysorean power. Crushed between two great military powers, and with possessions which made its title of a presidency only pathetic, Bombay could hope for little from the future. Whether the Company would retain any hold at all in western India was, in 1784, much in doubt.

It seemed that the East India Company's political position might be established with its military and territorial power based on Bengal and with a subsidiary settlement at Madras. The most that could be hoped from the western coast was the survival of Bombay as a naval station with a factory at Surat. There seemed no good reason for preserving the other stagnant little trading settlements on the coast. This was no sudden decline in the presidency's fortunes. Throughout the eighteenth century it had laboured under one difficulty and disaster after another. The Marathas were an ever watchful enemy and until the middle of the century the Moghul's admiral, the Sidi, and the Angria pirates committed almost daily depredations on Bombay's trade. Its climate had the reputation of killing off Europeans more quickly than any other settlement, helped by the malarial swamps on the island and the custom which survived up to 1750 of manuring the cocoanut trees with decaying fish. This had affected the wells and gave rise to a most unsavoury smell. The settlement had a reputation for vice, corruption and turbulence in its earlier history, and the poor salaries of the civil servants made a nomination to its establishment a matter of commiseration. Although the directors always sent out more men than the settlement needed, even in 1798 the whole European population, including seamen and soldiers, was not more than a thousand. Locked on their swampy peninsula in a town which only measured about a mile in length and a quarter of a mile in breadth, the tight little Bombay society lived a dull and demoralised life throughout most of the eighteenth century. Not for them were the rich pickings of Bengal or the plums of Arcot, but dull conversation at formal dinner parties where the guests invariably sat next to the same neighbours in an unvarying order of precedence.[1]

In 1775 Bombay had tried to break out of this backward existence by fishing in the muddy waters of Maratha politics. In return for the promise of territory in Gujarat which yielded an income of £350,000 Bombay sent an army to support Raghunath Rao, a claimant for the peshwaship. Success offered the hope of financial independence for the settlement, profitable employment for the civil servants and opportunities of private gain. But the army marched incompetently to disaster. Warren Hastings tried to retrieve the situation by sending a force from Bengal, but defeats followed early successes, and in the end the Marathas had to be bought off. Bombay had to surrender all its gains apart from the islands in its harbour. The bitterest blow was the loss of the rich district of Broach which the English had possessed since 1772. On top of this came the war with Mysore and the humiliating treaty of Mangalore which added bitterness and despair to the problem of the presidency's survival.

Even in peace-time the settlement had only carried on its business by means of heavy financial help from Bengal, but war had added hugely to its debt. In 1786 it stood at two crores and thirty-six lacs, and public credit had vanished.[2] No interest was paid on the debt, and the Bombay government's paper would only pass at a discount of 40 per cent. There was an estimated difference of nearly forty lacs between the receipts and expenses for the following year.[3] Every department of government was deeply in arrear and the civil servants went unpaid.[4] So stricken was the presidency that trade on the Company's account almost ceased, as there was no capital to provide any investments. Large sums were owing to the Malabar merchants and the king of Travancore for pepper,

---

[1] Spear, *The Nabobs*, 77.
[2] An unsigned document which Cornwallis received with a letter from Alexander Dalrymple, dated in London, 29 April 1786; PRO 30/11/8, f. 17.
[3] *Ibid.* ff. 17–19v.
[4] *Letters from Bombay* VIII, 232; 26 March 1785.

and they would not make further deliveries without payment.[1] To
the north foreigners were capturing the piece-good trade of Surat.[2]
Three ships from England called at Bombay early in 1785 to load
cargoes for China, but the Company could provide nothing for
two of them and their freight was let to private merchants. The
third was mainly filled with saltpetre.[3] The almost complete
annihilation of the Bombay marine made more perilous what little
traffic was carried on.[4]

With such heavy burdens to bear and such disastrous results of
their attempts at territorial expansion the prospects for the
Company's servants at Bombay were gloomy. With scarcely any
territory of its own to manage and little revenue, the settlement had
never been able to provide employment for all the men sent out
by the Court of Directors. In 1782 sixty-two, of whom twenty-
seven were senior merchants, were unemployed,[5] and the numbers
increased as civil servants returned to Bombay from the lost
possessions in Gujarat. The memoirs of James Forbes give a vivid
account of the distress and despondency of these men. 'To them
the Presidency offered neither pleasure, profit, nor usefulness; nor
was there any provision for them at the southern subordinates.
Our hopes in India being thus extinguished, we looked forwards to
England.'[6] The reduction of the Bombay government with that of
Madras, to a governor, two civilians and the commander-in-chief
further affected the prospects of the senior merchants.[7] The demand for passages home was such that captains of Indiamen were
asking £1,000 for the single voyage.[8]

For those who stayed behind there was no possibility of improving their lot by further military adventures. The appointment of a
resident at Poona in 1785 closed the avenue by which the Bombay
government was accustomed to seek an increase of its own power.
The only consolation was that the appointment was given to a
member of the Bombay establishment, Charles Malet, who from

---

[1] *Ibid.* 235–6.
[2] PRO 30/11/8, f. 17.
[3] *Letters from Bombay* VIII, 228–32; 26 March 1785.
[4] Rylands English MSS, Pitt Papers 929, 48; 18 April 1782.
[5] Personal Records XI, 395.
[6] James Forbes, *Oriental Memoires* (London, 1814) III, 433.
[7] HMC 74 (Palk MSS), 368: R. H. Boddam at Bombay to Sir Robert Palk at
Madras, 12 March 1785.
[8] Forbes, *Oriental Memoires* III, 403. See also Spear, *The Nabobs*, Chapter IV,
on the general unpopularity of Bombay.

1774 had been the resident at the Company's factory in Cambay. Nevertheless the resident was responsible directly to the governor-general, and the Company's policy to the Marathas was henceforward to be decided in Bengal. The sense of humiliation and impotence ran deep.

But beneath the surface of stagnation and despondency were hidden currents of change. Firstly, the political balance between the Marathas, the English and Mysore was an uneasy one. The Maratha confederacy was a loose and unstable unit led by five chieftains, under the nominal headship of the peshwa whose capital was at Poona. But the other four, the gaikwar of Baroda, Sindhia of Gwalior, Holkar of Indore, and the bhonsla raja of Berar were in reality independent princes, and as ready to war against each other as against their common enemies. Under strong leadership, such as that provided for a time by Nana Farnavis, the peshwa's minister, their predatory armies were a threat to the whole of India, but split by internal feuds, the Maratha empire could crumble. If that happened Mysorean power could dominate India. Whereas the East India Company from its weakness on the western coast had acquiesced in Haidar Ali's conquest of Malabar, it could not idly look on while the Mysorean empire further increased and threatened Madras. Another fear was the possibility of French intervention. The most powerful Maratha chieftain, Sindhia, had a body of able French officers, and Tipu, too, was known to have dealings with French agents. Any one of these political currents threatened to disturb the stability of western India. But they were not necessarily incapable of diplomatic solutions.

There was, though, another current of change moving below the surface. Less obvious than the shifts of politics, it was in the end to prove more powerful. This was the expanding network of private British trade. This development, which was to raise Bombay out of insignificance to the position of the greatest port in India, is, through the lack of private commercial records, difficult to analyse. The Cochin records of the Dutch show that between 1724 and 1742 the English country shipping which visited that port doubled in terms of tonnage, and that the number of English country ships and captains increased from seventeen to twenty-eight.[1] It is clear, though, that for the first half of the century this

[1] H. Furber, *Bombay Presidency in the Mid-18th Century* (1965), 44. 'Country' ship is the contemporary term for vessels trading in Asian waters.

growth of English private enterprise was comparatively slow and had by no means outdistanced the local Indian trade that made Surat and not Bombay the great port of the west coast. In the 1720s two-thirds of the trading ships which called at Surat were owned by Asians,[1] and even in 1750 it was estimated that no more than one-third of Surat's trading capital was under European protection.[2] The two great trades of the west coast, to the Red Sea and the Persian Gulf, were in the 1740s firmly in Indian hands.[3] It was not until 1735 that Lowji Nassarwanji Wadia emigrated to Bombay and began shipbuilding there. Surat came to suffer as a commercial centre from the city's misgovernment and the silting-up of its river. Gradually the Bombay marine established some protection against pirates for vessels carrying English passes, and the Parsis began to invest their capital with the English rather than with the Dutch, whose naval power had decreased.[4] Merchants began to move from the mainland to Bombay in search of greater security for their business. In 1728 the Mayor's Court had been created to enforce commercial law, and eight years earlier a bank had been founded.[5] These developments partly explain why Bombay began to attract trade, but not why this trade became concentrated in the hands of the English.

The available evidence suggests that the process was a slow and hard one, and that the greatest obstacle to English expansion was the shortage of capital in the English merchant community.[6] The young William Monson, newly arrived at Madras in 1725, stressed to his father that the man without capital or rich friends to give him credit could not hope to build up a fortune or do more than make a shift to live.[7] Monson's brother Charles sent him over 20,000 ounces of silver from England during the period 1726–47,[8] but even this support could not guarantee success. Interest rates were high, averaging about 12 per cent per annum, and the risks of trade were considerable. Poor market information, heavy overhead costs and losses at sea meant that a man often did not recover his

---

[1] *Ibid.* 8.
[2] *Ibid.* 64.
[3] *Ibid.* 32.
[4] *Ibid.* 65.
[5] S. M. Edwardes, *The Rise of Bombay* (1902), 155–6.
[6] LAO, 3 Ancaster 9/21/1, f. 11v. 'For if yᵉ Gentlemen resideing here [Bombay] had Stocks to launch into Trade, they cou'd not but find a very reasonable accᵗ.' No date, but early eighteenth century.
[7] LAO, Monson MSS LIII, letter 1: W. Monson to Lord Monson, 22 August 1725.
[8] *Ibid.* CCIV, no. 1.

premium.[1] At Bombay there were few who could draw on wealthy relatives to start them in trade. It was the dumping ground for the poorest clients of the least important directors. A civil servant's salary was a miserable pittance which scarcely allowed a man to survive, let alone save. And if a man did acquire capital he could expect the stiffest competition from the long-established Parsi and Indian business community as well as from his fellow-Europeans. It took David Scott, a future chairman of the East India Company, twenty-five years to make his fortune at Bombay, and he was one of the lucky ones. An early death, or disappointed hopes, was the more common end.

But despite these difficulties there had grown up in Bombay by the 1780s several powerful English trading firms or agency houses, as they were known, which had amassed a large capital. Their origins and growth are obscure, but they were to play a vital part in the expansion of English power in western India. For this reason it is worth examining in detail the account books of Francis Pym which provide some of the sparse surviving evidence for the early history of these firms.[2] Pym was one of the civil servants at Bombay and his accounts run from May 1746 to March 1751. There were obviously earlier ones which were lost, and they end abruptly when Pym's affairs were disrupted by the Sidi's attack on Surat. The first two entries in May 1746 reveal that Pym had a balance of Rs 1,914 and that he received Rs 30 a month for his salary and diet money as a factor and deputy accountant in the Company's service. He notes his expenses scrupulously down to the 1 rupee he paid his barber. Money was obviously tight and only a careful man could hope to increase it. It emerges from a later entry that of the Rs 1,914 standing to Pym's credit, Rs 1,372 had been lent to him by a certain Mr Fowke. It is almost certain that this man was the well-known Madras merchant, Joseph Fowke, and it seems likely that Pym's initial capital came from this source. He first employed it in July by lending Rs 1,600 at interest to three Indians. By October 1748 Pym had increased his balance to the sum of Rs 3,793. He had done this by small sums from the sale of books, pieces of cloth and money won at cards. He also received five payments amounting to Rs 1,000 from an Indian to whom he had

[1] LAO, Monson MSS xcviii, No. 39: W. Monson to Charles Monson, 12 January 1735/6.
[2] Bedfordshire Record Office, PM 2749.

lent money at interest, and another Rs 443 from the three to whom he lent Rs 1,600 in 1746. With profits coming in from his money-lending Pym decided on a big commercial investment. In November 1748 he joined with a Parsi in buying a quantity of red lead. He lent the Parsi money for his share at ¾ per cent per month. The initial investment was Rs 3,000. While the profits from the sale of the lead were slowly coming in Pym was also selling small articles: scarlet stocking breeches, a table and china dishes, Madeira wine, tea and settees. He was also acting as agent for a ship's captain, James Fraser, by settling accounts for the goods which Fraser brought ashore and auctioned. In February 1749 Pym took on another type of investment, a respondentia bond for Rs 200. This was to finance a voyage which a Muslim merchant was making to Persia. The interest was high, 30 per cent per annum, but the risks were proportionate, and if the vessel was lost, so was the investment. English ships apparently commanded more confidence because in the same month Pym lent Rs 100 to an English captain at 25 per cent. In September 1749 he lent another Muslim merchant Rs 500 and in the following month he was able to pay back his debt to Fowke.

Shortly afterwards Pym's affairs took a different turn. So far it appears that he had been trading almost entirely on his own account and mostly with Parsi and Muslim businessmen in a modest way. But in January 1750 he was given a post in the Company's factory at Surat, which was then undoubtedly the best place in the Bombay presidency for trade. There, with a capital of just over Rs 3,000, he entered into partnership with Robert Hunt and began to deal with some of the most prominent people on the Bombay establishment. The arrangement with Hunt permitted the partners to deal with their clients either as a firm or separately as individuals, and from this point Pym's accounts become much more complex. His dealings with the Parsi, Hindu and Muslim merchants multiplied, and several members of the English community at Surat used him as their agent, among them Thomas Hodges and Charles Crommelin, Brabazon Ellis and a future East India Company chairman, Laurence Sulivan.

Sulivan had gone to Bombay as a factor in 1741 and returned to England with a fortune in 1752. Like his fellow Bombay merchant, David Scott, Sulivan became a director, and in 1758, chairman of the Company. He was an extremely able man and played an important part in the affairs of the Company until his death in 1786, the year when Scott followed him to England.[1] It is curious, if not significant, that the two most influential chairmen in the second half of the eighteenth century had acquired all their experience of Indian affairs and of trade in the small community of Bombay. In Pym's account books some of that experience comes to light. Sulivan's name first appears in December 1749 when Pym lends Rs 2,000 on his behalf in the form of a respondentia bond to Captain John Watson for a voyage to Mocha. In February 1750 he received Rs 10,000 from a Parsi house on Sulivan's account, and through the latter he entered into trade with the English resident at Cambay. Sulivan's contacts were many and wide and his transactions figure prominently in the accounts. Pym's accounts give only some of his activities but they show him investing in respondentia bonds, trading with ships' captains, buying and selling shawls, vermilion, foreign coins, pearls, tutenag and cochineal. Sulivan's chief associate appears to have been a ship's captain, Samuel Hough.

Through these contacts Pym's business expanded rapidly. In March 1750 the sums passing through his hands reached Rs 50,000. His chief investment that year was over Rs 27,000 in raw cotton. This initial expansion and the cotton purchases were financed by short-term borrowing from two Hindu financiers. Using Sulivan's credit he borrowed Rs 20,000 from the house of Monackjee, and on his own credit over Rs 30,000 from Gopaldass Lolldass. The latter continued to have a close association with Pym. The contrast between the ease with which Pym could get money at Surat and its tightness at Bombay point to the importance of Surat's financial pre-eminence for English trade. The sophisticated financial system built up by Indian merchants and bankers was essential to English enterprise. Without the facilities which enabled money to be exchanged and transferred to different parts of the country, bills to be cashed and credit given, English enterprise would have been shackled.

The characteristic of this enterprise as it appears in Pym's books is its variety. Pym and his associates seized on any opportunity which offered a profit. But at this stage they were acting chiefly as agents for ships' captains and local merchants. They financed voyages, provided ships with cargoes and sold the goods

[1] L. Sutherland, *The East India Company in Eighteenth Century Politics* (1952), *passim*.

they imported, but their role was essentially that of the middleman, not the entrepreneur. To understand how the agency house of Pym's day developed into the giants which dominated the economy of western India by the turn of the century, one must look at the enterprise of the small country trading vessel with its English owner–captain and officers, who went from port to port in the eastern seas picking up a quick profit wherever it could be found. In Pym's books they can be seen trading chiefly from Bombay to Bussorah, Persia, Mocha and Cambay. This trade yielded much-sought-for returns of foreign coins; dollars, crowns, venetians, zelotas and piastres, as well as gum arabic and dates. But they also brought up cargoes from Malabar: cardamoms, pepper, rice, cochineal, cocoanuts, coir, and the products of Malabar's trade with the Dutch: cloves, nutmegs, ginger and sugar. In return they exported Surat's piece-goods and raw cotton to Madras for transhipment to Bengal or China. It was these men who were the real entrepreneurs of the private English trade. It was they who explored markets, judged profits and faced the risks of storms and piracy which often kept their Indian rivals nearer home.[1] That they were more successful at their business than their competitors is shown by the lower interest rates of their respondentia bonds. Gradually their association with their agents became closer and more permanent, and they became partners in one enterprise. It appears from Pym's papers that this was the sort of partnership which had become established between Laurence Sulivan and Captain Samuel Hough. David Scott's and John Forbes's agency houses grew from their careers as ship's officers. Once the partnership between agents and captains had become regular it was possible to organise trade more systematically and to explore markets more intensively.

By the time that Pym's business at Surat came to an abrupt end in 1751 the foundations had been laid on which English trade could expand. Behind the agents was the network of Surat financiers, brokers and merchants who could provide the capital and productive and retail organisation which English enterprise could exploit. The agency houses themselves had a variety of business contacts with other houses in Madras, Calcutta and Canton which gave them information about markets and exchanges, while their partnerships with country-trading captains enabled them to direct

[1] LAO, 3 Ancaster 9/21/1, f. 4.

trade into the most profitable channels. Given the right markets and products, the whole was capable of being knit into an efficient organisation for the expansion of English trade.

That it was the English who built up this organisation and not the local merchants was due primarily to the conditions of Indian society which inhibited local enterprise. The insecurity and arbitrary government with which businessmen had to contend under the Marathas and the petty nawabs and rajas made short-term money-lending to peasants preferable to long-term or commercial investments. It was fully recognised by the English that the Surat capitalists preferred to lend their money out at interest rather than employ it first hand in commercial enterprise.[1] This reluctance to invest in long-term prospects and the natural conservative outlook of society, as well as the hazard of piracy, kept the local merchants to the well-tried trades near at home. Only in the security offered by the settlement of Bombay could local, particularly Parsi, enterprise come into its own, and then it was natural that it should do so in partnership with the English.

By the 1780s the emigration of Parsi businessmen to Bombay had occurred on such a scale that the centre of trade had swung there from Surat, and with the influx of capital the second stage in the development of Bombay's agency houses began. This was the building of large ships for the China trade. While Bombay's commerce had been mainly with the Red Sea and the other ports of India small coasting vessels had been adequate, but with the opening of markets for raw cotton in China, vessels capable of the long voyage and of carrying a bulky cargo were needed. If the Bombay firms were to profit from the trade and not see it fall into other hands they had to build their own ships. This they proceeded to do, largely with Parsi capital, slowly in the 1770s, but feverishly in the 1780s.[2]

The third change which marked the transition from the firm of Hunt and Pym to the three or four great houses which dominated Bombay at the end of the century was a movement towards consolidation and specialisation. As Bombay's trade grew and commercial organisation became more complex, a civil servant of

---

[1] LAO, 3 Ancaster 9/21/1, f. 12. The banians 'dare not play ye Merch^ts but rest contented wth ye Buissinesse of Broker immediately passing it from one hand to the other'.

[2] Rylands English MSS, Melville Papers 686, 1465: W. G. Farmer to James Sibbald, 17 December 1789.

Pym's rank with only a small capital could not hope to compete with the well-established firms. It was safer to bank one's money with an agency house at 6 per cent interest and let the agent with his specialised knowledge of markets invest it at his discretion. Business ceased to be a matter of picking up commissions and profits from a wide variety of small enterprises; instead it demanded skill, knowledge, wide contacts throughout the commercial world of Asia and a large capital. The loose association of Pym's firm gave way in the face of complexity and competition to an efficient organisation in which usually one man became the dominant influence. Hence economic power in Bombay became concentrated in the hands of a few men who were shipowners, merchants and bankers for the settlement.

The power of these agency houses increased markedly from the 1780s when a 'commercial revolution' gave western India a key position in Asian and European trade.[1] By 1789 raw cotton had ceased to be exported in any quantity from Gujarat to Bengal, but it went instead in bulk to China. The great increase in the trade began about 1784 when Pitt's Commutation Act caused the East India Company to increase enormously its purchases of tea at Canton.[2] The problem of paying the Chinese for their tea in the absence of any profitable exports from Europe could only be met by sending from India raw cotton which the Chinese were prepared to take in ever-increasing quantities. But it was the agency houses of Bombay, and not the East India Company, that built the ships and invested the capital for this trade which was to be the foundation of Bombay's greatness. When David Cuming was at Canton in 1760 the only big ships there from Bombay belonged to the Company. But in 1787 he counted forty sail of large, privately owned ships from Bombay which had imported 60,000 bales of cotton, and carried cargoes representing £1,125,000 of private property.[3] In 1789 the Chief of Surat estimated that about 68,000 bales of cotton were exported from the northward, but only 4,500 bales had gone on the Company's account in 1787, 1,448 in 1793 and 2,000 bales in 1796.[4] The rest was the property of private merchants. These men now had a key role in Britain's vital China

[1] H. Furber, *John Company at Work* (1948), 162–6.
[2] Pritchard, *The Crucial Years*, 145–7.
[3] Rylands English MSS, Melville Papers 676, 522–3: David Cuming to Henry Dundas, 27 December 1788.
[4] BCP, range 414, II, 249.

trade, for they transferred the proceeds from the sale of their cotton and Indian spices to the East India Company's treasury at Canton in return for bills on Leadenhall Street or the Indian government revenue. Without this arrangement the China trade could not be financed.

This was the basis on which the Bombay agency houses built their prosperity, and wealth gave them political power, both in London and in the government of Bombay. Laurence Sulivan died in 1786 at the head of a considerable interest in the East India Company, but in the same year David Scott retired to England with a fortune. He was elected one of the Company's directors in December 1788 and soon won the complete confidence of Henry Dundas, the President of the Board of Control, and of Pitt himself.[1] Until 1803 Scott was in an unrivalled position to influence the policy of the East India Company and to protect the concerns of his friends at Bombay where he continued his interest in the agency house of Scott, Tate and Adamson.[2] During his last years in India Scott had been the most influential man in Bombay for it was his capital which helped to finance the settlement. In 1784 the Bombay government owed him on his private account £191,254 and on the accounts of his constituents £208,870. On his credit rested that of the Bombay government and the stability of the whole settlement's financial system.[3] When Scott returned to England his firm and the other agency houses continued to act as bankers for the Bombay government. Without the support given by the firms of Forbes and of Bruce, Fawcett and Company between 1802 and 1804, Bombay could not have kept an army in the field during the Maratha wars.[4]

But the power of the private traders in Bombay did not rest solely on their role as bankers to the government. Throughout most of the eighteenth century the private traders in Bombay were the government. This was true as well of the other presidencies, but whereas Bengal and Madras were purged by Cornwallis's reforms, Bombay was extraordinary in that its civil servants were allowed to trade until 1806.[5] This meant that men who held high

---

[1] Philips, *The East India Company*, 71–2.
[2] Furber, *John Company at Work*, 222.
[3] CSCB, range D, LXXI, Scott to the Bombay government, 5 October 1784.
[4] J. Douglas, *Bombay and Western India* (1893) I, 254–68. Cf. Furber, *John Company at Work*, 219–20.
[5] *Revenue Lettters Received from Bombay* I (1803–13), 79.

office in the presidency and were responsible for its policy, were deeply involved in private trading activities which could conflict with the Company's public policy. Of the twenty-two members of the Bombay Insurance Society in 1792, to which all the principal merchants belonged, at least twelve were civil servants.[1] Of these, several were very prominent men. Bruce, Fawcett and Company, with Forbes and Company, and Alexander Adamson, were the most powerful agency houses in the settlement at that time. John Forbes and his nephew Charles were never in the Company's service, but Henry Fawcett was the accountant-general, and his partner, P. C. Bruce, was mayor of the town. This one agency house therefore controlled the government's financial policy and was in charge of the judiciary.[2] Alexander Adamson, the partner of David Scott,[3] was in 1792 the transfer master and assistant to the treasurer. Cornwallis heard of him as 'a great monopoliser' of remittances as 'without his patronage no man's proposals however advantageous can be accepted', and he stated his opinion that Mr Adamson's 'official and Commercial situations must often stand much in each other's way and the duties of the former will often interfere with the interests of the latter'.[4] This could have been said of many more servants than Adamson. James Smith, the assistant accountant, was from 1793 to 1800 a partner in the house of Forbes.[5] John de Ponthieu, a partner of Bruce, Fawcett and Company, was Adamson's assistant in the transfer department in 1792 and secretary of the acting governor in 1797.[6] Taylor and Agnew, described in *The Bombay Directory* of 1792 as European merchants, held important positions in the Malabar province, Taylor as the chief of Tellicherry and Agnew as the resident at Calicut.[7] James Stevens, another member of the Insurance Society, was to become superintendent of the southern province of Malabar in 1793.[8] Rivett and Wilkinson, the owners of four ships,

[1] *The Bombay Directory*, 1792, 55.
[2] The mayor's court administered justice in Bombay until 1798 when a recorder's court was established in its place. The mayor and aldermen were civil servants or leading merchants and had had no legal education. See *The Memoires of Sir James Mackintosh*, ed. R. J. Mackintosh (1836) I, 269–71, for the difficulties of administering justice.
[3] Furber, *John Company at Work*, 221–2.
[4] Cornwallis to Abercromby, 17 September 1791; PRO 30/11/181, f. 79.
[5] BSPP, range 381, XIX, 370.
[6] Home Misc. CDXXXVIII, 213: W. Ewer to Henry Dundas, 10 September 1797.
[7] *The Bombay Directory*, 1792, 56.   [8] BRP, range 366, XV, 180.

with their partner, Richard Torin, were appointed members of the Malabar commission in 1797.[1] Robert Henshaw, another merchant with interests in the cotton trade and owner of two ships, later became the custom-master of the settlement.[2] For all these men trade was not just a sideline. To own four ships as Bruce, Fawcett and Company did in 1792[3] meant the management of a great deal of capital, much of which they got by acting as bankers for the members of the settlement. Public and private finance were inextricably intertwined. Jonathan Duncan, when governor of Bombay, left his private fortune to be managed by John Forbes,[4] while in his public capacity he asked for and received enormous loans from Forbes, and Bruce, Fawcett and Company, notably from 1802 to 1804 during the Maratha wars when the Bombay treasury was empty.[5]

But apart from the agency houses and shipowners nearly all the civil servants had some private interest in trade, if only a concern to remit their fortunes to England without loss. This frequently involved them in illicit trade with foreign ships. Even Duncan, one of the most honest of men, confessed to dealings with the Portuguese through his agent, J. H. Cherry, on the Malabar Coast.[6] Many who took their official duties seriously engaged in trade in a smaller way to supplement their incomes. When Charles Malet took up his post as the resident at Poona in 1785 he gave up his interest in eleven small vessels.[7]

In these circumstances private trade inevitably led to corruption. But such things were not talked about openly, as Henry Dundas's nephew, Philip, found when he began to show an interest in these matters.[8] Bombay gave him a new name, 'the Spy', and George Barnes reported that he was much disliked at the settlement.[9]

---

[1] Home Misc. CDXXXVIII, 86; CO 77/26: List of ships compiled by James Tate, Bombay, 24 December 1789.
[2] Personal Records X, 163; CO 77/26. [3] *The Bombay Directory*, 1792, 58.
[4] The records of the Guildhall Library muniment room, London—Michie Papers, MSS 5881, file 2: J. Duncan to J. Michie, 17 June 1799 and 7 July 1803.
[5] Douglas, *Bombay and Western India* I, 254–68. Cf. Furber, *John Company at Work*, 219–20, on David Scott and Stephen Iveson.
[6] Michie Papers, MSS 5881, file 2: J. Duncan to John Michie, 14 March 1784; Cherry was on the Surat establishment.
[7] *The Poona Residency Correspondence* II, ed. G. S. Sardesai, 11 and 50.
[8] Home Misc. CDLVI e, 180–3 and 217: Philip Dundas to John Bruce, 10 January 1795 and 17 January 1796.
[9] IOL, European Photostats XII, the letters of George Barnes, f. 42: 17 December 1795.

In Bengal and Madras similar circumstances had brought about public scandals like the nawab of Arcot's debts. But Bombay had few opportunities on that scale as its only dependent princeling was the nawab of Surat. Nevertheless, although the corruption was less spectacular, it took many forms. The most innocent was the peculation of money and stores.[1] The commercial men in high position made sure that they obtained the best government contracts. In 1797 Bruce, Fawcett and de Ponthieu, owning 'the worst ship in India' which was constantly pumping water even in harbour, secured a contract to carry wheat to the Cape, although the owners of sound ships had made lower tenders.[2] Some of the Bombay servants with commercial interests had dubious relations with the neighbouring Maratha pirates; in one such case Henshaw incurred the censure of the supreme government for his correspondence with the raja of Malwan.[3] But generally corruption only came to light when visitors from Europe or the other settlements were there to report it. A former director of the Company, Walter Ewer, was horrified by what he saw and heard at Bombay. He reported to Henry Dundas from Bombay in 1797:

At present, most of the Civilians are in Trade, & seem to be more employed in their own Counting Houses, than in the publick offices. A proof that there is not much to do in their publick Stations, or, that they neglect them. It ought to be an invariable Rule, that no Person enjoying the above Offices, shou'd be allowed to Trade. As it is not to be expected, they can give disinterested Advice to the Governor, in cases, where they are most probably concerned themselves.[4]

Jonathan Duncan discovered in 1796 that the presidency required 'reform in all parts', especially 'the sores' of Surat and Malabar. He laid bare, he told his uncle, 'villainy...and such a scene of it is opened, as may appal Mr. Dundas, and the Court of Directors'.[5]

The character of governors varied, although military men were preferred before Duncan was sent from Bengal. But Bombay

---

[1] Rylands English MSS, Melville Papers 686, 1467: W. G. Farmer to Holmes, Bombay, 17 December 1789. Home Misc. CDLVI e, 180–3: Philip Dundas to John Bruce, 10 January 1795.

[2] Home Misc. CDXXXVIII, 213–14: Walter Ewer to Henry Dundas, 10 September 1797.

[3] *Ibid.* DCVI, 296–7.

[4] *Ibid.* CDXXXVIII, 77–9: W. Ewer to Henry Dundas, 16 April 1797.

[5] Michie Papers, MSS 5881, file 2: J. Duncan to John Michie, 24 December 1796.

society was too well-knit and united in its interests for the reforming efforts of one man to make a deep impression. General
Medows began some military reforms in 1789 to root out peculation,[1] but under the government of George Dick the presidency
was at its nadir. The governor himself kept a Maratha woman and
permitted her to parade about the streets with all the pomp and
show of power. Ewer reported that she was responsible for many
acts of oppression against the local population and she was suspected of sending intelligence to the Maratha pirates. At this
time, Ewer declared, it was notorious that 'a sum of money
properly applied could obtain anything'.[2] So oppressed was
Jonathan Duncan by the difficulty of his task when he was sent as
governor to reform Bombay, that he declared the reward he sought
'would be to remove me to Madras, or anywhere in an honorable
way from this sad scene of things...'.[3]

The scene of Bombay's interests extended from the peninsula
of Kathiawar in the north to the kingdom of Travancore at the
southern extremity of the west coast. The presidency's actual
possessions, though, were few. To the north, apart from Fort
Victoria, which was used to provide cattle and wood for Bombay
and served as a military recruiting station,[4] the Company possessed
only a factory at Cambay and its share in the government of Surat.
There had been an English factory at Cambay from 1616, and the
city had once been the emporium of Gujarat. But the sea had
retreated from its walls, and Surat had risen in its place as the
centre of commerce. The troubles following the breakdown of
Moghul rule had added to its decline and the cruel and oppressive
government of Mohoman Caun, the then reigning nawab, had
completed its ruin.[5] In 1787 Dr Hove described it as 'a heap of
ruins' as the nawab had pulled down the houses of those subjects
who could not afford to pay his exorbitant taxes.[6] Charles Malet
had passed his years as resident at Cambay in efforts to preserve

[1] Rylands English MSS, Melville Papers 686, 1467: W. G. Farmer to Holmes,
17 December 1789.
[2] Home Misc. CDXXXVIII, 19–22: Walter Ewer to Henry Dundas, Bombay, 30
November 1796.
[3] Michie Papers, MSS 5881, file 2: J. Duncan to John Michie, 24 December
1796.
[4] BSPP, range D, LXXIV, 60–70: W. G. Farmer to Bombay, 23 January 1787.
[5] Forbes, *Oriental Memoires* III, 87.
[6] A. P. Hove, 'Tours for scientific and economical research made in Guzerat
Kattiawar and the Conkuns in 1787–88...', *Bombay Selections* XVI, 50 and 388.

the English influence over a nawab whom he had found oppressive, cruel and deceitful. To this end Malet had striven to remove the Maratha chauth, or levy, of Rs 40,000 and to get it transferred to the Company.[1] Apart from the material advantages, Malet pleaded the cause of 'a miserable city, that under the influence of our authority would experience that relief which it never can expect under the oppressive hand of necessitous despotism unchecked by the mild influence of English interposition',[2] and he declared that he had daily proofs how passionately the inhabitants wished to become subjects of the Company.[3] The Company's factory was there to provide an investment of piece-goods for the English market, but Malet said that the Company drew no article of trade from it under its existing government,[4] and a slight trade in cornelians and agates was all that Cambay could boast of.[5]

Very few of the Bombay servants had travelled further than Cambay in 1784,[6] but Kathiawar, the peninsula lying on the west side of the Gulf of Cambay, forced itself on their notice as the home of pirates who seriously menaced the northern trade. From the creeks and inlets of the rocky coast the pirates of Porbander, Beyt and Okhamandal, tribes who had lived by piracy for generations, swept out to prey on boats carrying cotton to Surat and Broach.[7] The Kathiawar peninsula could grow fine cotton from its fertile soil,[8] but the depredations of the Maratha mulkgiri army were not conducive to cultivation and the villages sought protection by putting themselves under the rule of petty chieftains.[9] One of the most powerful of these was the raja of Bhaunagar who paid tribute both to the peshwa and gaikwar. Half of his country was black-cotton soil, and a large part of the cotton imported at Surat came from his port.[10] The Company had acquired the right to a

---

[1] *The Poona Residency Correspondence*, 'Selections from Sir C. W. Malet's letter-book, 1780–84', ed. R. Sinh (Bombay, 1940), letters 7–8: Malet to General Goddard, 1 February 1780.

[2] *Ibid.* letter 8.

[3] *Ibid.* letter 15: Malet to R. H. Boddam, 8 April 1780.

[4] *Ibid.* letter 63: Malet to David Anderson, 21 February 1782.

[5] Hove, *Bombay Selections* XVI, 386.   [6] *Ibid.* 415.

[7] Home Misc. CDLXXII, 108.   [8] Hove, *Bombay Selections* XVI, 379.

[9] *The Imperial Gazetteer* XV, 176. The mulkgiri army was the force employed to collect the Maratha levies.

[10] BCP, range 414, IL, 299: John Griffith, chief of Surat, to Bombay, 22 August 1789. Bhaunagar exported 12,500 of the 34,000 candies of cotton exported yearly from Gujarat.

quarter share of Bhaunagar's customs from the Sidi of Surat[1] in 1759, but the Bombay government farmed them out annually.

West of Kathiawar lay Cutch, and beyond it Sind. The Company knew little of either in 1784. The great salt ranns made Cutch almost an island, and it was the scene of disorder and rival factions from the middle of the eighteenth century.[2] The Company had withdrawn its factory from Tatta in Sind in 1775 as trade was only possible with the protection of a naval and military force against the predatory chiefs.[3]

But east of the Gulf of Cambay was familiar territory to the Bombay servants, and it had been the scene of their ambitions in the Maratha war. The great rivers Mahi, Narbada and Tapti watered one of the most fertile regions in India, and the fifty-four-mile-long stretch of black-cotton soil which made up the Broach district was one of the richest parts.[4] The cession of the city and its 162 villages to Sindhia in 1783 was to Bombay the most bitter part of the peace, and was recorded as 'a death blow to our hopes in Guzerat'.[5] Charles Malet described the city as 'one of the shackles of Guzerat'.[6] About nine thousand candies of the best cotton were exported from it annually,[7] and the Company insisted on maintaining a commercial resident there after its cession. But it could not compare with Surat in size and population. There the Company had enjoyed a joint government with the nawab since 1759 and provided a large piece-good investment for Europe. But Surat, like the other towns of Gujarat, was in decline by the latter half of the eighteenth century. The oppression of the nawab's government, and the corruption and mismanagement which came from divided authority, left the city little power of recovery from natural disaster. The great storm of 1782 and the famine of 1790 brought devastation. George Barnes found it in 1793 'a shabby Dirty City Governed by a Nabob under the English who make a tool of him for Extortion on others it is still a place of trade but not to be compar'd to what it was formerly'.[8] Dr Hove thought that trade

---

[1] The Moghul admiral, not to be confused with the nawab of Surat.
[2] *The Imperial Gazetteer* XI, 78–9.
[3] J. Bruce, *Historical Plans for the Government of British India* . . .(1793), 568.
[4] *The Imperial Gazetteer* IX, 18–19.
[5] Forbes, *Oriental Memoires* III, 433 and IV, 221.
[6] *Poona Residency Correspondence*, 'Selections from Sir C. W. Malet's letter book, 1780–84', ed. R. Sinh, letter 32: Malet to General Goddard, 15 October 1780.
[7] BCP, range 414, II, 249.
[8] Letters of George Barnes, IOL, European Photostats 12, f. 37.

could be considerably increased if the Company would protect it between Surat and the neighbouring places, and remove the monopolies in the city.[1] But the population of Bombay rose steadily as more and more people from the continent sought security for themselves and their property under the Company's government.[2] And with the rise of Bombay proceeded further the decline of Surat.[3] The Company's Surat piece-good investment had been worth £91,300 in 1771, but in 1789 its value was only £33,357.[4]

Decline from former wealth to a state of poverty, insecurity and, in many parts, desolation, was the general picture given of Gujarat after the Maratha war. English observers discovered the principal cause in Maratha government. In the eighteenth century Gujarat had been divided between the gaikwar and the peshwa in such a way that their districts frequently intermingled.[5] The gaikwar, the most independent prince of the Maratha confederacy, held his lands in jaghir: he paid an annual tribute of eight lacs to Poona, and furnished 3,000 horsemen on demand. But the system of government, both at Poona and Baroda, was the same. Malet charged it with the responsibility for:

the present drooping Commercial state of all those Provinces of Hindostan that have been subjected to the Maratta Power, under which the Provincial monied Men, not to mention the substantial Landholders, have been subjected to oppressions, and exactions. Personal property has become insecure, Industry has failed, an Aristocratical Wealth, arising from the Soil and the Labours of the Peasantry, has succeeded which is confined to the conquerors...[6]

The gaikwar collected his revenue every year from his tributaries by means of a military expedition, the mulkgiri circuit, and was often met by armed resistance. Hove reported that an army of 20,000 was sent to Kathiawar, where it was fought by the inhabitants.[7]

---

[1] Hove, *Bombay Selections* XVI, 515.
[2] Forbes, *Oriental Memoires* III, 436; and Court's letter to Bombay, 26 March 1775, Bombay Dispatches I, 28.
[3] *Imperial Gazetteer* XXIII, 156 and 165.
[4] W. Milburne, *Oriental Commerce* I, 290.   [5] Forbes, *Oriental Memoires* II, 84.
[6] C. W. Malet, Appendix no. 6 of *Reports on the Export Trade from Great Britain to the East Indies*, 8 August 1788. BT 6/42. This analysis is accepted by R. D. Choksey in his introduction to *A History of British Diplomacy at the Court of the Peshwas*, ix.
[7] Hove, *Bombay Selections* XVI, 476.

The failure of the Marathas to cope effectively with problems of law and order encouraged brigandage and lawlessness. Trade and agriculture suffered severely from the depredations of the Bheels and Girasias. The Girasias had gained power through brigandage in the seventeenth and eighteenth centuries, when local rulers had surrendered land to them in an effort to stop their marauding. Many had considerable landed possessions and others exercised claims of feudal authority.[1] But with the growth of disorder in Gujarat many Girasias collected bands of robbers round them and terrorised the countryside, murdering and looting. Their internal family feuds added to the instability.[2] Also, there were bands of Bheels and Kolis to contend with. The Kolis did some sporadic cultivation, but the Bheels, whom Forbes described as 'wild mountaineers, under no regular government, and almost in a savage state', lived by plunder alone.[3] Gujarat also suffered from the incursions of the Kathies, marauding tribes from across the border in Kathiawar. It was not safe to travel any distance from the capital without armed escorts. Dr Hove took seventeen horsemen with him in 1787 on a journey from Broach to Surat, and on the way there he found that a notorious robber, with a band of two hundred men, had seized one of Fateh Sing's customs posts and was ransoming the baggage of travellers.[4] When he continued his journey to Jambusar, Hove was robbed and pursued by further gangs. He was forced to provide himself with twenty-six archers to travel to Cambay, and then an escort of sixty men to go through Kathiawar to Dholka.[5]

The trade that survived these hazards on land had further dangers to contend with at sea. If the shipping between Kathiawar and Surat escaped the notice of the Okhamandal pirates and the Kolis, it might be seized on between Surat and Bombay or Bombay and the Malabar Coast by fleets of Maratha pirates. The most dangerous of them was organised by the raja of Malwan.[6] Even when the Bombay marine was at its full strength it could not prevent almost daily acts of piracy. Malet summed up the situation when he declared that the Maratha government had persistently shown 'a spirit Hostile to Commerce...', and he added his con-

[1] W. Hamilton, *The East Indian Gazetteer* (1815), 386.
[2] A. K. Elwood, *Narrative of a Journey Overland from England to India* (1830) II, 280–1.
[3] Forbes, *Oriental Memoires* III, 68 and 213.   [4] Hove, *Bombay Selections* XVI, 370.
[5] *Ibid.* 386, 393.   [6] Home Misc. DCVI, 296–7.

viction that were its fleet equal to the end it would be 'instantly converted to the same predatory purpose at Sea as its Armies [were] by Land'. He concluded that any attempts by the Company to increase its trade with the Maratha dominions would be useless, as 'the Common course of causes arising from the state of the Society has already operated its utmost effects and will continue so to do'.[1]

But Bombay's chief anxiety after the peace in 1784 was the second branch of its commerce, with Malabar, whence it drew the pepper and spices for Europe and China. The Malabar kingdoms had first been invaded by Haidar Ali in 1766, but they were only fully occupied by him in 1773. With the exception of Cannanore the rulers and the dominant part of the population were Hindu. The kingdoms of Chericul, Cotiote, Cartinaad, and Cannanore which was ruled by a Moplah family, lay in the northern part of Malabar with the small taluks of Irvenaad, Corengotte and Randaterra. The latter district was subordinate to the English settlement at Tellicherry. To the south lay the kingdom of Coorminaad and the territories of the Zamorin.[2] The raja of Cochin was a tributary of the Dutch, but the kingdom of Travancore was independent and had been built into an important state by Martanda Varma in the first half of the eighteenth century.

In the Malabar kingdoms there was an almost feudal structure of society. The most prominent class was the Nayars who exercised local political power under the rajas, based on the feudal tenure of land and compulsory military service.[3] All the agricultural work was done by slave castes. Outside the main Hindu community there were two other important groups, the body of local Christians and the Muslim population led by Arab merchant princes. They lived almost exclusively in the coastal towns and most of the spice trade was in their hands.[4]

It was the spice trade which had first drawn European powers to the Malabar coast and had led to the Portuguese and Dutch attempts to win political power and enforce a commercial monopoly. Although they had given up this policy, the Dutch still clung to their settlement at Cochin and the French to Mahé,

---

[1] C. W. Malet, Appendix No. 6 to *Reports on the Export Trade from Great Britain to the East Indies*, 8 August 1788, BT 6/42.
[2] *Malabar Report*, 10–11.
[3] K. M. Panikkar, *A History of Kerala* (1960), 10.　　[4] *Ibid.* 15.

while the English company maintained its establishments at Tellicherry and Anjengo. But the expense of these establishments was beginning to outweigh the returns as they felt the effect of the Mysorean conquest on trade. The continued resistance of the Nayars to Haidar's and Tipu's rule and the savage reprisals which were enacted, brought cultivation to an end over large tracts of the country. Malabar was never at peace for twenty-six years. Before the Mysorean conquest the districts between Cavai and Chetwai yielded 20,000 candies of pepper, and the price was between Rs 70 and 80 a candy. In 1784 the same area provided only 11,000 or 12,000 candies and the price had leapt to Rs 130.[1] But the demand for pepper remained high. The Court of Directors wrote in 1783 to Bombay asking the government to increase its pepper purchases as the article was so profitable at the London sales.[2] The several factories and private adventurers competed for the diminishing supply and the Tellicherry servants were finding that the restriction on prices which the directors imposed was making the provision of an investment increasingly difficult.[3]

This was an unfortunate position for the Company and for the private merchants, as more than ever in 1784 they wanted trade to expand, not shrink. The demands of the Canton treasury were urgent, and in the face of defeat and bankruptcy trade was Bombay's only hope of survival. Before 1775 commercial interests had always played a leading part in Bombay's relations with the west-coast powers.[4] This was particularly marked in the presidency's policy towards Haidar Ali. The settlement of Tellicherry had made alliances with some of the rulers of the spice-growing kingdoms, and had promised them help if they were attacked. But the Bombay government calculatingly deserted them when Haidar Ali promised in February 1766 that the Company should have the sole purchase and export of all the pepper, sandalwood and cardamoms in Malabar.[5] The same considerations governed Bombay's decision to supply Haidar with arms and to send him support in 1765 when his country was in danger of being overrun by the Marathas.[6] The Bombay government had also made efforts to extend the area

---

[1] *Malabar Report*, 241.   [2] Despatches to Bombay VII, 93: 15 January 1783.
[3] BCP, range 414, LXV, 351: March 1800 (R. Taylor to the Court of Directors, 3 April 1794).
[4] B. Sheik Ali, 'English Relations with Haidar Ali, 1760–82', an unpublished Ph.D. thesis (London, 1960), 91.
[5] *Ibid*. 102.   [6] *Ibid*. 86.

of its settlements on the coast in attempts to secure the trade.[1] But in 1784 it was a question of trying to retrieve what commercial interests they could at a peace-making where they had only failure on their side. On the security of Bombay's trade depended the whole future of the presidency. The peace and its aftermath were to be crucial to its survival.

[1] *Ibid.* 86.

CHAPTER 3

THE SURVIVAL OF THE PRESIDENCY, 1784–92

The Bombay government was determined to fight for its interests in the peace negotiations with Tipu, and not trusting the Madras commissioners to speak for them they appointed two of their own men to make their claims. Their principal object was to increase the Company's commercial privileges in Malabar with a renewal of the ancient grants of factories at Carwar, Onore and Calicut. They were to secure the privilege of exporting rice from Mangalore, preferably with an increase in the quantity, and permission, if possible, to establish a factory there. The commissioners were also to provide for the Company's privilege of buying masts, timber and planks at Onore, Mangalore and Calicut and in other parts of the country. Then, in the hope that they could bribe Tipu into acquiescence by offering to supply him with arms, the Bombay government gave its opinion that Carwar would be a valuable acquisition because of its nearness to the pepper-growing districts and because of its good harbour. They considered the peace negotiations a good opportunity for obtaining a permanent grant of the port from Tipu.[1]

But the agents never delivered these demands to Tipu, as the supreme government directed the Madras commissioners to negotiate the peace alone. Bombay sent off a long and heated letter of protest to the governor-general complaining of the neglect of the presidency's commercial interests and expressing the hope that in the hands of the Madras commissioners their 'more valuable privileges of Trade and Commerce (all that this Presidency have now to look up to)...would not be sacrificed for less useful advantages on the other Side of India.'[2] Although the supreme government replied that it had expected Bombay to inform Madras of its

---

[1] Home Misc. CLXXXVIII, 276–83; 'Instructions intended to have been given by the President and Select Committee at Bombay to Messrs Callander and Ravenscroft, 18th Jany 1784'.

[2] CSCB, range D, LXXI, 61–3: Bombay to Bengal, 19 January 1784. A copy of the protest was also sent to the Court of Directors; Home Misc. CLXXXVIII, 130.

interests without an invitation, the peace was in fact concluded without Bombay finding much satisfaction in it. There was a formal recognition of the trading privileges which Bombay had possessed under the treaty made with Haidar Ali in 1770, Mount Dilly and the factory at Calicut were restored, but Bombay secured no new concessions and the Malabar princes were left without any protection.[1]

Despite this failure there was at first considerable optimism about Tipu's conduct and the prospects of trade with his dominions. Tellicherry reported to Bombay that Tipu had sent orders to receive the English resident at Calicut, and that he was encouraging trade between his ports and their settlement.[2] But early in 1785 relations began to deteriorate. The Bibi of Cannanore refused to surrender Mount Dilly to the Company according to the terms of the treaty of Mangalore, and it was feared that her refusal had Tipu's support.[3] Then in November of that year the suspicions and rumours of the previous months had their first confirmation. Tipu laid an embargo at his ports on the export of pepper, sandalwood and cardamoms.[4] It was not immediately obvious that the embargo was directed principally against the English. John Beaumont, the chief of Tellicherry, thought its purpose was either to raise the price or to 'fleece the merchants' and that it would soon be removed. But in January 1786 the Company found that it could no longer trade from Onore. Tipu had razed the place to the ground and removed the inhabitants.[5] The general embargo continued.

The effect on trade was soon felt. One of the first to experience it and to express his indignation was George Smith, a private merchant on a speculative voyage from Calcutta to the Malabar Coast and Bombay. Smith was a country trader of long experience in Indian and Chinese waters.[6] From 1783 to 1791 he wrote a series of letters to Henry Dundas giving commercial information and expounding the merits of a plan which he had proposed to the supreme government for supplying the Canton treasury through trade in the products of western India.[7] In November 1785 he set

[1] William Logan, *Malabar* (2nd ed., Madras, 1951) III, 83–4.
[2] CSCB, range D, LXXI, 633–4: Tellicherry to Bombay, 18 November 1784.
[3] *Ibid.* LXXII, 77: Bombay to Tellicherry, 9 March 1785.
[4] *Ibid.* 329: Tellicherry to Bombay, 12 November 1785.
[5] *Ibid.* LXXIII, 59 and 164: Bombay to Bengal, 13 January 1786.
[6] Pritchard, *The Crucial Years*, 184.
[7] Home Misc. CDXXXIV. Pritchard, *The Crucial Years*, 232.

sail in a vessel for the Malabar Coast, with the intention of proving by a voyage of his own that cargoes from the west coast could yield rich profits at Canton and so end the necessity of exporting specie from India.[1] But at Calicut Smith found that Tipu's embargo was very much in force. He could under certain conditions dispose of his own cargo, but he could not carry off any pepper, sandalwood, cardamoms, planks or timber.[2] The final proof of the severity of its enforcement came in a letter which Smith received from Murdock Brown. Brown had spent the best part of his life on the Malabar Coast. In his youth he had been employed by the notorious William Bolts in trading adventures, but had settled at Mahé and there changed his nationality as it suited his convenience. Born a Scot, he became successively a Dane, an Austrian and a Frenchman, and wherever smuggling or illicit trade was carried on he was sure to be involved.[3] Even his detractors admitted his intelligence and unparalleled knowledge of Malabar, and if anyone had the influence or initiative necessary to overcome Tipu's prohibition, it was he.[4] But on the 30 January 1786 he wrote to Smith from Mangalore that it would be 'imprudent and at best unprofitable' for him to go there, as there was 'no possibility of having immediate returns, because nothing can be bought without advising the sovereign, which occasions a delay of at least fifteen days without any certainty of the Goods being taken'. Furthermore, if Smith wished, despite these regulations, to dispose of his cargo, he could only do it safely by assuming French colours and then could not hope to get any pepper or sandalwood in return.[5]

It was becoming obvious that the embargo was aimed principally at the English trade and that it was part of a scheme by Tipu to drive them out of Malabar. In January the Bibi of Cannanore had sent a threatening message to the Moplah merchants at Tellicherry warning them to migrate to her dominions or suffer the consequences of Tipu's wrath.[6] The threat was made more real when the prince of Cherika with Tipu's support claimed the return of Randaterra from Tellicherry. The place had been assigned by the prince to the Company in 1765 as security for the payment of a

[1] Home Misc. CDXXXIV, 201–2: G. Smith to Dundas, 25 November 1785.
[2] *Ibid.* 235: G. Smith to Dundas, 12 March 1786.   [3] Personal Records II, 17.
[4] Home Misc. CDXXXVIII, 148–50: Walter Ewer to Henry Dundas, 17 July 1797.
[5] *Ibid.* CDXXXIV, 253–5: Murdock Brown to George Smith, Mangalore, 30 January 1786 (enclosed in Smith's letter to Dundas of 12 March 1786).
[6] BSPP, range D, LXXIII, 73–4: Tellicherry to Bombay, 12 January 1786.

debt.[1] Bombay protested to the Sultan, but the government was in a very difficult position. It was still crippled by enormous debts on which it could pay no interest, and the only hope that the bondholders had of recovering their fortunes was for the presidency to remain at peace. So impressed was the government by the necessity of this course that when it was informed of the probable outbreak of war between the Marathas and Tipu in August 1785, its reply was

when we consider the Condition of our Honble Employers Affairs under this Presidency & the intolerable Load of unprovided Debt with which it is now burdened, we must look upon the Honble Company being forced to become parties in any War between these Powers as a very unfortunate Event & which we must sincerely hope & wish may be avoided.[2]

Therefore, five months later it was in no position to resist any attempt which Tipu might make against its possessions in Malabar, and appeasement was its only possible course. Tellicherry was told to offer no resistance if the prince of Cherika seized Randaterra by force.[3]

But the threat to Tellicherry brought a reaction from Macpherson, the governor-general, and his council. They wrote to assure Bombay in March that they considered the preservation of Tellicherry of great importance to the commercial interests of the Company on the west coast of India and that the inhabitants had a just claim to the Company's protection. Macpherson wrote to Tipu and asked him to remove the embargo on trade. He also ordered that reinforcements and supplies should be sent to Tellicherry.[4]

The home government was kept informed of the situation in public and private letters. George Smith expressed his indignation to Henry Dundas at the Board of Control and did not hesitate to declare that Tipu was trying through the embargo to force the Company into withdrawing its settlements from the Malabar Coast. Already Tellicherry had become 'a dead loss'. Smith lamented that the Company's military and naval weakness made

---

[1] *Ibid.* 90: Bombay to Tellicherry, 24 January 1786.
[2] CSCB, range D, LXXII, 229: 19 August 1785; and CO 77/25: Edward Ravenscroft to Sir Edward Hughes, Bombay, 7 March 1786. Little of the debt was actually outstanding.
[3] BSPP, range D, LXXIII, 91: Bombay to Tellicherry, 24 January 1786.
[4] *Ibid.* 359–62: Bengal to Bombay, 9 March 1786.

them unable to counter this infringement of the treaty of Mangalore by helping merchants to force their way into Tipu's ports.
His final interpretation of the situation was that Tipu was 'virtually
at war' with the Company, since

> by the Embargo on the Productions of his Countrys, & the prohibition
> of Intercourse between it, & Tellicherry, the Co. cannot load their ships
> from hence for Europe, nor can any public or private supplies be thrown
> from his Countrys as before, into China, which proves in effect as
> injurious to the Commercial Interests of the Co. as if actually at War with
> him...[1]

Smith's answer to the situation and the course which he urged
on Dundas was the adoption of an aggressive policy towards Tipu.
Dundas, according to Smith, should see to it that Tellicherry was
made into a military base, and that a corps of 5,000 men was always
kept there. This he maintained would overawe Tipu, as he could
never attack the Carnatic without opening the provinces of Malabar
and Bednure to the Company's army. Moreover the force at
Tellicherry could always march to join the Madras troops through
the Palghaut gap.[2] A further advantage of this policy would be
that the rajas and landowners who were suffering under Tipu's
conquest and tyranny would be encouraged by the presence of a
large body of British troops to rebel against him, an event
which promised political and commercial advantages for the
Company.

In April 1786 Smith further advanced his argument for making
Tellicherry into a military base by reporting a conversation which
he had held on the subject with Governor Boddam at Bombay.[3]
Boddam had been the chief of Tellicherry for seven years and was
'well acquainted', according to Smith, 'with the political, local, &
mercantile situation of that Place, the Temper, and disposition of
the different Princes now Tributary to Tippoo Saheb, and their
Inclination to throw off his Iron Yoke, if protection was near to
them, and that Protection secured to them on application to it, and

---

[1] Home Misc. CDXXXIV, 235–8: G. Smith to Henry Dundas, Bombay, 12
March 1786. Edward Ravenscroft expressed the same opinion to Sir Edward
Hughes, but stressed Bombay's helplessness because of the heavy load of debt.
Hughes sent the letter to Lord Sydney: CO 77/25 enclosed in a letter dated 21
August 1786.
[2] Home Misc. CDXXXIV, 238–41.
[3] Rylands English MSS, Melville Papers 926, 1: G. Smith to Henry Dundas,
Bombay, 13 April 1786.

which a respectable Force at Tyllycherry would always afford them...'[1] This insight into Boddam's own opinion is strengthened by examining the information which he gave to Smith. He told him that the principal pass from Malabar into Mysore could be seen from Tellicherry House and could be easily taken by surprise, and a clear passage opened to Seringapatam. Furthermore, Tipu had himself built a road from Seringapatam to Calicut which was only 130 to 140 miles distant from Tellicherry.[2]

In association with this aggressive policy towards Tipu, Smith proposed that the Company should strengthen its relations with Travancore.[3] By this course, he contended, the effect of Tipu's embargo would be nullified and the Company could provide pepper cargoes for Europe. It would be profitable to pay more attention to the settlement of Anjengo in the Travancore kingdom, 'which grows the best pepper in great Abundance'. The king of Travancore, he reported, was under contract to deliver 3,000 candies of pepper annually to the Dutch, but in fact he only provided a third of it as the Dutch paid a fraction of the current price. Since, Smith maintained, the king was friendly to the English and courted their protection, he would readily enter into a contract with the Company provided they paid him the five or six lacs of rupees for which they were indebted. If this were done the Company might procure a quantity of pepper sufficient to load two or three ships annually for Europe. Anjengo would then become a profitable factory and the Company would also benefit from its cloth manufactures which at that moment went, like those of Tinnevelly, to enrich the Dutch instead of the English.[4] Smith concluded with the hope that his information had convinced Dundas of the advantages of the west coast possessions to the Company and nation, 'and that they ought to be retained and supported'.[5]

George Smith's letters to Dundas provide valuable evidence of the effect of Tipu Sultan's policy on British commercial interests. These interests demanded the expansion of the trade from Malabar to China, and when Tipu prohibited it altogether the natural reaction was to demand that commerce should be supported by

---

[1] *Ibid.*   [2] *Ibid.*: George Smith to Henry Dundas, Bombay, 15 April 1786.
[3] Home Misc. CDXXXIV, 241–3: G. Smith to Henry Dundas, Bombay, 12 March 1786.
[4] *Ibid.*
[5] *Ibid.* See Pritchard, *The Crucial Years*, 232–4, for the importance which Henry Dundas attached to Smith's information and views.

political and military action. Smith's conversations with Governor Boddam indicate that his views were shared, at least to some extent, by the Bombay government.

However, Bombay had not the means or power to pursue such a policy. But Smith's other suggestion of strengthening the association with Travancore was taken up. In June 1786 the Bombay government declared that if Tipu continued his embargo on the export of pepper, they had no way of completing their cargoes except by applying to the king of Travancore, in the hope that the supreme government would by that time have answered their pleas and paid off the Company's debt to the king.[1] Some such arrangement was becoming urgent as the Bombay government was under pressure from the Court of Directors and Canton to provide cargoes of spices. The Court had emphasised that it was relying on the good management of its commercial concerns to rescue the Company from its financial difficulties, and Bombay was ordered to provide an increased investment, especially of cardamoms, in as large a quantity as possible.[2] The supracargoes at Canton had also made plain their disappointment at receiving no sandalwood or pepper from Malabar and pointed out that sandalwood would have proved very profitable.[3]

The merchants at Tellicherry put forward their own proposals. They insisted that the situation would be remedied if the Company could again take possession of Randaterra, which the prince of Cherika had occupied in the previous January.[4] Tellicherry continued to press this point, assuring the government that once possessed of Randaterra, 'the Key to the pepper countries', they would undertake to deliver as much pepper as was required.[5] Some support for this aggressive proposal came from Bengal, where Macpherson was thinking on the same lines as George Smith. He assured Bombay that the supreme government saw the necessity of defending Tellicherry for commercial and political reasons and that it should be made into a military base with a large number of troops stationed there. Furthermore, he asserted, should the prince of Cherika not discharge the remaining debt to the Company for which Randaterra had been the security,

---

[1] Letters received from Bombay VIII, 455: 23 June 1786.
[2] Despatches to Bombay VIII, 267–85 and IX, 591–639.
[3] BCP, range 414, XLVII, 119: Canton to Bombay, 19 December 1786.
[4] *Ibid.* 21: Tellicherry to Bombay, 6 October 1786.
[5] *Ibid.* (1787) 9: Tellicherry to Bombay, 12 January 1787.

the Company should at the opportune moment recapture the district.[1]

But before the Bombay government could take up this point with Macpherson, the arrival of Lord Cornwallis in India in October 1786 brought a fresh mind and different ideas to the problems of the west coast. Cornwallis's first aim was to restore the Company's finances by ridding it of corruption in India and keeping it out of further wars. By profession a soldier, he looked with a somewhat distrustful eye on commercial men,[2] and soon acquired a contempt and hatred for Macpherson and his policies.[3] Himself upright, honest and conscientious, he began a new era in the Company's government in India by attacking the system which had brought about the subservience of public policy to private interests.[4] Although he saw Bengal as the chief field of his activity, Cornwallis took up his post with some knowledge of the Company's interests in western India. Henry Dundas had sent him a copy of a long paper which George Smith had written for him on the Company's possessions in that quarter and their commercial and political interests.[5] The fact that Dundas sent it to Cornwallis is an indication of the importance which he attached to Smith's views. It emphasised the value of Bombay to the Company and in language almost identical with that of his letter to Dundas of 12 March 1786 Smith pointed out the importance of Tellicherry to the Company's trade in providing pepper and other spices, as well as its value as a base from which to attack Bednure and Seringapatam.[6] He also gave an account of the Company's commercial interests in Travancore and proposed as in his letter from Bombay that the Company should press the raja of Travancore to transfer his pepper contract from the Dutch to the English.[7]

---

[1] BSPP, range D, LXXIII, 666–7: Bengal to Bombay, 23 June 1786.

[2] PRO 30/11/150, f. 97 and 97v: Cornwallis to Dundas, 8 November 1788.

[3] C. Ross (ed.), *The Correspondence of Charles, First Marquess Cornwallis* (1859), I, 371 and 415.

[4] P. E. Roberts, *History of British India under the Company and Crown* (3rd ed., 1952), 222.

[5] PRO 30/11/7, ff. 270–2: 'Observations on the English Possessions in India, their Government, Population, Cultivation, Produce and Commerce. Privately communicated to the Right Honorable Henry Dundas' (unsigned but dated at Calcutta on 20 September 1785). In the Harvard Melville MSS (IOL micro-film reel 647) the paper is listed in a catalogue of Dundas's private correspondence as enclosed in a letter from George Smith dated Calcutta, 1 October 1785.

[6] See above, p. 41.   [7] PRO 30/11/7, f. 272.

But when Cornwallis came to consider his policy towards Tellicherry and Malabar it was the financial position of the Company which governed his attitude. He told Dundas that Tellicherry could only have security and importance if a large force were stationed there and much money spent on building new fortifications. His conclusion was, 'In the present state of our finances, nothing but the appearance of an emergency could induce me to think of either; for the constant drain of pay for the troops, and particularly the engineers bills for the works, would totally demolish the effects of all my labours and economy in this country.'[1] The same concern led him to view the possibility of a war against Tipu with abhorrence, as it 'could be of no use to us, and would totally derange all our economical plans'.[2] Yet Cornwallis was quick to do whatever could be done through peaceful means to improve the Company's commercial position on the Malabar coast. He instructed the Madras government to pay off the Company's debt to the king of Travancore, which enabled the resident at Anjengo to make a contract for the delivery of 1250 candies of pepper.[3]

This was not enough, though, for the Bombay government. Governor Boddam was receiving information about the progress of Tipu's great road from Seringapatam to Calicut, and rumours reached him that Tipu was meditating an attack on Travancore. To Boddam there was more than loyalty to an ally at stake.[4] In a letter to Malet he went to the heart of the question. Were Tipu, he said, 'ever to get Possession of the Travancore Country our Interest on the Coast of Malabar would be annihilated and the total loss of the pepper trade follow'.[5] Malet sent the warning to Cornwallis.

At the same time Malet supported the governor-general in his refusal to spend money in fortifying Tellicherry and making it into a military base. He argued with Boddam that, as the stationing of the entire Company's force at Tellicherry could not procure a grain of pepper or sandalwood if Tipu chose to blockade the inland trade routes, then such a policy would be useless from the commercial

---

[1] Ross (ed.), *The Correspondence of Cornwallis* I, 251: Cornwallis to Dundas, 5 March 1787.
[2] PRO 30/11/188, f. 45: Cornwallis to Charles Stuart, 28 August 1787.
[3] BCP, range 414, XLVII, 135: Bombay to Anjengo, 20 August 1787.
[4] Travancore had been mentioned as an ally of the Company in the Treaty of Mangalore; Logan, *Malabar* III, 83, article 1.
[5] PRO 30/11/20, f. 272: Boddam to Malet, 21 October 1787 (enclosed in Malet's correspondence with Cornwallis).

point of view. Moreover in a military light Tellicherry was a bad choice as an arsenal. The place was very difficult to defend and its garrison would be cut off from the main force at Bombay. Malet thought it would serve rather to provoke than to deter Tipu[1] and in his opinion it would be best to reduce the place to a mere factory.[2]

Cornwallis determined before coming to any final decision to seek for more detailed information, and he commissioned Captain Kyd early in 1788 to go to Tellicherry and make a first-hand report on the fortification and its military possibilities.[3] In March Henry Dundas wrote to give his opinion that Tellicherry should be retained as a military station, although in fairness to the contrary opinion he enclosed a paper written by John Sulivan who denied that the place had any military value.[4]

Cornwallis could not make a decision about Tellicherry without taking into consideration the future of Bombay's commercial interests on the coast. The presidency had brought to his attention the question of renewing the trade in fire-arms with Tipu, and had expressed its hope that by this means, 'the Company may again ensure to themselves the valuable productions of Tippoo's Country in which Foreign European nations have so successfully Supplanted them and from obtaining which we have of late years been so effectually precluded, as to find it impracticable to furnish Cargoes for two ships annually from this Coast'.[5] The request showed the measure of Bombay's desperation. Clearly if Tellicherry were abandoned the presidency would be left with pitiful resources, and there would be scarcely adequate reasons for its preservation. Furthermore Cornwallis would have to justify his policy to the Court of Directors who continued to send orders to Bombay for investments from Malabar. So keen were they to have consignments of pepper that they went so far as to give Bombay permission to offer Rs 145 a candy, and expressed their indignation at receiving no cardamoms on the Company's account.[6] Moreover Malet had repeated his warning on 5 May that Tipu's

---

[1] PRO 30/11/23, f. 357–357v: Malet to Boddam, 12 November 1787 (enclosed in Malet's letter to Cornwallis of 19 April 1788).
[2] PRO 30/11/21, f. 391: Malet to Cornwallis, 16 November 1787.
[3] PRO 30/11/22, ff. 193–5: Kyd to Cornwallis, Madras, 7 February 1788.
[4] PRO 30/11/113, f. 44: Henry Dundas to Cornwallis, 29 March 1788.
[5] BSPP, range D, LXXIV, 424–6: Bombay to Bengal, 29 October 1787.
[6] Despatches to Bombay IX, 591–639: 21 November 1787.

schemes against Travancore might mean that he would gain the exclusive possession of 'the valuable Commercial produce of the Malabar Coast', and could reward the French with it if he chose.[1] It was perhaps these considerations which led the governor-general to order on 4 July that if Tipu gave open support to the prince of Cherika's campaign of insults against Tellicherry, the settlement was to defend itself and Bombay was to make alliances with the Malabar princes and prepare for a general offensive.[2]

But four months later Cornwallis had drastically changed his policy. On the basis of Kyd's report he came to the definite conclusion that Tellicherry was useless to the Company as a commercial station because of Tipu's prohibition of trade, and that militarily it was indefensible.[3] The natural conclusion was that Tellicherry must be abandoned. But this plan was only part of a more radical and comprehensive scheme which Cornwallis had resolved on: the reduction of Bombay from a presidency to a factory. What use, he asked Dundas on 4 November 1788, was the parade of governor and council and a large establishment of merchants and factors, supported by all and more than the surplus revenues of Benares and Bihar, when they did little more than load one ship a year and collect an insignificant revenue. A small factory at Bombay, and another at Surat, would be fully adequate for the Company's needs.[4] So seriously did Cornwallis hold these views that he repeated them in a letter sent two days later to Pitt, in which he declared that the only obstacles to the abolition of the Bombay civil establishment was the unwillingness of the Court of Directors to lose any field of patronage and the difficulty of overcoming prejudice and old habits of thought.[5]

Before any reply to this radical proposal could arrive from England, Cornwallis took the first step towards abandoning Tellicherry. In March 1789 he formed an alliance with the king of Travancore by which the latter agreed to pay for two battalions of Madras sepoys to defend his kingdom. The troops were to be

---

[1] PRO 30/11/24, f. 237 and 237v: Malet to Cornwallis, 5 May 1788.
[2] BSPP, range D, LXXV, 248–50: Bengal to Bombay, 4 July 1788.
[3] PRO 30/11/150, f. 95v: Cornwallis to Henry Dundas, 4 November 1788 (printed by Ross in *The Correspondence of Cornwallis* I, 375).
[4] PRO 30/11/150, f. 101 and 101v; Ross (ed.), *The Correspondence of Cornwallis* I, 377–8: Cornwallis to Henry Dundas, 4 November 1788.
[5] PRO 30/11/175, ff. 5v and 6: Cornwallis to Pitt, 6 November 1788; Ross (ed.), *The Correspondence of Cornwallis* I, 378–9.

stationed within the Travancore border. In this way Cornwallis got his alternative military station on the Malabar coast.[1] Unaware of the threat to its future, Bombay agreed with the governor-general that Tellicherry provided little of commercial value to offset its enormous expense, but clinging to hope they added, 'if through some fortuitous Event the Malabar Rajahs should shake off the yoke of Tippoo and circumstances should justify our forming alliances with them, we might venture to predict that Tellicherry would become a possession highly valuable to our Employers in point of commerce and of great political weight'.[2] But Cornwallis had already set on foot an enquiry into the value of the presidency's other possessions of Surat and Fort Victoria,[3] and by the end of the year he had acquired the firm conviction that there was 'nothing to gain on the Malabar side' that would not bring more embarrassment than good.[4] The presidency seemed to be doomed.

The future of Bombay lay in the hands of Henry Dundas, the president of the Board of Control. Dundas had always made clear to Cornwallis his conviction that Bombay was important as a military and naval station for the defence of all India and as a base for controlling the Marathas and Mysore.[5] He possessed considerable information of the value of Bombay's dockyard and harbour,[6] and also of its situation as a centre of trade. This he passed on to Cornwallis.[7] It was the military argument which he first used in reply to Cornwallis's demand of 4 November 1788 that the presidency should be abolished. He was not in favour of engaging in another Maratha war, he declared, in order to increase the Company's territories on the west coast, but

at the same time it is obviously our Interest to make the most we can of the Possessions we have, or even to enlarge by Negotiation if we can, our Possessions in that Quarter, for in no given State of our Indian Empire is it possible for us to be without a large Military Establishment

---

[1] PRO 30/11/150, f. 124: Cornwallis to Henry Dundas, 8 March 1789.
[2] BSPP, range E, I, 308: Bombay to Bengal, 16 June 1789.
[3] *Ibid.* 306–8: Bengal to Bombay, 5 May 1789.
[4] PRO 30/11/157: Cornwallis to the Court of Directors, 1 November 1789; Ross (ed.), *The Correspondence of Cornwallis* I, 439.
[5] Ross (ed.), *The Correspondence of Cornwallis* I, 526.
[6] Rylands English MSS, Pitt 929, 48: R. Smith, 'Observations on the Establishment of the Company's Marine Force in the East Indies', 18 April 1782.
[7] PRO 30/11/7, ff. 270–2: 'Observations on the English Possessions in India.'

on the West of Hindostan. A respectable Force in that Quarter is essential to our Interest both on the Coast and in Bengal.[1]

He assured Cornwallis that he was aware of the inconvenience of supporting such an establishment from Bengal or Madras but drew the opposite conclusion to that of the governor-general. Instead of abolishing the presidency he thought it should have a revenue of its own equal to its needs.[2] Furthermore, he told Cornwallis that he was not used to treating the possession of Tellicherry as such an unimportant place as Cornwallis considered it.[3] In conclusion Dundas expressed his wish for a whole chain of military posts along the west coast of India, but he left the final decisions to Cornwallis's own judgment.[4] But later in the summer before he received Cornwallis's reply, Dundas changed his mind about Tellicherry. He wrote to Cornwallis saying that he was ready to abandon the place whenever another convenient military station could be found as a substitute.[5] In fact in August 1789 the future of Bombay seemed to be lost. Dundas in a secret memorandum proposed that the government should negotiate with the Dutch for Cochin, which with its good harbour and fortifications could be made into a first-class military station. The Company could then abandon Tellicherry and keep Bombay merely as a military station, with a commercial residency there and at Surat.[6]

Before this reached Cornwallis he replied on 7 November to Dundas's earlier letter. He repeated his conviction that there was no possibility of providing Bombay with territory which would not threaten to increase the remittance from Bengal to fifty lacs rather than reduce it to thirty. He further expressed his surprise that Dundas should be thinking of new acquisitions on the western coast when he himself wished to abandon it completely.[7] At the same time he flatly delivered his opinion to the Court of Directors that the Company had no prospects of improving its position in western India.[8]

Dundas reacted to Cornwallis's opinions by collecting together

---

[1] PRO 30/11/114, ff. 42v–43: Dundas to Cornwallis, 3 April 1789.
[2] *Ibid.* f. 43.   [3] *Ibid.* f. 43v.   [4] *Ibid.* f. 44–44v.
[5] PRO 30/11/115, f. 197: Dundas to Cornwallis, 8 August 1789.
[6] *Ibid.* ff. 154v–155; this memorandum was sent to Cornwallis.
[7] PRO 30/11/150, ff. 151v–152: Cornwallis to Dundas, 7 November 1789; Ross (ed.), *The Correspondence of Cornwallis* I, 446.
[8] PRO 30/11/157, ff. 130–1: Cornwallis to the Secret Committee of the Court of Directors, 1 November 1789.

as many papers as he could which yielded information on the Company's west coast possessions and the importance of the Bombay presidency. He wrote to Cornwallis telling him that he would make his decision on the basis of this material, and he stressed the difficulty of the task.

> It is really matter of great moment to get rid of the immense load of expense which attends the Bombay Establishment. It has cost me more thought than any other subject whatever, I have never been able to form a decision satisfactory to my own mind. I must rest on the information of others and on no point is the opinions of men more contradictory.[1]

By 4 June 1790 Dundas had read all the information which his secretaries had collected from India House, as well as copies of the correspondence between Malet, the resident at Poona, and Cornwallis.[2] He then proceeded to deliver his opinion. First he considered the view that the whole establishment should be abolished. 'In revolving the subject in my own mind, I have repeatedly been disposed to go to that conclusion; but the difficulties which occur in opposition are so strong, I am not prepared to do it.'[3] His reasons were twofold. There was the political and military value of Bombay which he had already put before Cornwallis: if the Bombay establishment were abolished, he thought the Company's influence with the Marathas and Tipu would decline.[4] But the second reason was more positive and came from what appears to be Dundas's new comprehension of the important part which the Bombay presidency played in the eastern trade. Dundas suddenly saw Bombay and Surat with fresh eyes. His enlightenment came not only from reading the papers on his desk, but also from 'conversing with intelligent persons, well informed in the trade of India, either now or in former times'.[5]

> I am strongly impressed [he told Cornwallis] with a conviction that Surat is in that point of view, both in appearance, and substance, a most important Possession, and will be daily more so, if by just attention to the interests both of India and Britain, we can improve the internal Trade of India, and likewise its foreign Trade with the Chinese and Eastern Seas, or with the Gulphs of Arabia and Persia. These are objects of such extensive magnitude, they never can be lost sight of.

[1] PRO 30/11/116, ff. 37v–38: Dundas to Cornwallis, 16 May 1790.
[2] *Ibid*. ff. 84–6: Dundas to Cornwallis, 4 June 1790.
[3] *Ibid*. f. 85. [4] *Ibid*. f. 85v. [5] *Ibid*.

Dundas added that his reasoning would gain extra weight 'from applying more particularly what I have in general alluded to, respecting the Commerce of India'.[1]

This last remark referred to Dundas's long-held views on the importance of developing the trade between India and China, the value of which he had tried to drive home in his correspondence with Cornwallis. In July 1787 he had sent to Cornwallis a number of papers giving plans for an embassy to China.[2] Its mission was to improve the conditions under which trade was carried on at Canton. Dundas hoped that the outcome would be a commercial establishment to 'answer very valuable purposes, both in respect of providing China investments and in respect of the aid it would afford to the vent both of British and Indian Manufactures & Produce in the Empire of China and its Dependancies'.[3] He stressed to Cornwallis the significance which the trade between India and China had assumed particularly in helping to pay for the hugely increased investments of tea which the Commutation Act had brought about.[4] The embassy was not carried out as planned, but Dundas persisted with his policy and in July 1788 he admonished Cornwallis for not cooperating as well as he might.

From your Letters Publick and Private [he wrote] I am apt to think you are no great friend to the idea of supplying Canton from India. I shall write you in the course of the summer my ideas very much at large on that subject. I am clear it can never be attempted except through the medium of Commerce, between the two countries; and if Bengal is to be materially injured by it, the idea must be dropt, but as well in a Political as in a Commercial view, it would be of the utmost importance if the vast Tea Trade now carried on to this Country could be supplied from Indian Resources, without bringing any drain upon the Country. In short if China could be supplied by the sale of British and Indian Manufacture either directly or indirectly finding their way to China, it would render the benefit of our Indian Empire perfect, of course you will join with me in thinking that every exertion, and every ingenuity should be exercised to effectuate such a system, and it ought only to be departed from on the most unequivocal conviction that the system is impracticable.[5]

---

[1] PRO 30/11/116, f. 85v: Dundas to Cornwallis, 4 June 1790.
[2] PRO 30/11/112, f. 17–17v: Dundas to Cornwallis, 21 July 1787.
[3] *Ibid.* f. 17. Pritchard, *The Crucial Years*, 233–4.   [4] *Ibid.* f. 17–17v.
[5] PRO 30/11/113, ff. 125v–126: Dundas to Cornwallis, 13 July 1788. Cf. Barun Dé, 'Henry Dundas and the Government of India, 1773–1801', unpublished D.Phil. thesis in the Bodleian Library, Oxford (1961), 397: 'This after all was the main aim of Dundas's pattern of imperialism for India—a country

In August 1789 Dundas repeated the same views to Cornwallis,[1] who was therefore not ignorant of all the interests involved when Dundas referred him to this policy in support of the Bombay presidency.

This crucial decision for the future of the settlement was made, as Dundas explained to Cornwallis, on the basis of wide reading and personal conversations. It is important to know which men and which interests influenced Dundas in this decision. There is no means of positively identifying the people he talked with, but it is possible to deduce what some of the sources of his information were. He certainly read Charles Malet's letters to Cornwallis,[2] and also the letters of George Smith. The earliest paper written by Smith which came into Dundas's possession was dated 16 February 1783 and gave the outline of a plan which Smith was to press on the Bengal government and the Board of Control throughout the next seven years.[3] In it Smith emphasised the importance of the China trade to the nation and the need to make a treaty with the Chinese government which would allow the Company to increase its supplies of Indian produce to Canton and facilitate its trade there.[4] In January 1785 he pressed on Dundas a policy of expanding territory in order to finance the China trade and mentioned Trincomalee, Acheen and islands in the straits of Malacca as worthy of his attention. It was a policy which Alexander Dalrymple had first suggested,[5] but Smith followed it up with a plan for exporting produce from west India to China.[6] He had submitted

supplying resources to purchase a favourable British balance of payments in its inter-Asian and Asian–European trade.'

[1] 'I feel so much the importance of establishing a Commercial connexion with the great Empire of China, I am not disposed to be discouraged from the Plan by any trivial obstructions'; PRO 30/11/115, f. 21v: Dundas to Cornwallis, 1 August 1789. 'We understand each other so well on the importance of supplying China through the Medium either of British or Indian Manufactures or Produce, it is unnecessary for me to say any more on that subject'; *ibid.* f. 198, 8 August 1789.

[2] See above, p. 44–66.   [3] Home Misc. CDXXXIV, 11–30: 16 February 1783.

[4] These proposals influenced Dundas's decision to send an ambassador to China; see p. 50 above.

[5] Harlow, *The Founding of the Second British Empire, 1763–93* I, 70.

[6] Home Misc. CDXXXIV, 33–46. It is possible that Smith enclosed with this letter the unsigned and undated paper which appears in 'Mr. Dundas's Papers of Accounts' (*ibid.* CCCXL, 359–67). This paper seems to be of the same date as this letter as it refers to 'the great and singular advantages this Country is likely to experience from the Commutation Act' and gives details of the plan for developing the trade of west India.

it to the supreme government at Calcutta, which had apparently approved it in principle, but declared that it had not the means of financing it. Smith asked for Dundas's patronage and pointed out that his plan would stop the drain of specie from India to China.

The plan was for the Company to harness for its own benefit the extensive trade which Smith said was carried on by private individuals and foreign ships from the west coast of India to China. He estimated that the produce exported in this way amounted to between 16,000 and 20,000 bales of cotton, from 3,000 to 5,000 candies of pepper and from 1,000 to 2,000 candies of sandalwood, besides large sums remitted by pearl, putchuk and other articles. He believed that the Company had not profited from the trade because it had not the capital or ships to do so. His plan showed how it was possible. Six of the Company's China ships could call at Bombay with cargoes of staple goods to the value of at least £30,000 in each ship. From Bombay each ship would take 600 bales of cotton, 700 candies of pepper and 200 candies of sandalwood, which altogether, he believed, would furnish the Canton treasury with about £388,000. The funds for these cargoes would come from the sale of the English staple goods and from remittances from Bengal or bills on the Court of Directors.[1] Since Macpherson's government would not assent to the plan, Smith appealed to Dundas against 'the Supineness in our Government to the most Lucrative Branch of the Co.'s Commerce', and left Calcutta at the end of 1785 on the trading voyage to the Malabar Coast and China which involved him with Tipu Sultan's embargo on trade.[2]

Smith had sent a copy of his proposals to the Court of Directors in 1784,[3] and although it is not possible to assess its influence on the directors, in November 1786 the Court sent orders to Bombay to provide as many cargoes as possible for the China market as the supracargoes and Canton needed material help in providing their investments.[4] In May of the same year William Wright, the Company's auditor of Indian accounts, compiled statistics of Bombay's trade with Canton which showed how little was carried

---

[1] Home Misc. CCCXL, 359–67.
[2] *Ibid.* CDXXXIV, 140–2: George Smith to Dundas, 5 August 1785; *ibid.* 165: Smith to Dundas, 1 October 1785. See above, pp. 37–8.
[3] Home Misc. CDXXXIV, 34: Smith to Dundas, 27 January 1785.
[4] Despatches to Bombay IX, 31–7.

on the Company's account. The figures were sent to Henry Dundas.[1]

Dundas also received information on the subject from other private sources. He encouraged individuals to send him such reports and told Cornwallis about one particular source: 'I make it a Rule to receive information from everybody that offers it to me upon the subject of India. I get a great deal of information that way, which repays the time it consumes, although sometimes it consumes a great deal.'[2] The paper which he thought important enough to send to Cornwallis was written by David Cuming, a private merchant who was engaged in the eastern trade.[3] Cuming repeated the observations and proposals of George Smith on the need to expand the Company's trade with the Malay archipelago and to make new settlements there to benefit the China trade. And again, like Smith, Cuming emphasised the possibilities of the Malabar trade.

The Company should also increase their Investments from the Malabar Coast. It would be to their advantage to build six Ships of War at Bombay, to mount 64 Guns each, those ships could be employed for the Company in time of Peace to carry a Cargo once a year to China, and I am well convinced that they would in the course of four years pay for their building and stand a clear acquisition to the Company...[4]

The following year Cuming wrote again to Dundas.[5] He described the rich trade which the Bombay merchants were engaged in with China,[6] and complained that

A few of the Company's Serv^{ts}, Free Merchants and others, monied men Joining Interest to Wealth have long been accustomed to engross for themselves through the influence of the Company, the whole trade of the different Countries round it, The Court of Directors never once taking notice of the advantage which the Company might derive from this trade, were it properly managed in their own hands, considering how

---

[1] Home Misc. CCCXL, 331–40: No. 65 of 'Mr. Dundas's Papers of Accounts', 16 May 1786.

[2] PRO 30/11/112, f. 105: Dundas to Cornwallis, 27 July 1787 (enclosing a paper by David Cuming dated 18 February 1787).

[3] *Ibid.* f. 153.

[4] *Ibid.* f. 151.

[5] Rylands English MSS, Melville Papers 676, 523: David Cuming to Henry Dundas, 22 December 1788.

[6] See above, p. 23.

well it is situated for remitting money to China for the purpose of Tea investments.[1]

Cuming maintained that the Company's ships, which were normally sent out from England, could carry on this trade without any additional expense, and that as the freight costs should be less than with private shipping the Company should be able to capture the Canton market.[2]

The opposite view was held by David Scott, whom Dundas looked to for information and assistance in his relations with the Court of Directors.[3] Scott had left Bombay in 1786 after twenty-three years there as a private merchant, and after returning to England he continued his interest in the Bombay house of Scott, Tate and Adamson.[4] He therefore spoke on behalf of the private merchants when, in April 1787, he proposed to the Court of Directors that the Company should give up the export trade from England to India and from India to China, and should give their tonnage freight-free to the private merchants. By this means, he asserted, the merchants would increase the supplies of cotton, pepper and sandalwood which went from the west coast of India to Canton.[5] In response to Scott's proposals, the Court went so far as to order an increase of 2,500 tons in the shipping which they sent to China by way of Bombay. This could be taken up by the private merchants if the Bombay government could not use it.[6] Although Scott opposed the Company's increasing its own share of the trade from India to Canton, his almost daily association with Dundas could hardly fail to give the latter a keen sense of the trade's importance and the value of the western coast. Moreover Scott's influence with Dundas must have added weight to the

[1] Rylands English MSS, Melville Papers 676, 523: Cuming to Dundas, 22 December 1788.

[2] *Ibid.*

[3] Philips, *The East India Company*, 71–2. Dundas wrote to Cornwallis about Scott's being 'now one of the Court of Directors and intimately connected with Government. He is endeavouring to make the Court of Directors act in a very new Character, I mean to make them think now and then as Merchants, in place of viewing themselves only in the light of sovereigns and Great Generals' (11 August 1789); PRO 30/11/115, f. 93–93v.

[4] Furber, *John Company at Work*, 222.

[5] BT 6/42: 'Report on the Export Trade from Great Britain to the East Indies', 3 April 1787.

[6] PRO 30/11/115, f. 79: 'Report from the Special Committee appointed to take into consideration Regulations proposed by David Scott for improving the Company's Commerce', 22 July 1789.

views of his associates and acquaintances in India and England. Among those were men who played an important part in Bombay commerce and politics. Murdock Brown in his shady dealings at Mahé was prepared to do everything he could 'to serve any Friend of Mr. David Scott', and it was Dundas's assiduous correspondent, George Smith, who thus benefited from his claim to Scott's friendship.[1] In September 1787 Dundas himself told Pitt that James Sibbald who was one of Scott's associates in Bombay had won his favour 'by being the Person who suggested to me the propriety of aiding the China Trade through the Means of Cotton from Bombay...'[2] Moreover, Dundas's nephew, Philip, supplied his uncle with information of the valuable products of the Malabar coast in 1787.[3]

The evidence shows that Dundas's policy of developing the commercial connexion between India and China was influenced as much by the private trading interests as by the East India Company. The private traders hoped that he would use his power to break the Company's hold on the trade, while in George Smith's letters can be seen the beginning of pressure on the authorities to exercise political and military power in the interests of trade. The Court of Directors too between 1784 and 1789 became increasingly aware of the advantages of developing the connexion between western India and Canton, and had begun to press the Bombay government to provide larger investments for China. Together, these interests ensured the survival of the Bombay presidency.

Cornwallis's willingness to abandon it in the first place had perhaps something to do with his pessimism about the possibilities of supplying Canton from India. He had received George Smith's proposals in 1787,[4] but merely sent a copy of them to the Court of Directors without comment,[5] and on 14 August of that year he wrote to Dundas, 'We have been unfortunate in our China remittances, which after all I take to be perfectly useless, as the produce of every article that goes from hence to the China market,

---

[1] Home Misc. CDXXXIV, 253–5: Murdock Brown to George Smith, Mangalore, 30 January 1786 (enclosed in Smith's letter to Dundas of 12 March 1786).

[2] PRO 30/8/157, ff. 32v–33: H. Dundas to Pitt, 19 September 1787.

[3] Harvard Melville MSS, IOL microfilm reel 647: Philip Dundas to Henry Dundas, 4 July 1787.

[4] Home Misc. CDXXXIV, 293–6: G. Smith to Cornwallis, 26 July 1787 (enclosed in Smith's letter to Dundas of 10 September 1787).

[5] PRO 30/11/165, f. 9v: Cornwallis to Shore, 16 August 1787.

must be lodged in the hands of our Supracargoes', and he expressed his opinion that the latter were more concerned with their private interests than the Company's advantage.[1] He confessed to Dundas in November 1788 that he had 'few greater plagues than the remittances to China; & indeed I must be candid enough to acknowledge that I think I have not managed that business well; I have however learnt by experience that there is no believing the best of the mercantile people where their interest is concerned, and I trust I shall do better in future.[2] But in reply to Dundas's reproach that he was not cooperating fully, Cornwallis denied that he was unfriendly to the idea of supplying China from India and declared his willingness to undertake any proposition except that of sending specie, and on the subject of Bombay's part in the scheme he continued,

> Great quantities of cotton are sent annually to China from Bombay by private adventurers, but if that was to be paid for by our Indian or Bengal resources, for there are no resources anywhere else, we could only do it by encreasing the export of our silver to the Malabar Coast, which is already so great as nearly to ruin this country.

He assured Dundas that he knew the importance of the subject and had consulted the most intelligent merchants about it, but he was convinced that the remittances to China must depend on the export of opium from Bengal.[3]

Thus when Tipu Sultan attacked the territory of the raja of Travancore on 29 December 1789, Lord Cornwallis was still of the opinion that the Bombay presidency should be dissolved. He was bound in this by considerations of economy and by the conviction that Bombay could only pay its way if it acquired a territorial revenue. This could only be done through war and such a policy was expressly forbidden by act of parliament. He had not yet received Dundas's opinion that the presidency's value lay in trade. However, Tipu's attack on Travancore could only be met by war. The English were not only bound by treaty to defend the raja, but important interests were at stake.

Although Tipu had been intriguing with the French at Pondicherry there was no real threat from that quarter.[4] Dundas wrote

[1] PRO 30/11/150, f. 43v: Cornwallis to Dundas, 14 August 1787.
[2] *Ibid.* f. 97v: Cornwallis to Dundas, 4 November 1788.
[3] *Ibid.* ff. 125–7: Cornwallis to Dundas, 8 March 1789.
[4] PRO 30/11/24, f. 237–237v: Malet to Cornwallis, 5 May 1788.

to Cornwallis in August 1789 saying, 'It is impossible to feel any uneasiness from anything the French can at present do in India or anywhere else. Torn to pieces, as they are, by Civil Commotions, and a total dissolution of their Government.'[1] But if Tipu should conquer Travancore not only would he increase his resources and gain a new access to the Carnatic, but, as Malet had twice warned Cornwallis, the Company would be cut off from its last remaining pepper supplies.[2] Bombay saw the question almost exclusively in this light and put commercial interests well before political considerations. In April 1789 the Bombay government had even given Cornwallis its opinion that the king of Travancore's request to raise English colours on his forts should not be assented to 'Without conditioning for some reciprocal Advantages in a Commercial point of view: since in the Encouragement we are assured he has of late given to Foreign Traders we think he has not requited the Company as he ought, for the Signal Attachment they have shown him'.[3]

Plunged into war by Tipu, Cornwallis suddenly found that the policy of peace and economy for which he had worked throughout his tenure of office was utterly disrupted and that he must make a major change in his thinking. In his own mind he had abandoned western India, but Tipu's attack created new problems. The Company must defeat Tipu, but what considerations were to take first place in the making of peace called for deep and anxious thought. He had not to wait long before proposals came to him. Only a few weeks after the outbreak of war Malet sent his views to Cornwallis on the peace terms. The Company's aim, he thought, should be to drive Tipu from the Malabar coast and to 're-instate the Nair princes in their Ancient freedom and Tenures to secure such a Possession on the Coast as should be equal to their support to Purposes of our Commerce and to the supply of the deficiencies of the Bombay revenue...' In addition he proposed the strengthening of the Carnatic frontier.[4] Cornwallis's own views, which he instructed Malet in March 1790 to put to the Marathas, were that Tipu must give reparations to Travancore and an indemnity to the Company. As well as cessions to the Company's allies and an

[1] PRO 30/11/115, f. 198: Dundas to Cornwallis, 8 August 1789.
[2] PRO 30/11/24, f. 237–237v: Malet to Cornwallis, 5 May 1788.
[3] BSPP, range E, I, 155–7: Bombay to Bengal, 9 April 1788.
[4] PRO 30/11/34, f. 238–238v: Malet to Cornwallis, 5 February 1790.

improved frontier for the Carnatic, he instructed Malet, 'on account of the shocking barbarity with which he has treated the Nairs on the Coast of Malabar, to insist upon his setting those people free from future dependance upon him'.[1] At this stage it appears that Cornwallis envisaged the Malabar princes after the peace as independent powers subject neither to Tipu nor the Company. But by 31 May 1790 these rather vague ideas of restoring western India to its condition before the rise of Mysore had given place to a firm and definite policy of annexation. Cornwallis explained his new policy without reference to any military considerations; it was the Company's commercial interests which concerned him. He ordered the Bombay government on 31 May to win the Malabar princes to the Company's alliance

under the most solemn assurances that we will use our utmost efforts to force that prince [Tipu] to relinquish all future claims upon their allegiance and to agree to their becoming the dependants & subjects of the Honble Company to which we shall add that in order to secure a willing obedience from the Malabar Chiefs, we should be contented with their paying a very moderate Tribute provided they will give the Company advantageous privileges for carrying on a commerce in the valuable productions of their country.[2]

Apart from Malet's opinions there is no means of knowing what influenced Cornwallis in his decision, but it seems clear that he saw his old policy was ruined, and decided to gain every possible advantage from the new situation. His old policy towards Malabar was not made in ignorance of the country's commercial value; Malet and the Bombay government had seen to that. Cornwallis had only refused to provoke a war on those issues. But once the war had been made for him he saw in it a new answer to the problem of Bombay. The Malabar kingdoms could provide Bombay and the Company with the coveted spice cargoes for Europe and China. It seems, though, that Cornwallis thought this could be done without the Company's assuming administrative power in the area. His instructions only provided for the Malabar chiefs to pay 'a very moderate tribute', and to give commercial privileges to the Company. It appears that Cornwallis thought that the chiefs would retain political and administrative control of their kingdoms.

Doubts on this issue were soon raised at Bombay. In May 1790

[1] PRO 30/11/163, f. 8v: Cornwallis to Malet, 22 March 1790.
[2] BSP, range E, 11, 264–5: Bengal to Bombay, 31 May 1790.

the Tellicherry chief and factors made the first of the cowles, or agreements, with the rajas of Cartinaad and Chericul. They promised on behalf of the Company to give the rajas independence from Tipu in return for their military help.[1] The principal aim of the cowles was to ensure that assistance, but the Tellicherry servants were unhappy about the promise of independence. On 28 June they asked the Bombay government whether the rajas were, in fact, to be independent princes, or the 'Zemindars of the English'.[2] They revealed their own disposition by proposing at the same time that Cannanore should be reduced and annexed by the Company. The Bibi, they declared, was encouraging the Moplahs to disobey the orders of the Malabar rajas and to ill-treat the Nayars. If the Company took Cannanore, not only would the Moplahs be subject to British power, but, 'In another point of view the Reduction of Cannanore woud [sic] be very beneficial, by securing to the Company a considerable Quantity of Pepper annually exported by the Bebee in vessels of her own, & sold at different Ports in India on her own Account.'[3]

Another problem of territorial sovereignty in which commercial interests were involved arose over the district of Corengotte, which lay between Tellicherry and Mahé. Immediately after the Company's troops drove out Tipu's soldiers the French laid claim to the area, and maintained that the Corengotte Nayar was their tributary. The Tellicherry servants hotly denied the claim and pointed out to Bombay that if it were allowed the French would almost surround Tellicherry. Not only could they hinder the march of any military force, but they might easily encroach upon, if not altogether prevent, the trade by land between Tellicherry and Cartinaad.[4]

Tellicherry was preoccupied with pepper. In July Major Dow of that settlement reported to Bombay that he was about to set off to the southward to report on the area and to establish order. Two important objects of his mission were visits to the rajas of Cochin and Travancore. The Company, he claimed, had a good right to expect the first preference in the purchase of the pepper produced

[1] *Poona Residency Correspondence* III, ed. N. B. Ray, 125.
[2] Malabar Report, 48–9.
[3] PRO 30/11/37, ff. 430v–431: An extract of a letter from the chief and factors at Tellicherry to the Bombay government, 28 June 1790; see also the Malabar Report, 48–9.
[4] BSP, range E, II, 389–90: Tellicherry to Bombay, 1 July 1790.

in the Cochin raja's country, and his intention was to find out the quantity which the country exported and the best method of securing its exclusive trade to the Company. From Cochin he intended to proceed to a meeting with the raja of Travancore. Again his motive was to secure for the Company a preference in the trade of the country.[1] In August Tellicherry signed a preliminary treaty of alliance with the Bibi of Cannanore and inserted a clause in the agreement by which the Company was admitted to a free and uninterrupted trade with her port and country, and she agreed to supply an annual quantity of pepper at a favourable price.[2] In October the raja of Coorg entered into a similar alliance and promised the Company preference in purchasing cardamoms, sandalwood, cinnamon and nutmegs to the exclusion of other European nations.[3] The Bombay government immediately asked for contracts of sandalwood to provide cargoes for the China market.[4] Even Cornwallis expressed his hope to Dundas that the outcome of the Malabar chiefs' dependence on the Company would be that they would 'soon again provide for us ample Supplies of Pepper'.[5]

It came as a rude shock to the Tellicherry servants at the end of the year when they found, after these high hopes, that the merchants with whom they had contracted for supplies of pepper and cardamoms delivered quantities much below the required amount. Tellicherry blamed the settlement at Mahé for the deficiencies. There French and Imperial agents were paying from 170 to 180 rupees for each candy of pepper and were attracting all the supplies of the province.[6] The Company would not give more than 130 rupees a candy.[7] This was the first indication of the trouble which Mahé was to give to the Company's concerns in Malabar. Earlier in the century the French settlement there and the English factors at Tellicherry had cooperated to keep down the price of pepper in their mutual interest.[8] This cooperation had continued,

[1] BSPP, range E, v, 661: a minute delivered by Major Dow and sent to Bombay, 8 July 1790.
[2] BSP, range E, II, 399–400. The agreement was signed on 8 August 1790.
[3] *Ibid.* 537–9: 25 October.
[4] BCP, range 414, L, 254: Bombay to Tellicherry, 1 November 1790.
[5] PRO 30/11/151, ff. 54v–55: Cornwallis to Dundas, 9 August 1790.
[6] BCP, range 414, L, 275–6: Tellicherry to Bombay, 20 November 1790.
[7] *Ibid.* LI: Tellicherry to Bombay, 2 January 1791 (entered under 28 January 1791).
[8] Logan, *Malabar* III, 16, article 4: an agreement between Tellicherry and Mahé, 28 April 1728.

apart from the intervals of war, until about the year 1787, when the consequence of Mahé's being declared a free port by the French began to appear. Private merchants, the prince of whom was Murdock Brown, began giving higher prices to attract large quantities of pepper.[1] From that time the price climbed steadily throughout the province.

The Tellicherry Board suggested to Bombay in November 1790 that the Company's best policy in the situation would be to contract directly with the several rajas for the pepper in their dominions instead of relying on the merchants at Tellicherry.[2] They followed up this suggestion in the new year when they pointed out to Bombay that since the rajas were to be restored to power, they would undoubtedly consider as their own exclusive property all the pepper, cardamoms and sandalwood which were grown in their dominions. The merchants would have to make their terms with the rajas or take the risk of smuggling the pepper out, and the Company might benefit by making their own contracts directly with the rajas. Furthermore, relations with the Tellicherry merchants had become increasingly difficult as the price of pepper rose at Mahé, for the Company had used what amounted to compulsory methods to get them to deliver pepper at a low price. In this situation the plan of contracting with the rajas appeared in an attractive light—the more so as it was believed they would take arms, ammunition and rice in exchange for the spices. The only disadvantage of the scheme was that the Company would get no security from the rajas for the performance of their engagements.[3]

Tellicherry, in concert with General Abercromby, the governor of Bombay, who was then commanding the army in Malabar, thought that the advantages outweighed the other considerations. They wrote to Bombay on 12 January that they would use their 'best endeavours, under the influence of Major General Abercromby, to enter into as extensive Engagements with the Rajahs for the delivery of pepper, Cardamoms and Sandalwood, and that upon as moderate terms as possible'.[4] Abercromby obtained the support of the Bombay Council for his decision to adopt the

---

[1] BCP, range 414, LXV, 434: a report from Murdock Brown to the Malabar commissioners, 1 September 1799.
[2] *Ibid.* L, 276: Tellicherry to Bombay, 20 November 1790.
[3] *Ibid.* LI, 18–23: Tellicherry to Bombay, 2 January 1791.
[4] *Ibid.* 23: Tellicherry to Bombay, 12 January 1791.

plan.[1] There could be no clearer proof that the Bombay government accepted the Malabar rajas' claim to the sovereignty and
government of their kingdoms.

Abercromby, with his army at his back, used his influence with
the rajas, and by February Tellicherry was in possession of
contracts with the Cartinaad and Cotiote rajas for 700 candies of
pepper at 125 rupees a candy. To make up the necessary cargoes
the chief and factors had to buy pepper from the merchants, at
135 rupees a candy.[2] Clearly it was more profitable to use 'influence'. Tellicherry brought some energy to the task. The results
showed themselves in a lengthy protest from Mahé. A deputation
from the French settlement told Robert Taylor, the chief of
Tellicherry, that they had learnt with the greatest astonishment of
his activities in Corengotte. They accused him of intimidating the
prince of Corengotte and forcing him to send all his pepper to
Tellicherry. The French also said that 'he, Mr. Taylor, had forbid
the King of Cartinade & the Nambiers to permit any pepper to be
sent into Mahé & that these prohibitions put upon [our] Trade
were what only could be done by Enemies'.[3]

But the chief and factors were spurred on in their activity by the
instructions of the Court of Directors. These ordered Bombay to
show the 'utmost Vigilance' in securing 'as large a supply as the
state of circumstances will admit', and urged the government to
negotiate with the raja of Travancore to increase the quantity of
pepper he provided. The advantage of this course in the directors'
eyes was that it would reduce the Dutch share in the trade, and
prevent Imperial and country traders from obtaining such large
supplies as they were accustomed to get from the Travancore
country.[4] But the Court had in mind only 'a trifling Addition of
Price' for any deliveries beyond the 1500 candies which the raja
had contracted for.[5]

While these plans to engross the greater part of the pepper trade
were going forward, the Company's forces were still fighting Tipu
and peace was not in sight. But there was no lack of ideas on what
form the peace should take, and commercial interests received

[1] BSPP, range E, IV, 29–30: Abercromby to Bombay, 12 January 1791.
[2] BCP, range 414, LI, 57–8: Tellicherry to Bombay, 7 February 1791.
[3] BSPP, range E, IV, 288: a report of the Mahé deputation to Tellicherry, 28
January 1791.
[4] Despatches to Bombay XII, 491: 4 May 1791.
[5] BRP, range 366, XIV, 93: Tellicherry to Bombay, 26 July 1791.

considerable attention. Abercromby gave his approval to Tellicherry's demand that the Company should annex Randaterra. The
merchants had pointed out its importance to the pepper trade.
From London Henry Dundas wrote to Cornwallis recommending
that the Malabar rajas should have his particular attention. In
Dundas's opinion they should become the Company's tributaries
so that the English could enjoy 'the great political and commercial
benefits to be derived from a free, secure and uninterrupted intercourse with the Malabar Coast...' Like Cornwallis, at this time
Dundas seems to have envisaged that the rajas would keep the
government and administration of their kingdoms in their own
hands.[1]

Shortly after Dundas wrote to Cornwallis he himself received
the first of several letters from Captain John Taylor of the Bombay
military establishment, who was then in London pursuing certain
claims he had on the Company. Taylor, like George Smith, was a
friend of David Scott[2] and, apart from the influence which they
had on Dundas, his letters are important for the light they throw
on the views of the Bombay establishment. The most remarkable
aspect of them is that although Taylor was a military man he was
concerned as much with commercial interests in Malabar as with
military advantages. His letters say nothing about the desirability
of taking Malabar in order to cut off Tipu Sultan from contact with
the French. But they are eloquent on the subject of the Company's
trade to China. He thought Cochin a desirable acquisition because
its fine river and harbour would serve as a good station for a packet-
boat and even as a base for attacking Tipu, should his power
survive the war. But he did not neglect to point out its advantages
for shipbuilding, and its vicinity to the finest teak timber in India.[3]
In a letter written in November to Dundas, Taylor described the
way in which Tipu had interfered with the Company's commercial
privileges before the war, and claimed that they had a better title to
factories in Canara and Sounda than Tipu had to rule Malabar.[4]
He described the products which Malabar yielded, pepper, sandalwood, cardamoms, cassia, coir, rice, and the teak from the moun-
tains which was dragged to the rivers by elephants and floated to

[1] PRO 30/11/117, ff. 111–13: Dundas to Cornwallis, 21 September 1791.
[2] Home Misc. CDXXXVI, 225.
[3] *Ibid.* 119–21: J. Taylor to Dundas, 30 September 1791.
[4] *Ibid.* 149–53: 21 November 1791.

the coast. He put forward his opinion that 'the China Market might be supplied from the Coast of Malabar, together with cotton from the Northward, to half the amount of the Tea Investments of the Company. The Malabaris would willingly receive many European Articles, and return Pepper, Sandalwood, and Cardamoms to a large amount.'[1] The Company, Taylor declared, would make a profit of 60 per cent on its exports of pepper to China.[2]

In March 1792, Taylor submitted some radical proposals to Dundas. His friendship with David Scott perhaps accounts for some of them. He proposed that parliament should take over the responsibility for the government of India and establish a new commercial company. This would continue the monopoly of trade with China and be given, as well, an additional monopoly in the Indian products which were profitable at Canton. Otherwise private merchants and foreigners could share in the trade to and from India.[3] In this scheme the products of Malabar would be included in the Company's monopoly. This, in his view, was the only way for the English to win back the spice trade which had been lost to foreigners and to that 'nest of smugglers and thieves' who made up 'the defenceless and insignificant settlement of Mahé'. According to Taylor, Mahé had control of three-quarters of the trade.[4] He emphasised that the peace offered the Company a chance to make a commercial treaty with the restored rajas which would destroy all competition. The English could either buy the spices from the rajas with their own manufactures, or the princes could be induced to pay a subsidy for the maintenance of British troops and the protection of the British government. The subsidy would solve the problem of payment and would act as a lever in the interests of commerce, because according to Taylor, it would 'become the interest of the Rajahs to take special care that their respective subjects do not dispose of their most valuable articles to any others than the servants of the East India Company, and to use their Influence with their Subjects for the same purpose'.[5] If the Company would at the same time induce the Chinese to receive the staple goods of India in exchange for investments of

[1] Home Misc. CDXXXVI, 189: 21 November 1791.
[2] *Ibid.* 191: 21 November 1791.
[3] *Ibid.* 298: Taylor to Cabell, 11 March 1792.   [4] *Ibid.* 298–9.
[5] *Ibid.* 299–300: Taylor to Cabell, 11 March 1792.

tea, the Malabar monopoly would save the Company considerable annual exports of specie.[1]

Besides Taylor's letters, the Board of Control received similar proposals and information at much the same time. One letter proposed that the Company should acquire the province of Bednure and pointed out the commercial prospects of the district. The numerous rivers made it desirable for shipbuilding, and its products included rice, pepper, cocoanut and teak.[2] Colonel John Murray, the military auditor-general at Bengal, also received a lengthy paper on the subject which he later sent to Henry Dundas. The paper was written at the beginning of the war and had the title, 'On the Revenues and Trade of the Malabar Coast'. The writer described the commercial benefits which would accrue to the Company if they possessed such ports as Carwar, Onore and Mangalore and gave in great detail an account of the pepper, teak, sandalwood and cardamoms which made the province so valuable. At the conclusion of the paper he added 'Should we be successful in the present War, and the Malabar Coast become subject to the British Nation, we might hope to see it again restored to Cultivation and riches, the productions of it supplying Wealthy Cargoes for Europe, the sandal and surplus Cash throwing a considerable Sum into the Treasury at the Expenses of Government on *this* side India'.[3]

How far these proposals which came to the Board of Control were written purely from public-spirited motives, or how far they were stimulated by private interests, is a difficult question to answer. At first sight it seems strange that anyone with private commercial interests should advocate the Company's exercising a monopoly of trade in Malabar. But it must be remembered that at this period the Bombay servants scarcely saw the Company as a body with interests distinct from their own. They and their relations and friends at Leadenhall Street were the Company, and they served each other's pockets, not the financial interests of distant shareholders. The time was shortly coming when tighter control from Whitehall and the reforms of successive governors-

---

[1] *Ibid.* 303. These proposals also appear in Charters and Treaties XI (on East India Commerce).

[2] Home Misc. CCCLXXVII, 1–3. This letter has no date or signature, but was written before 1792.

[3] *Ibid.* CCCLXXXVII, 809–15: an unsigned paper enclosed in a letter from Colonel Murray to Henry Dundas dated 3 September 1792.

general who were not servants of the Company, would create a division of interests between the Company and the private trader. But in 1792 a Company monopoly of trade meant an English monopoly of trade from which the private trader expected to benefit by the exclusion of the French and Dutch. In 1789 W. G. Farmer had suggested to James Sibbald, one of the biggest merchants at Bombay, that there was no reason why the Company should not attempt to engross the trade of the settlement and 'pick up twenty lacks of profit yearly instead of leaving them to a Crew of Parsees in whose welfare the state has no Interest and who on every occasion have plucked the Company without mercy'.[1] One can hardly imagine his writing in this way to a private merchant if the Company's monopoly had meant the merchant would be deprived of his trade. Similarly, Taylor's plans for a monopoly in Malabar were directed not against the English private trader, but against the French, Dutch and Imperialists at Mahé. If, in the name of the Company, the English took the ports and pepper countries, then the private trader could rely on his own position in the Company's service or the influence of his friends to see that he flourished and grew rich on trade.

Indeed, before Dundas received Captain Taylor's letters General Abercromby had already made determined efforts to secure the exclusive pepper trade in Malabar. In December 1791 he sent a circular to the rajas of Cartinaad, Cotiote and Chericul and to the Zamorin calling upon them 'in compliance with express engagements they had entered into with Government, that the Company should have the exclusive right to the whole of the trade of their countries, whether of pepper or of any other article of commerce'. He demanded that the rajas should issue immediate orders to this effect.[2] The English were following the policy of the Portuguese and Dutch in using political control to further a commercial monopoly. It was the competition at Mahé which was responsible for this extreme measure. Cornwallis had only envisaged 'advantageous privileges' of trade as the fruits of the political connexion[3] and Major Dow had visited the rajas of Cochin and Travancore to procure 'a preference to all others in the purchase of the pepper'.[4] But like the Dutch before them, the Company clung to a policy of

---

[1] Rylands English MSS, Melville Papers 686, 1465: W. G. Farmer to James Sibbald, 17 December 1789.
[2] *Malabar Report*, 95–6.   [3] See above, p. 58.   [4] See above, pp. 59–60.

restricted prices.[1] They would not pay more than Rs 130 while the merchants at Mahé were offering Rs 175 a candy.[2] In this situation, monopoly or the reduction of Mahé was the only answer.

The problem of enforcing a monopoly of trade raised the question of the Company's political status in Malabar. So far there was no peace treaty with Tipu, and so no ultimate definition of the Company's relationship with the Malabar powers. But hitherto the governor-general and the Bombay establishment had acted on the assumption that the rajas had recovered their independent political power, apart from an obligation to pay tribute. The Company had given some legal confirmation to this status when General Medows invested the Zamorin in August 1791 'with the sole management of all the countries heretofore included in the province of Calicut which are or may be conquered by the British troops'. Although this was for the duration of the war only, the Company promised at the peace to examine the title of the Zamorin and of the other rajas and Polygars to determine 'the rightful inheritor agreeably to established custom and then also the Peishcush to be paid to the Honourable Company...'[3] There was no suggestion that the Company intended to assume administrative power or that it wanted more than tribute.

But by January 1792 several voices were expressing doubts about the wisdom of this policy. Besides the problem of how to enforce a commercial monopoly on the Malabar rajas, the eruption of violence in the province appeared to threaten the very organisation of the pepper trade. From the beginning of 1791 several members of the Zamorin's family had been responsible for organising attacks on the Moplahs. Their object was vengeance for the suffering of the Nayars under Tipu's government.[4] The violence spread to other parts of the province, and in January 1792 the Tellicherry merchants, who were themselves Moplahs, warned the government of the effect on the pepper trade. They protested that their efforts to collect pepper had been frustrated by 'the unhappy jealousy which has so long subsisted between the two prevailing casts of Inhabitants of this country'.[5] The Tellicherry Board told

[1] A. R. Das Gupta, *Malabar in Asian Trade* (1967), 25. In the 1750s the Dutch were paying up to Rs 125 a candy.
[2] *Malabar Report*, 95–6.
[3] Logan, *Malabar* III, 87–8.
[4] *Malabar Report*, 64.
[5] BCP, range 414, LII, 51: Tellicherry to Bombay, 20 January 1792.

Bombay that the country was suffering from 'the most unpardonable violences, very prejudicial to the commerce of the country & the interests of society in general'. They had remonstrated with the rajas against the impunity with which the Nayars committed murders, robberies and other crimes of violence, against which the rajas took no action. The pepper dealers were afraid to send out their agents at the risk of their lives to buy pepper, and consequently supplies to the Company were very uncertain. Tellicherry was deeply concerned. The Board was sure that the outrages would continue until the Company or their agents were empowered to impose a more effective restraint on the lawless inhabitants and they determined to represent the situation in the strongest colours to the Bombay government and the governor-general. They declared their opinion that

the General good absolutely demands the interposition of the Company's authority & some strong & drastic measures must be adopted to establish good order & tranquility among a race of men professedly devoted to war and bloodshed & enraged with the recollection of past injuries & oppressions. It must be further remarked that the Moplahs, though considered by the Nairs as innovators & only established by right of conquest on the coast, yet as an extensive & mercantile body are certainly deserving of encouragement & protection as a useful race their rights ought the more to be protected...[1]

Such protection, Tellicherry pointed out, was as much in the interests of the Company as to 'the general comfort of the Natives'.

On 22 February 1792 the Company signed the preliminary articles of peace with Tipu Sultan. The terms did not specify which areas of Tipu's dominions were to form the half which he ceded to the Company and their allies,[2] and on 29 February Abercromby wrote to his colleagues at Bombay that he thought it probable Malabar would be restored to the Nayar rajas, 'Under the Company's protection...'[3] Even at this late stage it appears that the governor of Bombay, who was in the governor-general's confidence, did not envisage that the Company would assume direct political control in Malabar. But on 17 March, the day before the definitive treaty with Tipu was signed, Cornwallis wrote to Dundas to explain the meaning of the final terms. 'The Rajahs on that coast are not

[1] BCP, range 414, LII, 50–5.   [2] BSPP, range E, V, 183–4.
[3] *Ibid.* 202: Abercromby to Bombay, 29 February 1792.

independent, but now become our subjects, and if we can put them in some degree on the footing of the Bengal Zemindars, and prevent their oppressing the people under them, the commerce of that country in pepper, spices, etc. may become extremely advantageous to the Company.' The revenue, he pointed out, would also be a great help to Bombay.[1]

This sudden reversal of policy from considering the Malabar rajas as independent princes paying tribute, to the consideration of them as 'Bengal Zemindars' was a crucial decision in the development of the Bombay presidency. For the first time the Bombay servants were to be made rulers of a province. It was a decision, moreover, as unexpected as it was sudden. The only explanation is that Cornwallis acted in the Company's commercial interests. He was aware of the difficulties which the Company was experiencing in securing its pepper supplies, because of the competition from Mahé.[2] And he was informed by Tellicherry of the violent attacks which the rajas condoned against the Moplah merchants.[3] Tellicherry had pleaded with the Company to exercise political power for the sake of its commerce, and it appears that Cornwallis made the decision on these grounds.[4] He wrote to Abercromby on 23 March 1792:

I feel a peculiar satisfaction from knowing that you see as clearly as I do the importance of the acquisitions we have made by the late treaty on the Coast of Malabar. And that you are no less anxious than I am to introduce & establish, with as much dispatch as may be practicable a system for their future Government that shall be calculated to prevent internal dissentions amongst the Chiefs and to procure under a regular administration of justice, all Advantages to the Company, which their situation & valuable productions are capable of Affording both in revenue and Commerce.[5]

[1] PRO 30/11/151, f. 113–113v: Cornwallis to Dundas, 17 March 1792.
[2] See below, p. 70.
[3] See above, p. 68, and PRO 30/11/155, f. 210. Cornwallis told the Court of Directors on 5 April 1792 that 'the two great and inimical classes of the People the Nairs and Moplahs [were] almost at open war with each other'.
[4] Cf. BM Add. MSS 13,695, 143 (Duncan to Wellesley, 27 September 1798): 'there were strong reasons in corroboration of the purport of the recent Instructions for our assuming the sovereignty; the first Commissioners general Report of Oct. 1793 will I think sufficiently demonstrate were it only to be a more powerful Check on the ever-operating baneful & bloody feuds, between the two Classes of Hindus & Mopillas, which constitute the Population of the Province, in nearly equal numbers'.
[5] BSPP, range E, v, 253–5: Cornwallis to Abercromby, 23 March 1792.

He told Abercromby that the first essential was to establish peace and order and to make a temporary settlement with the rajas for the payment of one year's revenue in money or kind. Cornwallis promised that when he returned to Bengal he would draw up a plan for managing the commerce and revenues of the newly acquired territories and for the administration of justice in them by the Company's servants. He instructed Abercromby to appoint two commissioners from Bombay, who, with two from Bengal, would be responsible for investigating the resources and produce of the province and would report on the best means of governing it. His concern for the Company's commercial interests is further apparent in the orders he gave about Travancore. The Malabar commissioners should include that country's commerce in their enquiries and 'suggest whatever means may occur to them for securing the share of it to the Company, that former engagements, and still more the recent exertions in the Rajah's favor give them so good a right to expect'. And, more significantly, the commissioners were to reflect 'whether the illicit trade so detrimental to the Company's Interests which has long been carried on at Mahé, could be effectually prevented by our obtaining a tract of Country adjoining to that settlement, in Jaghir to the Company, in lieu of part of the Tribute of the proprietory Rajah...'[1]

Two days before Cornwallis sent these instructions to General Abercromby, the Bombay council, which was unaware that the peace had been signed, hastened to send a letter to Charles Malet in which they expressed their hope that he would use his influence to provide for the political and commercial interests of the presidency at the peace.[2] They also prepared to send information to Abercromby on their interests in 'a country valuable in every respect of situation produce revenue & commerce'. Contrary to their customary concerns they pointed out that if the Company possessed all the Malabar ports, Tipu could be cut off from French supplies and military stores. Whether this was purely a concern for the national interest or the result of Bombay's ambition to displace the French in that trade, one cannot say.[3] But that Bombay was chiefly interested in the commercial prospects of the province appears from the minute which the council sent to

[1] BSPP, range E, v, 255: Cornwallis to Abercromby, 23 March 1792.
[2] *Ibid.* 193–4: Bombay to Charles Malet, 21 March 1792.
[3] See above, p. 45.

Malet.[1] It was written by Mr Lewis, a former chief of Tellicherry. He described at length the Malabar kingdoms and the amount of pepper, sandalwood and cardamoms which each produced. He then submitted a plan 'to make these Princes Territories as beneficial as possible...always supposing however that the Malabar princes are to be heavily tributary to us'. He proposed that the rajas should deliver quantities of pepper at low prices in payment of their tribute and that the Company should have the preference in buying the surplus. Furthermore he advised the annexation of the Corengotte district, 'as we could thereby in a great measure deprive the French and others trading under them at Mahé from being supplied with pepper and cardamoms'. Cochin and Travancore should be made to provide the Company with pepper, the Zamorin had great resources of timber and cardamoms and Coorg could supply cardamoms and sandalwood.[2] The minute was written too late to influence the peace, but its sentiments were echoed when Lord Cornwallis congratulated the Directors on securing territory which promised to open 'sources of Commerce in Pepper, Cardamams, Teak, Sandal Wood etc. that may be looked upon as a great importance both to the Company and to the Nation'.[3]

It was left to General Abercromby to see that the Company extricated itself, in a rather tortuous piece of reasoning, from the promises which had been made to the Malabar princes. Most of the rajas believed that the agreements which they had made with the Company at the outbreak of the war had restored them to independent power. But as the governor-general had indicated 'interior arrangements practicable only where the Sovereignty lay', Abercromby had to do his best in interpreting the treaties which, he declared, 'were not as comprehensive as could now be wished. They provide for the Emancipation of the Country from Tipu but do not as clearly express its dependence on us'. This, said Abercromby, had to be taken as implied, but he counselled the newly appointed Malabar commissioners to use mild language with the chiefs and to claim tribute in return for protection. He reminded them that the Company had one powerful argument on their side. The rajas could not very well insist on a literal interpretation of the treaties when they had broken 'the most essential Article—The

[1] BSPP, range E, v, 204: 27 March 1792.   [2] *Ibid.* 206–13: 30 March 1792.
[3] PRO 30/11/155, f. 204: Cornwallis to the Court of Directors, 5 April 1792.

exclusive trade of the Country'. Most of their pepper had gone to Mahé. Abercromby concluded his instructions by pointing out that it would be more advantageous to the Company if the tribute were paid in pepper, sandalwood and cardamoms.[1] Sovereignty and commerce went hand in hand in Malabar.

The Bombay presidency had survived. It had overcome the dangers which had threatened its existence since 1784. Bankruptcy, the embargo on the spice trade, the military threat from Tipu and Cornwallis's determination to reduce its status to a factory had menaced it in turn. But it had survived and extended its territory because of the importance of its commerce. Dundas had saved the presidency because he was convinced of its importance to the China trade as well of its military value. And Cornwallis had decided on the acquisition of Malabar for the same reason. It was, too, because disorder threatened the spice trade that the decision was made to assume full political and administrative powers in the province. How this power was used in the interests of commerce leads to a study of the Bombay government's administration of Malabar.

[1] BSPP, range E, v, 340–4: Abercromby to Major Alexander Dow and W. G. Farmer, 21 April 1792.

CHAPTER 4

THE PEPPER TRADE AND THE ADMINISTRATION OF MALABAR, 1792–1800

Between April and December 1792 the province of Malabar was under the exclusive control of civil servants of the Bombay presidency. This period, although short, is important not only because it set the pattern for the subsequent administration of the province, but because it shows clearly some of the factors which were shaping Bombay's policy quite independently of Bengal. The policy, which in letters to the Court of Directors or to the Bengal government was expressed in terms of the national interest, can in Malabar be traced to private and self-interested motives. For the first time the roots of imperialism begin to appear. What slowly clarified in Henry Dundas's mind and passed from him to Cornwallis and Wellesley as a coherent policy, grew from the network of private commercial interests, often crossing and conflicting, which flourished on the west coast of India among the friends and acquaintances of David Scott.[1] Fortunately for the long-term interests of the Company on the west coast and for the territories they were to rule, those same roots were capable of producing a Charles Malet and an Alexander Walker, whose vision was not guided by the prospect of retirement with a nabob's wealth to Tunbridge Wells or Cheltenham.

William Gamul Farmer and Alexander Dow were the two members of the Bombay presidency who were appointed by General Abercromby to serve on the Malabar commission. Neither of them was peculiarly fitted by talents or experience for the post, a reflexion perhaps more on the calibre of the senior servants Abercromby had to choose from, than on the governor himself. Dow had been the military commander at Tellicherry since 1789, without distinguishing himself, but Farmer had no experience of the province. His ambition had been the lucrative chiefship of Surat

---

[1] Cf. Barun Dé, 'Henry Dundas and the Government of India, 1773–1801', 432, 439.

and he complained bitterly when his junior, John Griffith, was appointed to it over his head.[1] Farmer's career of almost thirty years in the Bombay presidency had brought him only the residency at Fort Victoria and the chiefship of Tannah, neither of which were particularly desirable rewards.[2] After the bitterness of losing Surat, the Malabar appointment came to him with prospects of power and emolument which, until that time, Surat alone had dangled before the hungry eyes of the Bombay servants. Farmer was not alone in hastening southwards. Malabar was soon to have the reputation of making its civil servants as 'rich as Crœsus', for money earned interest rates of 15, 20 or 30 per cent a year.[3]

On 22 April 1792 the Bombay commissioners met at Tellicherry to discuss the task which was entrusted to them. They had three objects to guide them in their administration of the province. Cornwallis had left instructions that they were to make a temporary agreement with the rajas to deliver one year's revenue to the Company, and they were to consider the means of transferring all judicial power in the province into the hands of the Company's servants. In addition the commissioners were to discover how best to enforce a monopoly of the pepper trade in the province which as far as possible was to include the Travancore produce.[4]

These instructions were precise and scarcely admitted of alternatives. But at their first official meeting Farmer and Dow recorded their opposition to the policy of the governor-general. They protested first against the plan of introducing British administrators into the province. Tipu, they pointed out, had never fully subjugated Malabar and had left behind no machinery of government or trained officials which the Company could use in its own administration. There were not even records to rely on, as according to Tipu they had all been destroyed. The rajas had returned to their countries determined to reassert their old authority and it was unlikely that they would willingly give the commissioners the information they needed. It was conceivable that they would do everything to obstruct the commissioners' enquiries and would falsify their revenue returns so that their tribute to the Company

[1] NLS, Melville MSS 1072, ff. 60–63v: W. G. Farmer to George Johnstone, Fort Victoria, 21 February 1787.
[2] Personal Records II, f. 83.
[3] Manuscript copies of Forbes's correspondence from Castle Newe: Charles Forbes to William Harvey, 25 November 1794.
[4] See above, pp. 69–70.

should be small. In these circumstances, Farmer and Dow insisted, it was essential that the Company should maintain the power of the rajas and leave the administration of the country in their hands.[1]

Cornwallis's plan of making a temporary agreement with the rajas suited these views, and at Calicut the commissioners lost no time in vesting the raja of Cartinaad with all the powers of government in his country for one year, subject only to the control of the Company if he abused this authority by oppressing the inhabitants. The commissioners further agreed that the raja and the Company would each appoint two officials to estimate the revenues and the size of the pepper crop. The raja promised to deliver his own share of the pepper to the Company in payment of his tribute, and the Company claimed the right to appoint merchants who would act as agents to buy up the rest of the pepper produce for them, with the help of government protection.[2] The ease with which they concluded this agreement gave the commissioners greater confidence, and they repeated their demand that instead of attempting to force the Bengal system of government on Malabar, the Company should make the power of the raja the pivot of its administration in the province.[3] The agreement with the raja of Cartinaad was in their intention 'a trial how far the authority of the Rajah can subsist consistently with the good and security of the subjects' and they went on to explain in detail why the Company should leave the powers of government in the hands of these princes. The Company, they maintained, was bound in the first place by the promises which they had made to the rajas at the outbreak of the war to restore them to at least some of their old authority. But secondly they insisted that this policy provided the only hope which the Company had of establishing order and prosperity in the province. Unless the Company won the loyalty and friendship of the rajas the province would be plunged again into the chaos and rebellion which had defeated Tipu.[4]

In support of their views Farmer and Dow brought forward arguments which were based on fundamental criticisms of the Company's system of government in India. They declared that the rajas would rule the province far more effectively than the English

[1] BSPP, range E, v, 365–9: minute of Farmer and Dow, Tellicherry, 22 April 1792.
[2] *Ibid.* 371–4: minute of Farmer and Dow, 28 April 1792.   [3] *Ibid.* 374–6.
[4] *Ibid.*

could even hope to do for some time to come. This was not only because the Company was temporarily short of trained administrators and was inadequately informed about the province. Their criticisms went deeper. In their opinion,

if the power of the Raja is destroyed the interior protection and defence of the Inhabitants is at an end—Experience proves that with the mildest and most humanised Inhabitants the legal powers of the British Government are so much too weak that our Police is a Mockery and neither Person or Property is safe even in Bombay whilst at Poonah by the terrors of instant and certain Punishment no disturbance is heard. Where there is no principle in the human mind but fear we know that amongst the most subjected People the terror of a Despotick Government is requisite...

In Malabar, therefore, where according to them even the labourers in the fields were armed and murder was a daily occurrence, the commissioners did not hesitate to pronounce 'that the despotick Powers of the Rajah and the prompt and unimpeded exercise of them are and for a long time will be alone efficient for the due protection of life and property'.[1]

It is possible to see the commissioners' arguments as an enlightened enunciation of the principles of indirect rule or as a sound practical approach to the problem of governing a lawless province. One of these interpretations would be acceptable if the commissioners had based their conclusions on greater experience, and if they had not coupled their political proposals with a more radical economic one which again challenged the express policy of Lord Cornwallis and suggested a revolution in the East India Company's affairs.[2] The Company, they proposed, should give up their plans to monopolise the pepper trade and should stop considering pepper in a commercial light. The attempt at monopoly had failed and would continue to fail because the private traders at Mahé offered prices for pepper far in advance of those given by the Company. Murdock Brown was engrossing the trade of the province. While Tellicherry with great difficulty scratched together only 700 candies of pepper, five large ships were laden at Mahé.[3] The Company could not hope to outbid the Mahé traders

---

[1] BSPP, range E, v, 374–6: minute of Farmer and Dow, 28 April 1792.
[2] *Ibid.* 377–8.
[3] Brown declared later that the average annual exports of pepper from Mahé between 1789 and 1793 exceeded 4,000 candies (BCP, range 414, LXV: a report from Murdock Brown to the Malabar commissioners, 1 September 1799).

as it was burdened in its commercial dealings by the heavy annual cost of freight and factory charges, whereas the merchants at Mahé paid only customs dues and were able to finance their purchases by importing goods for which they were paid in pepper. For these reasons they could afford to pay much higher prices than the Company which had no import trade of any value. When the Malabaris could get Rs 175 a candy for their pepper at Mahé no threats or coercion could make them sell it to the Company at Rs 130. The commissioners pressed in conclusion that 'since... the charges of the Company will not bear a Competition on a Mercantile footing it might be expedient to consider Pepper merely in the light of a remittance to Europe of the surplus revenues of India...'[1] The Company should give up its policy of enforcing a monopoly by coercion and pay higher prices instead.

These proposals challenged the very basis of the policy which the Company had hitherto pursued in Malabar. They were opposed to all the intentions of the Court of Directors and the governor-general, and were put forward by the commissioners before they had attempted to carry out their instructions. Even so, it would be possible to see them as a response to the economic realities of the situation and as a courageous attempt to modernise the Company's thinking, were it not for one significant piece of evidence. Writing in 1799 during the course of an enquiry into the pepper trade, Murdock Brown expressed his opinions on the commercial policy which the Company had pursued after their acquisition of the province. He declared that when the Company became the sovereign their interests demanded 'a total change of the principles hitherto adopted in their mercantile transactions in the article of pepper. It was not now their interest to reduce, but to raise the price as much as possible so long as there were foreign competitors to purchase it'.[2] The Company, he insisted, should have looked to the revenues of the province to reimburse them for the higher price they had to pay for pepper, and by these means defeated the competition of foreign merchants. Brown then went on to say,

Soon after the late Mr Farmer came as one of the Commissioners to settle the affairs of the Province, he asked me how the Merchants of

---

[1] BSPP, range E, v, 377–8: minute of Farmer and Dow, 28 April 1792.
[2] BCP, range 414, LXV, 437–8: Murdock Brown to the Malabar commissioners, 1 September 1799.

Mahé managed to draw so great a proportion of the Pepper produce to that place...I then explained to him my opinion on the subject & though much against my own interest at that time endeavoured to convince him of the truth of what I have above said, that it was the interest of the Company instead of endeavouring to depress, to raise the price of Pepper as high as possible, *not, however, with the intention of taking more than a certain portion*, but to oblige all others to pay for it as dear as possible.[1]

Whatever Murdock Brown did it was never against his own interest as events will show.

The extraordinary point is not the soundness or otherwise of Brown's argument but that Farmer who was entrusted with the settlement of Malabar in the Company's interests should consult and urge on his superiors the views of a man who had been Tipu's ally in the embargo which he had laid on English trade. It was Brown who at the very time when Farmer met him was chiefly responsible for receiving the rajas' pepper which should have gone to the Company. For Farmer to discuss the Company's pepper policy with him and then to reproduce Brown's opinions as his own was a circumstance which was highly suspicious in the state of the relations which then existed between Mahé and the Company in Malabar. Apart from this instance of a connexion between Farmer and Brown there followed others which show that the Imperial Consul had considerable influence with Farmer.[2] When a former director of the Company, Walter Ewer, visited the Malabar coast in 1797, he threw some light on the nature of Brown's association with members of the Bombay establishment.[3] Ewer reported of him ''Tis said he was concerned in the War before last, with some Merchants of Bombay, in Supplying the Enemy with Provisions or Stores; this is not so much to his Discredit as to theirs; & I only introduce it, because it is said to have given him considerable Interest, both at that Place & in England'.[4] David

---

[1] My italics.

[2] Personal Records II, 17–31: W. G. Farmer on Murdock Brown, 5 January 1798.

[3] Walter Ewer was introduced into the Court of Directors by Henry Dundas in 1790. He was a member of the City interest, but was disqualified in 1795; Philips, *The East India Company*, 62n. and 336. He then went out to India, probably for financial reasons, but it was as Henry Dundas's friend that he made his reports on Malabar and Bombay. For his career in Sumatra see J. Bastin, *The Native Policies of Sir Stamford Raffles in Java and Sumatra* (Oxford, 1957), 80–2.

[4] Home Misc. CDXXXVIII, 148–50: W. Ewer to Henry Dundas, 17 July 1797.

Scott was certainly Brown's friend and this connexion gave him powerful support in England.[1] There is no evidence to show that Farmer himself ever had commercial dealings with Brown, but he was making his fortune by lending money at respondentia, that is by lending it to merchants for the purchase of ships' cargoes, and in 1789 he had lent as much as a lac of rupees in this way.[2] When Farmer was the supervisor of the province Ewer thought him guilty of profiteering from the minting of Malabar coins from which prominent Bombay merchants also made considerable sums.[3] But there is no means of knowing whether these private interests involved Farmer in any partnership with Brown or predisposed him to propose a policy favourable to the private merchant. He might innocently have adopted Brown's views. The only hint which suggests otherwise is the fact that Farmer was later to deny that he had ever met Brown before the arrival of Jonathan Duncan in the province in December 1792.[4] But Brown's own statement and the details of Farmer's minute of 28 April, which show considerable knowledge of the Mahé trade besides corresponding with Brown's commercial ideas and interests, point to this denial being false. If the association was purely for the benefit of the Company it seems strange that Farmer should have lied about it. His subsequent relationship with Brown after unmistakable proof of the ways in which Brown was damaging the Company's commercial interests, makes it improbable that he innocently adopted the latter's ideas and supported him from public-spirited motives.[5]

Whatever was the nature of the association there seems little doubt that the policy which Farmer put forward for the administration of Malabar was based on Brown's ideas, and that it was designed to leave the rajas in effective control of the province and to encourage the Company to drop their plan of a pepper monopoly. Why Brown should advocate this policy is a further question on which there is no clear evidence. It is the more surprising as it

[1] See above, p. 55.
[2] Rylands English MSS, Melville papers 686, 1467: W. G. Farmer to Holmes, 17 December 1789.
[3] Home Misc. CDXXXVIII, 197–9 and 118–20: W. Ewer to Henry Dundas, 10 May 1797.
[4] BSPP, range E, 533: Farmer to Bombay, 30 October 1793.
[5] Alexander Walker said of Farmer that his 'integrity was doubtful'. Harvard Melville MSS, IOL microfilm reel 650: Walker's report on Malabar, 24 August 1799.

79

was based on serious misapprehensions of the position of the rajas. The power which Farmer and Dow ascribed to the chieftains was not theirs by right in Malabar society. Before the Mysorean conquest the Malabar rajas had no political and military power based on a regular land revenue. They had a customary share in the produce of their demesne lands like the Nayars and could call on the latter for military service. They had also certain judicial rights, but unlike the far stronger ruler of Travancore they had no military power independent of the Nayars and no rights of taxation.[1] It was the Mysorean conquerors who first established a strong centralised government over Malabar within modern times. Haidar and Tipu assessed the whole country and levied taxes which fell exclusively on that share of the land produce which belonged to the landholders, the Nayars and rajas. The percentage taken by the conquerors varied from 10 per cent on wet lands in some areas to 100 per cent on garden lands in all south Malabar where the landholder's share was entirely expropriated.[2] Sometimes pepper was taken in kind.[3] In the south the landholders were forced to flee and, as rebellion and repression succeeded the conquest, most of the northern rajas and Nayars followed them into exile in Travancore. When the rajas returned to their countries after the Company's victory they had acquired an added prestige as leaders of the rebellion against Tipu, but they were not entitled to take over Tipu's system of revenue and administration against which the Nayars had revolted. The rajas could cooperate with the British in exercising their judicial powers, although these were not unlimited as Farmer and Dow asserted,[4] and in supplying pepper from their own demesne lands, but they could not levy any general taxes to provide a tribute either in pepper or money for the Company.

Murdock Brown had lived on intimate terms with Malabar society over a long period, and he must have been fully aware that the rajas did not possess the power which the commissioners ascribed to them. If he was responsible for urging that administrative power should be concentrated in their hands he was advocating a revolution in Malabar society. This is not unlikely as he stood to profit by it. What he had to fear, with perhaps many Bombay

[1] Logan, *Malabar* I, 599–605. [2] *Ibid*. 608–9.
[3] *Ibid*. 629.
[4] *Ibid*. 172–4.

servants, was the introduction into Malabar of the kind of administration which Cornwallis was establishing in Bengal: an administration where the civil servants were denied the opportunities of
private trade, where corruption and profiteering were being purged
away, and where the most valuable commodities like opium were a
government monopoly. For the Bombay servants the acquisition
of Malabar meant their arrival in the promised land. After decades
of impoverishment, debt and failure, they had acquired a province
rich in opportunity. If, as Cornwallis seemed to intend, the Bengal
system of government were to prevail their fortunes would remain
unmade, and a pepper monopoly enforced by an efficient bureau-
cracy would end their own commercial concerns and Murdock
Brown's reign as the principal merchant in the province. If the
Company left all administrative powers to the rajas and looked to
tribute instead of to commerce for their profits, Brown's position,
and that of his associates, would remain secure.

Although for these or other reasons the commissioners declared
their opposition to the governor-general's policy they could not
openly flout his instructions. Cornwallis had ordered them to see if
the Company could stop the smuggling to Mahé by obtaining a
tract of territory next to it, and for this reason the nambyars or
ruling landowners of Randaterra and Irvenaad were not restored to
their possessions. The Company took over the direct administration of the territory and its revenues and put them under the
control of Robert Rickards of the Tellicherry establishment.[1]
This measure did not stop the smuggling. The more difficult it
became, the higher the price of pepper climbed at Mahé and so the
greater became the profits and the incentive.[2]

This did not favour the private commercial interests of all the
Bombay civil servants. The rivalries of trade like ambitions for
office divided what was to the outsider the solidarity of the Bombay
interest. Whatever Farmer's relations were with Murdock Brown,
by no means all of the Bombay servants in the Malabar province
had favourable feelings towards him. Brown was too successful in
engrossing the pepper trade for that to be so. John Agnew, the
commercial resident at Calicut, and Robert Taylor, the chief of
Tellicherry, both of whom traded in pepper on their own account,

[1] *Malabar Report*, 62.
[2] BCP, range 414, LXV, 435: Murdock Brown to the Malabar commissioners,
1 September 1799.

had every reason to fear Brown's operations.[1] While Brown offered high prices at Mahé all the English private merchants had to pay high prices for their own supplies if they were to get any pepper at all. If the competition from Mahé and Murdock Brown were removed, those company servants with private trading concerns which were not connected with the French settlement stood to gain enormously. John Agnew, who was later to describe Murdock Brown as his 'bitterest foe',[2] wrote on 11 May 1792 to Robert Taylor warning him that a ship from Mahé under Danish colours had arrived at Calicut with the intention of re-establishing the Danish factory there. Agnew gave his opinion that it was done at Murdock Brown's instigation and was an attempt to extend his field of operations. The Company, declared Agnew, must watch Brown carefully and 'attend particularly to his Machinations & false assertions'.[3] Indeed, some information which Farmer received from the raja of Cartinaad appears to have made the commissioner think so too. On 17 May Farmer reported on the information of the raja that Murdock Brown and the French traders had shut up their rice granaries and were refusing to let supplies into the province. Malabar relied on Tipu's port of Mangalore for considerable supplies of rice, and since Tipu's prohibition of trade with the English, which he still continued after the peace, the rice trade had been in the hands of the Mahé traders, particularly Murdock Brown. Brown's action was therefore a serious threat to the economy and the revenues of the province, particularly as the shortage of grain in Bengal and Madras meant that little could be imported to supply the deficiency. Farmer interpreted it in one way: it was Brown's method of trying to monopolise the whole of the pepper trade for himself. Brown could either force the Malabaris to take their pepper to him by threatening them with scarcity of rice unless they complied, or he could use his control over the supplies to offer rice to the Malabaris at a cheaper rate than the Company.[4] Farmer urged the Bombay government to bring pressure to bear on Tipu to open his ports and trade to the Company.

[1] Rylands English MSS, Melville Papers 670, 30: John Agnew to Henry Dundas, 4 April 1797 and Personal Records II, 261-3.
[2] See below, p. 109.
[3] BSPP, range E, v, 418-9: John Agnew to Robert Taylor, Calicut, 11 May 1792.
[4] *Ibid.* 400-2: W. G. Farmer to Bombay, 17 May 1792.

Whatever mutual interests might have bound Farmer and Brown together on the commissioner's first arrival on the coast, the bond seems to have been shaken by this evidence of Brown's pursuit of his exclusive self-interest. If Brown followed this course the private as well as the public concerns of the Bombay servants would be defeated and they would reap nothing from the conquest of Malabar. Perhaps it is significant that shortly after reporting Brown's conduct to Bombay the commissioners began to change their opinions about the administration of Malabar. On 27 May Farmer gave a detailed criticism of the Zamorin's government and declared that it should not be restored to power. He thought it feudal and oppressive, guilty of violence against the Moplahs, and likely to oppose the continuance of the Company's authority in the country.[1] This was a marked change from the opinions he and Dow had expressed in their minute of 28 April, although he still did not see his way to a speedy establishment of the Company's administration. But by 9 June Dow was repeating Farmer's criticisms of the Zamorin's government, and he declared that if it were restored to power a civil war with the Moplahs would follow. But prominent among Dow's accusations was the fact that the Zamorin smuggled pepper to Mahé. If his power were restored,

The produce of the Country so much desired for the Company would be promised but for a small encrease of Price would be secretly carried to Mahé as was experienced this year...the same total want of good faith and performance has prevailed in all they have promised and we have reason to believe from their avidity to benefit by the present Hour regardless of future consequences that it always will prevail.

The Company would have to make a settlement with the Zamorin and rajas for one year but Dow looked forward to the time when 'our Instruments the Rajahs may be laid aside and pensioned as they have been at Bengal and for this reason the Agreements with them should be only temporary'.[2] Two days later Dow went further. The northern rajas, he declared, were themselves pepper merchants and had sold their pepper to private traders and foreigners instead of fulfilling their obligations to the Company. For this reason, he maintained, the Company would be justified in

---

[1] *Malabar Report*, 78–9.
[2] BSPP, range E, v, 446–62: Major Dow to Bombay, 9 June 1792.

dispossessing them.[1] The change of policy, though sudden, was complete.

The commissioners had discovered that if the Company left the government of the province to the rajas neither the private interests of its servants nor the treasury at Leadenhall Street would benefit from the pepper trade of Malabar. The judicial powers and influence of the rajas and their position as landowners gave them considerable control of the pepper supplies. As landowners, the rajas received pepper from the cultivators in payment of rent and in return for money advanced to them to provide food and the necessities of life. They used their power and influence to purchase at low prices the greater part of what was left. In this the rajas worked closely with the merchants of the province, who bought the pepper from them and disposed of it to foreign traders, Arabs and merchants from Gujarat and the north. The merchants also collected supplies in small parcels from individual cultivators to whom they advanced money, and who were not under the direct influence of the rajas.[2] Between them the rajas and the merchants of Malabar, almost all of whom were Moplahs, held the pepper trade in a tight grip. And while the European merchants had a base at Mahé and competed with the English company for supplies the Malabar rajas and merchants made large profits. Moreover, it was obvious that Mahé was far more successful than the Company in engrossing the trade, and that Murdock Brown was taking measures to increase his share. Shortly after the news that Brown had closed his rice granaries Robert Taylor reported from Tellicherry that the French and the Imperial Consul were making attempts to claim the overlordship of the Corengotte district, despite the terms of the peace treaty which put it under English control. This, Taylor declared, was all part of Brown and the Mahé traders' scheme 'to establish settlements in the Malabar Country which is become a matter of so much more consequence now that the country no longer appertains to Tippoo, from whom they constantly received the preference in the way of Trade in the purchase of its productions...'[3]

In response, the Malabar commissioners determined to tap two

---

[1] Home Misc. DLXXXV, 76–7: 'Proceedings of Mr W. Gamul Farmer & Majr Alex. Dow, Malabar Commissioners', 11 June 1792.

[2] BCP, range 414, LVI, 663–7: J. Stevens to Bombay, 6 May 1795.

[3] BSPP, range E, v, 499–504: Robert Taylor to Bombay, Tellicherry, 21 June 1792.

of the richest sources of Mahé's supply, Cochin and Travancore. On 8 July, Major Dow set off on an expedition to the south, with the object of securing a preference for the Company in the pepper trade of Cochin and Travancore.[1] On 21 July, Dow reported that the raja of Travancore had contracted to supply large quantities of pepper to Mahé, and the Cochin raja had already sent 200 candies to the French settlement. Dow estimated that if this traffic to Mahé could be stopped the Company could send six complete cargoes of pepper to England at a profit of £40,000 on each.[2] Although the Travancore raja was warned against trading with Murdock Brown and other foreigners, Farmer was doubtful whether this would have any effect, as it was unlikely that gratitude would influence the raja's commercial dealings when the menace of Tipu had gone.[3] At Cochin Dow had no success at all. He estimated that the country produced from 2,500 to 3,000 candies of pepper, but the raja and his ministers pretended that it yielded only 100 candies, and the raja's subjects were forbidden under pain of death to give Dow any further information.[4]

These fresh failures indicated that a new policy towards the rajas was necessary. Farmer began at the court of the Zamorin. With some perception he discovered that the position of the Zamorin's chief minister, Shamnauth, was increasingly threatened by private enemies at court. Using this knowledge he offered Shamnauth the bribe of the Company's support if the minister would secure the Zamorin's pepper at a cheap rate for the Company. Farmer also hinted that the Zamorin's tribute might be reduced provided the Company received his pepper.

The Argument with regard to the Tribute he seemed to feel very much ad hominem with regard to his Durbar and I further observed to him that in this Durbar he had many Enemies whose efforts to his prejudice would be useless if by making himself the Instrument of so desirable an object he thus recommended himself to the English and became the Karricar of the Company.[5]

The method was effective and Farmer got his Instrument.

---

[1] Home Misc. DLXXXV, 128–9: 'Proceedings of Mr W. Gamul Farmer and Maj. Alex. Dow, Malabar Commissioners', 8 July 1792.
[2] *Ibid.* 160–1: Major Dow's minute which he sent to Cornwallis, 21 July 1792.
[3] BSPP, range E, v, 604–6: W. G. Farmer to Bombay, 14 August 1792.
[4] *Malabar Report*, 106–7.
[5] BSPP, range E, v, 718–21: W. G. Farmer to Bombay, 6 September 1792.

Shamnauth offered to deliver pepper from the southern part of the province to the Company at Rs 100 a candy by using the Zamorin's officers to collect it at the vines. To encourage the further planting of vines Farmer agreed with Shamnauth to free them from taxes for seven years. Farmer was jubilant at the success of his methods. He wrote off to the Bombay government,

If the Pepper can thus be secured at the Vine by means of the officers of Government and at so low a price as one hundred without any oppression to the people it will in future be a very great object to the Company and render this Coast a very valuable acquisition both in a territorial and Commercial light and be more effectual in preventing the interference of Foreigners than any other mode whatever...[1]

In this way the struggle for pepper was drawing the commissioners more and more to advocate the intervention of the Company in the administration of Malabar. Farmer saw the agreement with Shamnauth for collecting the pepper at the vine as an experiment for the time when the Company's own revenue officers would replace those of the Zamorin.[2] This was very different from the view he had expressed in April. Robert Taylor and Major Dow were urging the necessity of offering a price higher than the Company's limit of Rs 130, but at the same time Dow asked for one or two gun-boats to cruise in Travancore waters to compel the raja to fulfil his contract with the Company. He recommended that the Company should also enforce an embargo on trade with Travancore until the raja carried out his contract.[3] By September this new policy of intervention had matured into a scheme for enforcing a complete monopoly of all the pepper grown in the province. The time for delicacy in dealings with the rajas was over. The commissioners decided that in the interests of the pepper monopoly the Company must intervene and exercise power. In Farmer's words

The most repeated experience having evinced the Mercantile impracticability of engrossing the Mallabar pepper, under the formidable rivalry in Point of price which we have to contend with from foreign Nations, there seems no mode left but to exert the influence we now possess as sovereigns of the country, which will in time equally advance our Revenues & our Commerce.[4]

[1] BSPP, range E, v, 718–21: W. G. Farmer to Bombay, 6 September 1792.
[2] *Ibid.* 721.
[3] BCP, range 414, LII, 330–3: Dow to Bombay, 12 September 1792.
[4] *Ibid.* 327–8: Extracts of a meeting held in the Chericul country on 30 Septem-

In the interests of trade the Company was finally led to exercise its sovereign rights in Malabar.

The northern rajas, the most important pepper producers, were told bluntly that all the rights of sovereignty which Tipu had exercised were transferred to the Company, and that henceforth the rajas could act only as agents of the Company.[1] Therefore, if the commissioners

perceived that the produce of their Country went in Aid of the commerce of the French they would attribute it to some vice in the administration of the Rajahs, and direct that the Collection of the Revenues with every other Circumstance of Government should be taken from the Rajahs and Conducted immediately by their own Servants as practised in Bengal and other Parts.[2]

Under this threat they forced the northern rajas to agree to a new system, whereby all the pepper which was grown in their countries was collected at the vine and delivered to the Company. This meant that instead of the Company's receiving half of the total produce in revenue, which allowed the rajas to sell the other half (as well as what they fraudulently withheld of the Company's share) at Mahé for high prices, the Company bought every grain which the province produced at the rate of Rs 100 a candy. It was the system which Farmer had first devised with the cooperation of Shamnauth at Calicut, but in the case of the northern rajas the commissioners were dealing with far stronger and more independent princes whose revenues depended to a large extent on the sale of their pepper. For the first time the Company claimed a total monopoly. Pepper not bound for the Company's warehouses was contraband, and any merchant found carrying it would be expelled from the province.[3] It was a system which the commissioners themselves declared was 'totally adverse to the Interests of the Rajahs'.[4] They were to receive a price for their pepper which was Rs 60 to 70 a candy less than they could get at Mahé.

This meant that strong measures were necessary to enforce the

---

ber 1792 between W. G. Farmer and William Page. The minutes were sent to Bombay on 4 October 1792.

[1] BRP, range 366, XIV, 193: W. G. Farmer and William Page to Robert Taylor, 31 October 1792.

[2] BCP, range 414, LII, 325: extracts of a meeting held in the Chericul country on 30 September 1792 between W. G. Farmer and William Page.

[3] *Ibid.* 416: Bombay to the Malabar commissioners, 7 November 1792.

[4] BRP, range 366, XIV, 191: W. G. Farmer and William Page to Robert Taylor, 31 October 1792.

system. Besides the threat of depriving the rajas of the government of their kingdoms and of expelling those merchants from the province who were found guilty of smuggling, the commissioners imposed penalties of Rs 400 a candy for any deliveries short of the assessments. But they went further to lay down regulations which were the first step towards bringing the administration of the province under the Company's control. The rajas could not appoint revenue officers without the permission of the Company, and the Company's own officers were to join those employed by the rajas in making the assessments of the pepper crop.[1] In the case of the raja of Cotiote whom the commissioners thought 'weak, ignorant, and unfit for Business', they reserved the right of appointing officials of their own to collect his pepper.[2] Cotiote was the country which the commissioners found 'beyond all others in the province of Malabar abounds with pepper vines, the very jungles being...replenished therewith'.[3] Finally the commissioners proposed that another battalion of troops and armed cruisers should be sent to the Malabar coast to prevent further smuggling to Mahé. The Company's or the Bombay servants' commercial interests were bringing administrative powers into being. It was not primarily Bengal ideas about administration or abstract principles of government which decided that British officials and not the Malabar rajas were to rule the province. The period in which Bombay had exclusive control of Malabar suggests that the presidency's imperialism was the offspring of its private trade.

Nevertheless, the commissioners' plan for monopolising the pepper of the province acquired some support from Lord Cornwallis's instructions to the two Bengal commissioners, Jonathan Duncan and Charles Boddam, who were about to take up their duties in Malabar. The governor-general expressed his wish that as far as possible the revenues of the province might be received in pepper 'taken at a fair Market Valuation, instead of Money Payments; leaving whatever proportion cannot be secured in this Way, to be purchased by the Company's Commercial Agents on the Spot' according to the regulations of the Bengal commercial department. The commissioners were also ordered to turn their attention to Travancore and to secure for the Company as large a share of that

---

[1] BCP, range 366, XIV, 191: W. G. Farmer and William Page to Robert Taylor, 31 October 1792.
[2] *Ibid.*   [3] *Malabar Report*, 175–6.

country's pepper trade as possible.[1] Pepper was also high on the Court of Directors' demands to the Bombay government. The Court expressed its anxiety about the supplies as the price of pepper was 'more than Ordinarily high' in England. In reply the Bombay government gave its reasons for hoping that the new regulations would enable them to send large consignments of pepper and cardamoms to England.[2]

But the Bengal commissioners were to find when they arrived in Malabar in December 1792 that such hopes were not easily realised. They even found it impossible to get adequate information about the country as the rajas forbade their subjects to tell them anything. Accordingly, on 2 January 1793 Charles Boddam declared that the only way of making the new acquisition of territory 'very beneficial to the Company both in a point of Revenue and Commerce, by putting a stop to the extortions and enormities which are said to exist throughout the Country, and give general Satisfaction and encouragement to the inhabitants...' was by appointing civil servants from Bombay to take over the collection of revenue and the administration of justice.[3] That this course was essential if the Company's interests were to be upheld was emphasised by the rajas' failure to deliver their pepper to the Company within the time allotted to them. The commissioners gave a warning of six days before imposing fines of Rs 100 a candy for all short deliveries and declared that they would consider all who had sent their pepper to Mahé instead of to the Company to have thereby forfeited their future claim to the Company's protection, and that in the permanent arrangements for the settlement of the country which they were then making they would pass them by as totally unworthy of the Company's confidence.[4]

There was no serious division of opinion between the Bombay and the Bengal commissioners. The latter were predisposed by their own experience and the views of Cornwallis to introduce the Bengal system of government into Malabar. The Bombay men might have fought against it but experience had shown them that neither the Company's nor their own private trade could survive

[1] BRP, range 366, XIV, 210: Cornwallis to Duncan and Boddam, 16 November 1792.
[2] Letters received from Bombay X, 101, 24 December 1792.
[3] BRP, range 366, XV, 51–2: minute of Charles Boddam, 2 January 1793.
[4] BCP, range 414, LIII, 42–3: letter from the Malabar commissioners to Robert Taylor, collector-general for the northern districts, 28 January 1793.

unless they took over the full powers of government in the province. They had no difficulty, therefore, in agreeing on a system of government for Malabar. Under the leadership of Jonathan Duncan who had established himself in Cornwallis's favour first as a revenue expert and then as the resident at Benares,[1] they decided to divide the province into two administrative areas, each under a superintendent who was responsible for preserving order, administering justice, and collecting the revenues. Over the superintendents they placed a supervisor with controlling power. As in Bengal the Company's commercial interests were to be administered separately from the political and revenue concerns and they were put in charge of commercial residents. The supervisor was given charge of the mint. All interior customs dues were abolished in the province and the Company was to appoint its own customs officers to collect the duties on imports and exports.[2] General Abercromby appointed Farmer as the supervisor and James Stevens as the superintendent of the southern districts.

But it was left to the governor-general to provide fresh ideas on the Company's pepper policy. On 29 January he had warned General Abercromby that the only way to get pepper from Travancore was to pay the market price for it. Cornwallis obviously thought that this was worth while to stop the smuggling.[3] On 17 March he was more emphatic, and condemned the policy of forcing the Malabaris to accept low prices for pepper which, he said, was responsible for the Company's losing almost all the pepper trade to private merchants. He strongly advised that the Company should revert to the long-established custom of taking half the produce in revenue and allow the Malabaris to sell the rest.[4] That Cornwallis had the Company's commercial interests in Malabar chiefly at heart appears from a minute written at this time by Sir John Shore, his close adviser and appointed successor. Shore's minute was an analysis of the state of India, and he said about Malabar that it was more important to conciliate the Company's new subjects than to draw revenue from them. He

[1] V. A. Narain, *Jonathan Duncan and Varanasi* (Calcutta, 1959).
[2] BRP, range 366, xv, 171–4: minute of Jonathan Duncan, 11 March 1793.
[3] BSPP, range E, vi, 117–18: Cornwallis to General Abercromby, 29 January 1793.
[4] Letters received from Bombay xi, paragraph 25 of the letter of 25 September 1794, 'Extract of a Letter from Marquis Cornwallis to Sir Robert Abercromby', 17 March 1793.

gave his opinion that, 'By proper care and attention in establishing good regulations and in enforcing them, the new settlements may rise to great commercial importance, and to this we ought principally to look'.[1]

The commissioners had begun to realise that their policy was an impossible one. Pepper was being smuggled at the price of Rs 200 a candy. In February by employing well-informed native merchants supported by the Company's officials in the districts of Chericul and Cotiote they had secured less than half of the total crop of the province.[2] Only Mahé was profiting from their policy. Therefore they were not disposed to quarrel with the governor-general's opinion, and on 15 April 1793 the Malabaris were told by proclamation that the Company had relinquished the pepper monopoly and that it would claim in future only half the produce by right of its sovereignty. The cultivators were free to sell the remainder.[3] Mahé had defeated the monopoly.

But the acknowledged supremacy of Mahé was not to last long. The declaration of war against France provided an opportunity which the Company was quick to seize. On 11 June Lord Cornwallis sent off his instructions for the capture of the French settlements in India,[4] and on 25 June the Court of Directors sent orders for a large increase in the investments from the west coast in anticipation of the end of French trade.[5] On 10 July Mahé surrendered. The thorn in the Company's side was removed. Among the booty were 240 muskets, 96 iron guns and over 3,000 cannon-balls, the property of Murdock Brown.[6] Farmer wasted no time in impressing Cornwallis with the absolute necessity of the Company's retaining the settlement at the peace. He emphasised 'the perpetual bar which Mahé will be to any arrangement We may think fit to make for securing to the Company the greatest share of the Pepper Trade on this Coast', besides the part it played as a market for slaves and its possible use by the French as

---

[1] *The Poona Residency Correspondence* II, ed. Sardesai, 347; minute of Sir John Shore, 25 March 1793.
[2] BCP, range 414, LIV, under 8 September 1794: Bombay to the Court of Directors.
[3] *Ibid.* LIII, 99: a proclamation of the commissioners, 15 April 1793.
[4] BSPP, range E, VI, 382: W. G. Farmer to Lord Cornwallis, 17 July 1793.
[5] BCP, range 414, LIII, 318–20: the Court of Directors to Bombay, 25 June 1793.
[6] BSPP, range E, VI, 414–5: 18 July 1793.

an offensive base in war-time.[1] Furthermore, Farmer urged the advantages of the Company's using it as a commercial depot. The river made it easy to import goods from Corengotte, Irvenaad, Cartinaad and Cotiote, and there were fine warehouses at the water's edge. He suggested that the Company should make its commercial headquarters there while leaving the seat of government at Tellicherry.[2]

The Company, it would seem, had unchallenged power in Malabar to reap what advantages it chose from the province. In August the commissioners produced their plans for the future government of the country. The Company claimed four-fifths of the revenue for its own use and this was to be collected by its own agents. Although there was no attempt to renew the pepper monopoly the Company demanded half of the pepper produce of the northern districts in payment of revenue. The rajas had to be content with the one-fifth of the revenues remaining to them. The situation, as Farmer explained, was 'totally new, instead of a receiver of tribute each superintendent and the Supervisor in his Revenue division are become collectors in the first instance, in some districts jointly with the Rajahs, in others, and those very considerable ones, the Company collect wholly for themselves...'[3] Many of Tipu's old revenue officers were re-appointed by the commissioners to undertake the work of collection. Theoretically the power of the rajas was at last curtailed, and as the only large-scale buyer of pepper, the Company, it seemed, could enjoy the advantages they had looked for on their first acquisition of the province.

The activity of Murdock Brown and the private traders at Mahé had been the key factor in determining the Company's policy during the first sixteen months of its administration of Malabar. This was so from the first visit which Farmer paid Brown and which was followed by the commissioners advocating free trade in the province. After they changed their mind about Brown the existence of Mahé was responsible for their attempts to coerce the rajas and to

[1] BSPP, range E, vi, 384–5: Farmer to Cornwallis, 17 July 1793. Bands of armed Moplahs who lived in the jungle made money by abducting Hindus to Mahé where they were sold as slaves and taken to Mauritius by the French.
[2] *Ibid.* 384–7: W. G. Farmer to Lord Cornwallis, 17 July 1793; and *ibid.* 463–4: G. Parry to W. G. Farmer, 24 August 1793.
[3] BRP, range 366, xv, 438–43: W. G. Farmer to Bombay, 30 September 1793.

enforce a pepper monopoly, and then for the complete breakdown of this policy and its abandonment. But on the capture of Mahé the commissioners were free to pursue the Company's best interests. It is therefore curious to find that little over a month after the fall of the French settlement W. G. Farmer wrote to Bombay saying that he had appointed Mr Murdock Brown as deputy superintendent of police at Mahé. The supervisor justified this appointment as a mark of appreciation of Brown's 'zeal for the welfare of this province of which both myself and Mr Commissioner Duncan can bear witness in the very interesting information he has liberally & frequently afforded us, both as to Commerce Government and Revenue...'[1] With that amazing capacity of his for emerging always on the winning side Brown had survived what should have been the shipwreck of his fortunes. How exactly he did it is not apparent, but it is obvious that he had been preparing his course for some time. Whether he foresaw the eventual conquest of Mahé or whether he judged that a position of influence within the Company would be more profitable than his opposition to it which involved him in paying yet higher and higher prices for pepper, one cannot say, although the latter case seems more probable. But what is certain is that he managed to establish himself in the confidence of Jonathan Duncan before the fall of Mahé. Brown can only have done this with the cooperation of Farmer, which would seem to indicate that the two men had reached an understanding. Either Brown had convinced Farmer that he was zealous for the Company's interests or the two men had a more private bond. Duncan had 'heard Mr Brown described in Bengal as a Man possessed of very considerable Talents and of great experience of the language and Manners of the Coast...', but 'from the equivocal political Character that this Gentleman was said still to stand in the French Settlement of Mahé [was] at first deterred for some months after his arrival from seeking to derive advantage from establishing any Intercourse with him whatever...'[2] But Duncan was eventually led 'to avail himself of an opportunity that occurred of his becoming acquainted with Mr Brown' from his realisation of the inadequate knowledge which the Company's servants had of the province. From that time he seems

[1] BSPP, range E, VI, 465–7: W. G. Farmer to G. Parry, 27 August 1793.
[2] Letters received from Bombay XIII, paragraph 128 of the law department, 18 December 1796.

to have accepted Murdock Brown completely and never doubted his integrity. Before war with France was even declared Brown had written for the commissioners a lengthy paper on the commerce of Malabar which they included in their report to the governor-general.[1]

Jonathan Duncan, first as commissioner in Malabar and then from 1796 to 1811 as governor of Bombay, bore for several years the final responsibility for the Company's administration of the province. To understand the policy which was pursued and the interests which it served it is necessary to examine Duncan's own character and objectives. His close relationship with Murdock Brown and the subsequent part which Brown played in the government of the country raises questions about Duncan which must materially affect any judgment of him. The history of Duncan's early career in Bengal and Benares has been written to show Duncan as one of the first able and upright administrators of British India.[2] He emerges from the study in an ideal light as a man of science, a social reformer, a philanthropist, cultured, learned, an able economist and a fine revenue administrator. This judgment on him receives powerful support from the opinions of Lord Cornwallis who looked on Duncan with high favour and pressed the Court of Directors to give him a seat on the Bengal council.[3] Cornwallis's opinion contrasts curiously with William Hickey's who reported when Duncan was appointed to Bombay that, 'The partiality of Lord Cornwallis to Mr Duncan occasioned general astonishment: almost every person who knew that gentleman considering him a heavy, dull man, without a particle of genius...'[4] Hickey's criticism might be judged as a proof of Duncan's respectability, yet there remain some strange anomalies in Duncan's Bengal career which his biographer does not elucidate but which throw light on his career in Malabar. One curious fact is that Duncan retained a life-long friendship and admiration for John Macpherson, the man whose government Cornwallis condemned as 'a system of mean jobbing and peculation' and whose character was composed of 'flimsy cunning and shameless falsehoods'.[5] But such was Duncan's admiration for Macpherson that he told his

---

[1] *Malabar Report*, 247–9.
[2] Narain, *Jonathan Duncan and Varanasi*.   [3] *Ibid.* 20.
[4] A. Spencer (ed.), *Memoires of William Hickey* (London, 1925) IV, 129.
[5] Ross (ed.), *The Correspondence of Cornwallis* II, 415: Cornwallis to Henry Dundas, 8 August 1789.

uncle in 1787 that Macpherson had 'done more good to the Company for the time he held the government than any one of his predecessors ever did'.[1] Nowhere in Duncan's long career does one gain the impression that he himself was a time-server or involved in corrupt practices. His honesty and integrity were the qualities which appealed to Cornwallis and this was one of the reasons why he was sent to reform the abuses of Bombay.[2] But Sir John Shore made some interesting remarks about him to Henry Dundas. Shore was convinced of Duncan's 'Zeal, Abilities & Integrity'. But he added, 'in one point only I think him weak, in his Judgement upon Characters; his partiality to his friends does not permit him to see their Defects, and his Good nature requires a little check...'[3] Honest men are often incapable of seeing dishonesty in others, and in Duncan's case the failing had a long history. When he was a young man his uncle John Michie pointed it out to him. He had heard that his nephew was 'one of the most sensible and industrious young men in Bengal', but he warned Duncan of his suspicion that 'You have not (nor indeed can have at your time of Life) the necessary knowledge of mankind, to guard against their Arts'.[4] It was a failing which time did not seem to cure. Walter Ewer said of Duncan in 1796 that 'having lived long almost secluded from Europeans, he is very ignorant of the World'.[5] This was to cost Duncan dear. In 1799 he learnt that the man to whom he had entrusted his fortune in Benares had defrauded him of almost the whole of it, and that from having possessed £30,000 he was left with nothing to show for all his years in India.[6]

This inability to judge men was perhaps responsible for another weakness in his character, a lack of self-confidence and leadership among his fellow Europeans. Cornwallis wrote of him in 1787 that 'with all his honesty & ability I doubt whether he would have

---

[1] Michie Papers, MSS 5881, file 2: J. Duncan to John Michie, 17 February 1787.
[2] Rylands English MSS, Melville Papers 692, 2029: Henry Dundas to Jonathan Duncan, 14 January 1796.
[3] Harvard Melville MSS, IOL microfilm reel 648: Sir John Shore to H. Dundas, 31 December 1794.
[4] Michie Papers, MSS 5881, file 2: John Michie to Jonathan Duncan, 17 November 1784.
[5] Home Misc. CDXXXVIII, 13–14: W. Ewer to Henry Dundas, Bombay, 30 November 1796.
[6] Michie Papers, MSS 5881, file 2: Duncan to Jonathan Michie, Bombay, 31 March, 6 May 1799 and 19 July 1800.

sufficient authority over men of equal standing in the service'.[1]
In 1804 Sir Walter Ewer thought him afraid of responsibility, and
therefore untrustworthy.[2] James Mackintosh thought Duncan
'good natured, inclined towards good, and indisposed to violence,
but rather submissive to those who are otherwise'.[3] Duncan
himself confessed his inclination to avoid European society to
David Scott when he said he would like to pass the rest of his life
'in a small district with as many natives under my charge as I
could by attending to them make happy, which my schooling at
Benares renders me pretty competent to. . .'[4] David Scott repri-
manded him in 1797 for not ruling his establishment with a
sufficiently firm hand. Scott thought that what Duncan called
'conciliatory motives' would be ascribed to 'weak nerves',[5] and
when Duncan complained of his difficulties Scott grew impatient.
'If you had not too great a share of good nature you could have met
no difficulties which would not have vanished when you used the
great powers with which you was invested and supported as you was
at home by the friends attached to principle. . .'[6] Duncan was
always inclined to write lengthy reports on his problems and to
refer difficulties to his superiors instead of making attempts to
solve them himself. David Scott complained in 1798 that Duncan's
correspondence with the Court was at least ten times larger than
that of Bengal and he warned Duncan to curtail it if he meant it to
be read.[7] Duncan displayed a constant anxiety to have the appro-
bation of the directors and the governor-general,[8] and Scott showed
some irritation at his repeated self-justification.[9]

If this interpretation of Duncan's character is right it does much
to explain his relationship with Murdock Brown. Brown was
undoubtedly an able man, and he possessed many of the talents and
interests which Duncan admired and can rarely have found in his
colleagues in the Company's service. Duncan had been one of the
founder members of the Asiatic Society of Bengal and was keenly
interested in the language, history and architecture of the people

[1] PRO 30/11/150, f. 40: Cornwallis to Henry Dundas, 14 August 1787.
[2] Home Misc. CDXXXVIII, 29: W. Ewer to H. Dundas, 12 February 1797.
[3] Mackintosh (ed.), *The Memoires of Sir James Mackintosh*, 207.
[4] C. H. Philips (ed.), *The Correspondence of David Scott* (London, 1951) II, 422.
[5] *Ibid.* I, 114: David Scott to J. Duncan, 31 July 1797.   [6] *Ibid.* I, 115–7:
[7] *Ibid.* I, 141: David Scott to J. Duncan, 13 August 1798.
[8] Michie Papers, MSS 5881, file 2: J. Duncan to John Michie, 2 February 1798.
[9] Philips (ed.), *The Correspondence of David Scott* I, 140: David Scott to J.
  Duncan, 9 August 1798.

of India. Murdock Brown, too, possessed considerable knowledge and appreciation of Hindu laws and culture which apart from his understanding of the Malabar tongue and incomparable experience of the province must have endeared him to Duncan. The latter's 'Braminised' mind[1] must have rejoiced at finding a man who could write, 'The division of Mankind into Casts and the various Rules prescribed for the observance of each, if considered with due attention as a Political Institution will be found to be one of the most Sublime Efforts of human wisdom...'[2] It cannot have taken Brown long to convince Duncan of his rectitude and indispensability. Moreover, Duncan's ignorance of commerce in a situation where considerable commercial knowledge was necessary, gave Brown a great deal of influence over him. In 1796 Walter Ewer declared that the new governor of Bombay, though an upright, honest man, had constantly been employed in the revenue line and was 'too fond of Minitiæ & has not a Commercial Idea, having the Publick Welfare at heart he will make some Good Regulations but I am afraid they will be counterbalanced by others from his want of Knowledge. It would have been fortunate for him, had he never been removed from the revenue Line, in which he certainly shines...'[3] Duncan never questioned the commercial advice which Brown gave him, and he used his influence to defend Brown's appointment to a position in the Company's service.[4] In 1793 the Bombay government opposed Brown's appointment as deputy-superintendent of police at Mahé,[5] and ordered his dismissal or resignation.[6] But the Malabar authorities ignored the order and Brown kept his office.[7]

In this way after the capture of the French settlement at Mahé all was set for Murdock Brown to influence the Company's policy in the province. It was Brown's ideas on the commercial development of Malabar which the commissioners sent in their report to

[1] Mackintosh (ed.), *The Memoires of Sir James Mackintosh*, 207: 'The Governor, who has been very civil to us, is an ingenious, intelligent man, not without capacity and disposition to speculate. Four and thirty years' residence in this country have Braminised his mind and body.'
[2] See Murdock Brown's account of Malabar in Home Misc. CDLVIC, 353–491.
[3] Home Misc. CDXXXVIII, 13–23: W. Ewer to Henry Dundas, 30 November 1796.
[4] Letters received from Bombay XIII, par. 128 of the law department, 18 December 1796.
[5] BSPP, range E, VI, 467–8.   [6] *Ibid.* 533, 4 December 1793.
[7] Letters received from Bombay XIII, par. 128 of the law department, 18 December 1796.

the governor-general. These included his proposal that the commercial residents should be deprived of all political and coercive authority as they were in Bengal.[1] He did not intend to keep his rivals in power. He also advocated the abolition of all internal tolls and duties which were choking trade, and he fixed the import and export duties which the Company levied in the province.[2] But his influence went far beyond what appeared in official reports. Walter Ewer discovered his hand in everything when he visited Malabar in 1797.[3] His activities, moreover, were almost invariably designed to further his private interest. Either Farmer acted in collusion with him, or, like Duncan, he was blind to Brown's designs. Brown continued his trade in pepper, although according to Ewer the greater part of it involved smuggling immense quantities out of the province. Ewer even heard it whispered that Murdock Brown was to be employed in the customs, 'if it is on the Principle, that a reformed Thief makes a good Thief-taker, it may be very proper, & I will engage that the Customs will increase, as he will take Care that no one smuggles but himself'.[4] In 1796 the raja of Cochin was accused of not paying his revenue. The raja wrote to Bombay to say that Mr Farmer had told him to sell his pepper to Mr Brown who would pay the money to the Company and send him a receipt. Brown had paid part of the money to the Company but left Rs 15,000 outstanding. The raja said that he had continually written to Brown asking for a receipt or for the money, but without effect. Duncan replied from Bombay that when the raja dealt like a merchant he ought to take all suitable precautions, and proclaimed his trust in 'Mr Brown's known good and respectable Character within the Province...'[5]

One of the worst abuses in the province which Ewer reported and which he ascribed to Duncan's commercial ignorance,[6] was the debasement of the coinage. Farmer first brought this to Duncan's attention in September 1793 when the market value of the fanam in relation to the Bombay or Surat rupee had dropped from $3\frac{1}{4}$ to $3\frac{1}{2}$ since the new Malabar coinage was issued.[7] This meant that the

---

[1] *Malabar Report*, 246–7.　　　　　　　　　　　　　　[2] *Ibid.* 253–7.
[3] Home Misc. CDXXXVIII, 165: W. Ewer to Henry Dundas, 17 July 1797.
[4] *Ibid.* 159–60: W. Ewer to Henry Dundas, 17 July 1797.
[5] BRP, range 366, XVIII, 44–6: letter from the raja of Cochin to Bombay, 10 January 1796 and the governor's reply, 21 January 1796.
[6] Home Misc. CDXXXVIII, 176: W. Ewer to Henry Dundas, 17 July 1797.
[7] BRP, range 366, XV, 503–5: W. G. Farmer to Jonathan Duncan, 13 September 1793.

revenue which the Company was to receive in fanams was of less value than it should be, and the Company's soldiers were showing their discontent at their depreciated pay. Farmer accounted for the depreciation by saying that whereas before the peace the Calicut fanams had been current throughout dominions which were part of Mysore, Tipu's officers would no longer accept the new coins in payment of revenue except at a large discount, and as a result the fanams had poured back into the Company's districts.[1] Farmer did not say why the fanams were at a discount in Mysore, but Ewer supplied the reason. The fanams were exchanged at a discount everywhere except when they were forced on the Company's soldiers because they were so bad when they were issued that no one would touch them.[2] In 1797 the value of the fanam had dropped further so that 4 were worth only 1 rupee. Ewer drew up a table to prove the debasement of the coin. He showed that 3 venetians were worth Rs 15, but 27 gold fanams, which were equal in weight to 3 venetians, were worth only Rs 7-2-87. This debasement of the new coinage, according to Ewer, began when Farmer had charge of the mint and 'that he had a great Advantage from it, few People doubt'.[3] That the Bombay merchants also profited from it Ewer did not doubt either. He told Henry Dundas that the accountant-general of Bombay, Henry Fawcett, one of the partners of Bruce, Fawcett and Company, had used his position to make profits of at least 10 per cent by sending goods to Madras and remitting the produce of them in star pagodas to Malabar where the difference between the bazaar price of fanams in terms of the star pagoda and rupee and their official rate of exchange, yielded handsome profits to the remitter.[4] When Farmer first reported the depreciation of the coin Duncan told him to consult Murdock Brown,[5] but when Duncan became governor of Bombay he made the position worse by attempting to remedy it. The future duke of Wellington reported that Duncan, 'an excellent, well-meaning man, and with good abilities, but...sometimes misled', purchased at a low price a large number of rupees at Bombay which he sent to Malabar where they were circulated at a nominal price far above their real value.

---

[1] *Ibid.*
[2] Home Misc. CDXXXVIII, 118–20: W. Ewer to Henry Dundas, 10 May 1797.
[3] *Ibid.* 197–9: W. Ewer to Henry Dundas, 10 September 1797.
[4] *Ibid.* 119–20: W. Ewer to Henry Dundas, 10 May 1797.
[5] BRP, range 366, XV, 506–7: Duncan and Page to W. G. Farmer, 17 September 1793.

The merchants of Bombay thereupon saw the chance of making large profits and sent down 'oceans of rupees' to Malabar. The province was inundated with bad rupees and the exchange value depreciated accordingly.[1] In 1801 the situation remained unremedied.[2]

Duncan's aptness to be 'sometimes misled' caused the continuance under his government of another scandal in the province, the exploitation of its timber for private profit. In June 1793 Farmer first pointed out that the Company had inherited from Tipu the right to enjoy a monopoly of all the timber which was grown in the province. The demand for timber at Bombay for shipbuilding was considerable and the Company could profit from supplying it. But the difficulty lay in providing the elephants to carry the logs to the coast.[3] Shortly after pointing out the resources of Malabar, Farmer recommended that the Bombay government should accept the proposals of Alexander Mackonochie who wished to set up a sawmill on the Beypore river to supply the Company with planks. On Farmer's recommendation seconded by the Bombay government Mackonochie persuaded the Court of Directors in October 1794 to permit machinery to be sent out to Malabar, and he secured a loan of £10,000 from the Court for the enterprise.[4] Ewer reported that Farmer was supposed to be Mackonochie's partner[5] and that Murdock Brown was also concerned with him.[6] In 1796 the Bombay government refused to allow two Moplah merchants to pay Rs 65,000 a year for the privilege of cutting timber on the grounds that it would interfere with Mackonochie's operations.[7] But the Beypore mill and all of

---

[1] S. J. Owen (ed.), *A Selection from the Despatches, Treaties, and other Papers of the Marquess Wellesley during his Government of India* (Oxford, 1877): Arthur Wellesley to Major Macleod, Seringapatam, 19 October 1801.

[2] Cf. Narain, *Jonathan Duncan and Varanasi*, 209, 'The fiscal and commercial reforms enunciated by the Commissioners bear testimony to the skill and ability of Duncan', and 'By the introduction of a new coinage, the trading communities of Malabar shook off the economic disadvantage under which they had had to labour...'

[3] BRP, range 366, XXI, 701–3: W. G. Farmer to Bombay, 13 June 1793.

[4] Home Misc. CCX, 9–10: Mackonochie to the Court of Directors, London, 8 October 1794; and *ibid.* CDXXXVIII, 120–38: W. Ewer to Henry Dundas, 10 May 1797.

[5] *Ibid.* 120–1.

[6] *Ibid.* 167: W. Ewer to Henry Dundas, 17 July 1797.

[7] BRP, range 366, XX, 65–73: Mackonochie to the Malabar commissioners, 15 December 1796; and Home Misc. CDXXXVIII, 123–6: W. Ewer to H. Dundas, 10 May 1797.

Mackonochie's schemes were a failure. To begin with there was little timber on the banks of the river, and the mill would not do more work in one day than could be procured for Rs 85 by hand.[1] But the concern was not finally taken over by the government until 1800 when Duncan accepted it in order to recover the money which the Company had lent Mackonochie. As late as June 1799 Mackonochie had received Rs 100,000 from the Bombay government.[2] Meanwhile all the profits were reaped by private merchants including Moosa and Murdock Brown who rivalled each other in selling to the Company what was its own property. Ewer reported that trees were brought down the Beliapatam river at an expense of Rs 70 to 80 and were then sold for Rs 700 or 800.[3] Murdock Brown, he was informed, had cut down a thousand trees in Irvenaad.[4]

Murdock Brown's influence was, as Ewer said, felt everywhere in the province. The boldness of the man's schemes and his undoubted success was only possible because of Duncan's blind trust in him and because of the cooperation of those Bombay servants who administered Malabar. One further striking instance of his power is shown in the affair of the Randaterra plantation. In 1798 Duncan recommended to the Court of Directors that they should support Brown's application to grow pepper, coffee and cotton for the Company on a plantation in Randaterra. The plantation was to be of 200 acres and the Court was to supply the capital for its development on Brown's promise to provide annual investments worth at least seven lacs after January 1802. Duncan supposed that the directors would not object to the scheme and granted Brown a monthly salary of Rs 800 to act as overseer.[5] In February 1799 Duncan recorded in a minute that the plantation was suffering from a shortage of labour and that Brown was

[1] Home Misc. CDXXXVIII, 120–1: W. Ewer to Henry Dundas, 10 May 1797.
[2] BRP, range 366, XXVI, 393–414: 3 April 1800.
[3] Home Misc. CDXXXVIII, 125–8: W. Ewer to Henry Dundas, 10 May 1797.
[4] *Ibid*. 166–7.
In 1796 the Zamorin's minister reported that Brown had offered to advance the Zamorin money to pay his revenues in return for teak. Brown, according to the minister, promised to supply the necessary elephants but failed to do so, and the timber was not delivered. Brown then sued the Zamorin for the money and the profits which he had calculated on receiving. He had advanced Rs 6,150 and sued for Rs 11,100. Home Misc. CDLXX, 96–101.
[5] Letters received from Bombay XV, pars. 37–8 of the revenue department, 1 January 1798.

experiencing trouble from the local revenue collector who was a Malabari. Brown had suggested to Duncan

that he should himself be vested with the Charge of the Collections of Randaterra, subordinate of Course to the Superintendent, and with the same judicial & Revenue Authorities, and under the like Sanctions and Engagements on his part, for his faithful Administration thereof, as are now applicable to the assistants in local Charge throughout the Province...Mr Brown having on this occasion further observed that the District of Randaterra is so extensive and populous, that if he had Authority in it, he could, without detriment to its general Cultivation ensure for the Plantation, the labor of from 2 to 300 persons daily...

This incomparable piece of audacity by which Brown sought to acquire for himself the omnipotence of a magistrate and revenue collector in one of the richest pepper-producing districts of Malabar only met with Duncan's approval, and he had no objection to make to the request.[1] It was Duncan who took upon himself the responsibility in March 1800 of revoking the Directors' orders that Brown should bear the whole expense of the plantation and should repay the Company for what they had spent on it.[2] But when Malabar passed under the control of the Madras government Brown himself offered to assume the ownership of the plantation. This he did in 1802, and secured his exemption from the land tax at the same time.[3] But without his Bombay friends Brown soon found himself in difficulties. A new sub-collector of revenue discovered that Brown had added nearly 3,000 acres to his plantation quite illegally by usurping the property of the local inhabitants. Furthermore, the Company had not received the revenue which Brown had collected from the district and he paid nothing on the 150 candies of pepper it was estimated he produced. As late as 1811 the Madras authorities were investigating the traffic in slaves which Brown had carried on to supply his plantation for thirteen years. In resisting the manumission of his slaves Brown cited 'Authority from the Malabar Commissioners Messrs Spencer, Hartly, Smee to Mr Gillis to purchase Pooliars for the Rhandaterra plantation agreeable to the known customs & laws of Malabar relating to them', dated 20 October 1798. But the investigators found Nayars, Moplahs and

[1] BRP, range 366, XXIV, 211–13: minute of J. Duncan, 8 February 1799.
[2] Letters received from Bombay XVII, par. 8 of the public department, 15 March 1800.
[3] Personal Records X, 605–6.

natives of Travancore among the slaves on the plantation. Brown was undeterred by these discoveries and went on to petition the governor of Madras to be recompensed for his losses. The papers were finally referred to the Court of Directors and the case was not closed until 1817. Brown retained the whole of the plantation but paid the normal land tax on it.[1] The final outcome of this piece of private enterprise as put before the parliamentary commission of enquiry in 1830 was contained in the brief phrase, 'Successful, it is believed, as concerned Mr Brown.'[2]

This extraordinary history gives point to Ewer's reference to the influence which Brown had in Bombay and in England, and it reveals the measure of Jonathan Duncan's blindness. But its telling also throws some light on the policy which was pursued in the province after the fall of Mahé. After the capture of the foreign settlement the Company, it seemed, could look forward to an unrivalled enjoyment of the pepper trade at favourable prices. In September 1793 the Bombay government reminded the supervisor that the Company expected a greatly increased trade and asked somewhat impatiently for information. The Court of Directors continued to urge their servants at Bombay to make the pepper consignments as large as possible and to reduce them in price. They also hoped that the raja of Travancore would be more punctual in fulfilling his pepper engagements to the Company.[3] John Bruce, Henry Dundas's assistant, wrote in May 1794 to Philip Dundas for information on how much 'from our influence with the Coorga Rajah, an outlet for British produce may be expected in the Mysore country and what degree of spiceries &c may be expected in our encreased trade to the Malabar Coast'. The produce of the Malabar Coast, he pointed out, 'particularly its *Spiceries*, have, in every Age been considered, as the key to the Eastern Trade'. Bruce also asked Philip Dundas to tell him whether Tipu's remaining piece of coast-line gave opportunities 'to our rival European Companies, to

---

[1] Personal Records x, 610–62.
[2] Parliamentary Papers, 1830, VI, Report from the Lords, 245. In December 1818 F. C. Brown wrote to the Court to say that he had been instructed by his father, Murdock Brown of Malabar, to settle the balance due to the Company on account of the Randaterra plantation, because after forty-three years in India his father wanted to revisit his native land; Personal Records IX, 697–8. The descendants of Murdock Brown still held the Randaterra plantation when Logan was writing in 1888. See W. Logan, *Malabar* I, 495.
[3] BCP, range 414, LIV, 525–6: the Court of Directors to Bombay, 1 May 1794.

acquire a part in the Trade, and whether any measures can be devised, for securing it to the Company'.[1]

The Bengal government showed a similar anxiety to see the Company's trade prosper in Malabar. The governor-general, Sir John Shore, urged the Bombay government to encourage the growth of the pepper vines and cardamoms in the province[2] and he asked for Bombay's opinion on the expediency of making a commercial treaty with Tipu Sultan.[3] In October 1794 Shore expressed his hope that the abolition of the pepper monopoly had produced the desired effect of 'encreasing the Pepper Produce of our new Territories to the greatest possible extent'. In particular he wanted to know whether the Company's commercial and financial interests benefited most from the revenue arrangements by which the Company received half the pepper in kind from the northern districts, or from a money payment alone, as in the southern districts where the cultivator was left free to sell his pepper.[4] It is clear from these enquiries that neither the Court of Directors nor the governor-general considered that the ending of the pepper monopoly marked the ruin of the Company's plans to control the trade of the province. The new policy was adopted as the best way of achieving that aim, and after the fall of Mahé they expected the pepper trade to fall exclusively into the Company's hands.

But in January 1795 Philip Dundas reported to his uncle that the Company had to pay between Rs 180 and 205 for each candy of pepper while private merchants paid only Rs 150.[5] This was a reversal of what had happened when Mahé had commanded the trade. Then the private merchants had gained control of the supplies by paying a much higher price than the Company. It is interesting to see how this new state of affairs was brought about. In September 1793 Farmer told the Bombay government in reply to their enquiries about the pepper supplies that 'the system laid down is that for the benifit [sic] of the Company as Sovereigns of this Country, their Commercial Monopoly is distroyed, and they

[1] Home Misc. CDVIe, 69–70: John Bruce to Philip Dundas, 27 May 1794.
[2] BRP, range 366, XVI, 493–5: Bengal to Bombay, 6 October 1794.
[3] *Ibid.* 523: Bengal to Bombay, 27 October 1794. Shore had first asked Bombay's opinion on the subject in a letter of 27 March 1794.
[4] *Ibid.* 522: Bengal to Bombay, 27 October 1794.
[5] Rylands English MSS, Melville Papers 926, 4: Philip Dundas to Henry Dundas, Bombay, 6 January 1795.

must take the chance of the Market, like other Merchants...'[1] Under the new system, he told Bombay, the Company could only expect to receive 1,200 candies in kind as their half-share of the produce of the northern districts, and furthermore, the method of collecting the pepper at the vine was to be dropped in favour of contracting with the principal merchants for deliveries to the Company. The pepper, added Farmer, would make its own price according to the demand, and he concluded 'the more the Company wants, in course the dearer it will be'.[2] Arab merchants, he stated, were paying Rs 200 a candy for pepper, and there was no hope of loading four cargoes for the Company. Complaining that he was too busy to be bothered with the business at all, Farmer declared flatly that the Company must pay the market price for the pepper both of Travancore and Malabar. The tone was markedly different. Farmer, once the chief protagonist of monopoly, had swung round to be its chief opponent. It was he who, in opposition to John Agnew, the commercial resident at Calicut, was responsible for freeing the pepper trade completely in the southern part of the province, instead of taking half the pepper produce in payment of the Company's revenue.[3] Moreover, by ending the system by which the Company's agents collected pepper from the vine, the Company's commercial interests were left at the mercy of the pepper contractors, among whom was now numbered Mr Murdock Brown.[4]

It has already been shown how the rajas and pepper contractors united to keep the pepper trade in a tight grip which the Company could not break.[5] Robert Taylor, who had become the commercial resident at Mahé when the chiefship of Tellicherry was abolished, found that the hold of the rajas and merchants amounted almost to a monopoly and that 'the merchants and contractors have long been accustomed to take the produce of the poor ryot at a very inferior price & by confederating together sell it to the Company at as high a rate as possible...'[6] It now appears that Murdock Brown

[1] BCP, range 414, LIII, 220: Farmer to Bombay, 2 October 1793.
[2] *Ibid.* 218–21.
[3] *Ibid.* LXV, 349: John Agnew to Robert Taylor; and *ibid.* 290.
[4] *Ibid.* 362 and 446: report from Murdock Brown to the Malabar commissioners, 1 September 1799.
[5] See above p. 84.
[6] BCP, range 414, LXV, 302: 'Extract of a letter from Mr Robert Taylor, Commercial Resident at Mahé, 21 November 1794'.

joined this select group, and in so doing worked against the private interests of the Company's commercial residents, Agnew and Taylor, and other members of the Bombay establishment who had commercial interests in Malabar. Brown, with his long experience of the province and of its rajas and pepper merchants, found it easy with the cooperation of Farmer to become a large-scale pepper contractor. The fall of Mahé had not put a total end to foreign demands for pepper: Arab and Gujarat merchants still traded on the coast[1] and European merchants who had had their base at Mahé returned to the coast under neutral colours.[2] The rajas and contractors were therefore not dependent on the Company for their market and they could combine to sell it to the Company at the highest possible price. But for the purposes of their own foreign trade, Brown and Moosa could with the aid of the rajas extort the pepper at a low price from the cultivators and smuggle it out of the province without paying duty.[3] Brown still worked in association with the Frenchman, Dineur.[4] By these methods, as Philip Dundas observed, the Company was forced to pay up to Rs 205 a candy while the private merchants paid only Rs 150.

This situation was only possible while the rajas retained their full powers of government and control of their own land-revenues. But the Malabar commissioners under Duncan's leadership had completed their work by settling that in both the northern and southern parts of the province the Company was to take one-half of the value of the produce in revenue, from the north in pepper, and from the south in money. Of this half the rajas were to be allowed one-fifth for their maintenance. This was the revenue system which Tipu Sultan had established.[5] In November 1793 the rajas of Coorminaad and Cotiote expressed their discontent with this settlement and demanded that large shares of the revenue should be given to the service of their gods. The revenue collections were brought to a standstill and the raja of Cotiote would not

[1] BCP, range 414, LXV, 300–2: extract of a letter from John Agnew, 4 December 1794.
[2] *Ibid.* LIX 223–5: 15 December 1796.
[3] See above, p. 98. Half of the pepper produce of northern Malabar was smuggled; Home Misc. CDXXXVIII, 176–7: W. Ewer to H. Dundas, 17 July 1797.
[4] BCP, range 414, LV, 252–5: John Agnew to Bombay, 16 March 1795.
[5] *Reply of the Governor-General in Council to the Malabar Joint Commissioners' Reports*, 73 (Madras, 1879).

permit the Company's officials to inspect the pepper vines.[1]
Farmer had to deal with the situation. The northern rajas insisted
that the Company's revenue should be only one half of the rent
which the landholders received from the cultivators, and not one
half of the total produce. The rajas demanded that the Company
should receive their revenue in the form of tribute which they
themselves would collect from the landowners and cultivators,
whereas the commissioners had envisaged that the Company
would collect it directly from the cultivators.[2] What was at stake
in the dispute was the Company's whole future in Malabar. The
rajas wanted to preserve their authority and incomes in their own
countries and to limit the Company's functions to the receipt of
tribute. This was quite the opposite of what the commissioners
intended.[3] Farmer therefore set out on a tour of the northern
kingdoms to settle the issue. He took with him one companion,
Murdock Brown, who, Farmer said, had 'voluntarily offered to
accompany me during my tour of settlement of the Northern
Districts, which considering the magnitude and importance of his
own private Concerns, is a testimony of zeal that ought not to pass
unnoticed'.[4]

Whatever object attracted Brown's zeal Farmer ended his tour
having made large concessions to the northern rajas. He reduced by
a half the amount of revenue which the Company could collect
from those countries, and allowed the Cotiote raja, despite his
'weak and imbecile' character to collect the revenues of his
country himself.[5] There is no evidence to show what part Brown
played in these negotiations, but three years later Ewer reported his
belief that Murdock Brown was encouraging petitions against the
revenue settlements and was advising people to delay making
their payments. He was, said Ewer, 'the Chief Incendiary of the
Country'.[6] Whatever responsibility Brown bore for these concessions they were certainly to his interest. In Cotiote, the chief
pepper-producing country, the raja was left with his powers almost
undisturbed, and in the other northern countries the Company's

[1] BSPP, range E, VII, 18–28: W. G. Farmer to Bombay, 18 November 1793.
[2] *Ibid.* 58–66: the diary of W. G. Farmer, 4 December 1793.
[3] *Reply to the Joint Commissioners' Reports*, 81.
[4] BSPP, range E, VII, 80: the diary of W. G. Farmer, 9 December 1793.
[5] Home Misc. DLXXXV, 268–92: James Stevens to Bombay, 18 March 1794.
[6] *Ibid.* CDXXXVIII, 162 and 165: W. Ewer to Henry Dundas, 17 July 1797.

claims on the pepper produce were greatly reduced. Brown's activities could go on.

It is not possible to say whether Farmer conspired with Brown to this end, but between them they had gone a long way towards realising the policy which they had discussed at Mahé and which Farmer had advocated in April 1792.[1] Moreover, there was another curious action of Farmer's which seemed to favour the interests of Murdock Brown. Farmer had reported to the governor-general that the Dutch were negotiating the sale of Cochin to the raja of Travancore, but he had given his opinion that Cochin was of no importance to the Company and they should not concern themselves with its future. The Bengal government, and particularly Sir Robert Abercromby, told the Court of Directors on 17 January 1794 that on the contrary the possession of Cochin was of great importance to the Company, as a military station, a port, a source of excellent timber supplies and 'because it would contribute greatly to an exclusive Trade in Pepper in favor of the Company'.[2] It did not need the Bengal government to tell Farmer that, but perhaps Cochin's timber and pepper were the very reasons why he did not want the place to pass under the Company's control.

Shortly after Farmer's settlement with the northern rajas he left Malabar to become the chief of Surat, and he was succeeded as supervisor by James Stevens, formerly the southern superintendent.[3] Stevens had private commercial interests of his own. He was a member of the Bombay Insurance Society,[4] and was the relation and confidant of John Agnew and Agnew's friend Robert Taylor. He was involved with them both in charges of extortion from the Zamorin, which led to his suspension from the service in 1797 and a sentence ultimately of two years' imprisonment. Murdock Brown

---

[1] Alexander Walker said of Farmer's concessions to the rajas that they were 'effected by fear and corruption' and 'increased the spirit of independence among the Northern Rajas. The untimely and abject compliances on this occasion encouraged future resistance and diminished the respect for the Company's Government. Their authority was nowhere asserted with vigour and was in most places exposed to contempt or neglect...' Harvard Melville MSS, IOL microfilm reel 650: Captain Walker's report on Malabar, 24 August 1799.

[2] Home Misc. DCV, 594–5.

[3] According to Alexander Walker Farmer left Malabar 'Overcome by anxiety and apprehending it was said a legal enquiry...'; Harvard Melville MSS, IOL microfilm reel 650: report on Malabar by Captain Walker, 24 August 1799.

[4] See above, p. 25.

had much to do with bringing the charges against Agnew, and Stevens and Agnew wrote to Henry Dundas saying that Brown had suborned witnesses against him. It has already been seen that Agnew and Taylor regarded Brown with deep suspicion and hostility,[1] and the former described Brown to Dundas as 'my bitterest Foe...formerly the Company's great Opponent at the French Factory at Mahé...where he was one of the municipality and wore the national Cockade constantly but now the Bosom Friend of Mr Duncan and enjoying places of Emolument under him'.[2] The enmity which Agnew and Taylor felt for Brown was based on commercial rivalry. While Brown prospered their private commercial concerns suffered, and it seems likely that Stevens shared their interests. According to Alexander Walker he possessed 'neither private nor public virtues: Desirous of heaping up Money he cared not how he obtained it...'[3] Theirs was an ambiguous position. On the one hand too close a control by the Company threatened to affect their own private trade, but on the other, if the Company did not intervene the rajas and merchants would continue their own monopoly of the pepper trade. Thus Taylor opposed any schemes for the Company to purchase pepper directly from the cultivators on the grounds that it 'would create endless accounts in advance & perhaps frequent losses by the failure of crops, or other accidental circumstances', and he recommended that the Company should offer instead a fair market price to the merchants with heavy penalties for any deliveries short of the contracts.[4] He later made proposals which were designed to preserve a free trade in pepper and undermine the influence of the rajas and contractors. The scheme was for the Company to offer prices for pepper at their warehouses 'more considerable than they [the cultivators] could expect from interested merchants...it may be fairly inferred that in proportion to the increased confidence the inhabitants have in the safety of their property, so will the chance encrease of bringing the price of pepper to a just medium'.[5]

[1] See above, p. 82.
[2] Rylands English MSS, Melville Papers 670, 30: John Agnew to Henry Dundas, 4 April 1797. Agnew describes his commercial concerns in this letter. He was the sole agent on the Malabar coast for all the Madras agency houses, and he profited from the remittance of gold coins from Madras to Malabar.
[3] Harvard Melville MSS, IOL microfilm reel 650: Captain Walker's report on Malabar, 24 August 1799.
[4] BCP, range 414, LXV, 336–7: Robert Taylor to Bombay, 31 October 1793.
[5] *Ibid*. Robert Taylor to Bombay, 21 November 1794.

On the departure of Farmer the interests of this group of private merchants came to the fore, and Stevens did not wait long before bitterly criticising Farmer's new settlement with the northern rajas. He wrote to Bombay that

the Company's Rights have been with little limitation given up, and the Revenues sacrificed to a very considerable Amount...Their effect on the System of Government We are attempting to introduce may occasion more loss of power and Revenue than can now be estimated; for already the Southern Rajahs and particularly the Samorine avow their pretensions to equal concessions...[1]

Duncan himself was later to ascribe to Farmer's concessions 'a farther diminution of the respect due to our authority',[2] and the Bengal government immediately revoked the measures when informed of them on the grounds that they were extremely impolitic and would only lead to future disturbances.[3] In fact Chericul and Cotiote pursued a policy of almost open resistance to the Company after the visit of Farmer and Brown so that in May Stevens directed that the Company's revenue establishment there should be reduced as it was useless.[4] Farmer defended himself by saying that it would be necessary to defer making revenue settlements in the north for some years until the Company could establish its authority there,[5] but in September Stevens did succeed in making an agreement with the raja of Cartinaad for a revenue not far short of that estimated by the commissioners.[6]

Despite the energy which Stevens brought to the task of establishing the Company's political authority in the province, he advocated commercial ideas which were the same as Robert Taylor's. He gave his opinion that the Company would encourage an increased production of pepper if they levied a money tax on the vines in the north instead of taking half the produce in kind. He declared the impossibility of putting guards in every pepper garden to see that the Company gained its rightful share, and pointed out that the

---

[1] BSPP, range E, VII, 237–44: James Stevens to Bombay, 18 March 1794.
[2] *Ibid.* range 380, LXXIV, 4778–9: minute of Jonathan Duncan, 11 December 1798.
[3] *Ibid.* range E, VII, 464–8: Bengal to Bombay, 28 May 1794.
[4] *Ibid.* range 380, LXXIV, 4783: minute of Jonathan Duncan, 11 December 1798.
[5] BRP, range 366, XVI, 272–5: Farmer to Bombay, 11 June 1794.
[6] Personal Records II, 423: 'Narrative of Proceedings respecting the Concessions made by Mr Farmer', dated 2 September 1794.

produce would increase when the Company controlled the northern districts sufficiently to stop the rajas from extorting the pepper from the cultivators at a rate which was much below its real price.[1] On 12 February Stevens announced his intention of proceeding to the northern districts with an armed force sufficient to impose the Company's will on the rajas and to enforce the same financial and judicial regulations there as were imposed in the southern districts. Only by force, he asserted, could the Company hope to make any progress in the north.[2] He was not unsuccessful in his policy. He discovered that Cotiote was abounding in pepper and made a revenue settlement with the Coorminaad raja who, as head of the house of Cotiote, agreed to be responsible to the Company for its revenue. He found that the Moplah inhabitants of Cotiote had suffered from every kind of extortion and injustice from their ruler. Acting on his own proposal, Stevens settled for money payments of the revenue from Cotiote and Cartinaad on the grounds that the rajas used the system of giving half the pepper produce to the Company as a means of defrauding them and holding back a far greater share of the crop for their own use.

Stevens defended his policy and insisted that it was not practical to purchase pepper directly from the cultivator. He emphasised the hold that the rajas and merchants had on the pepper supplies, and repeated Robert Taylor's proposal that the Company should pay the merchants in cash for the pepper they delivered and levy high penalties for any failure to carry out contracts.[3] But Thomas Wilkinson, the new commercial resident at Mahé, asserted that these proposals would have no effect on the price of pepper as the power of the rajas and the merchants was so great that they could fix whatever price they wanted for the pepper.[4]

In these several ways the unbroken hold of the rajas and pepper merchants on the spice trade, the activities of Murdock Brown, and the private interests of the Company's servants in Malabar, combined to deprive the Company of the commercial advantages they looked for on the acquisition of the province. Continued disappointments in Malabar led the government to turn its attention to Travancore. The raja of Travancore supplied large quantities

[1] BRP, range 366, XVII, 28–9: J. Stevens to Bombay, 20 December 1794.
[2] *Ibid.* 57–9: J. Stevens to Bombay, 12 February 1795.
[3] BCP, range 414, LVI, 663–7: J. Stevens to Bombay, 6 May 1795.
[4] Home Misc. DLXXXV, 642–50.

of pepper to foreign merchants and made constant excuses to the Company for failing to provide the 3,000 candies for which he was bound. Murdock Brown was one of his most important customers.[1]

But in December 1795 Jonathan Duncan concluded on behalf of the governor-general a treaty of alliance with Travancore which provided for the country's defence against possible attacks by the French. Sir John Shore recommended that at the same time Bombay should revise its pepper contract with the raja and by paying the market price for pepper make sure that the contract was fulfilled.[2] Duncan supported this policy as the best means of increasing the Company's supplies and of 'rendering the port of London the common or general Emporium to Europe for the Commercial products of India'.[3] Despite Duncan's efforts, John Hutchinson, the resident at Anjengo, was again predicting in July 1796 that most of the raja's pepper 'will mistake the road to Leadenhall Street, and turn off to Marseilles, or Leghorn'. The raja would take only the market price or above it, and it had become his practice to fail in his engagements with the Company every second year. A better plan had to be found to secure his pepper.[4]

Thus by May 1796, four years after the end of the war, the Company had little success to its name in Malabar. It had failed to establish its authority in the northern part of the province where the revenue was largely unrealised,[5] and its commercial position was little better than that it had enjoyed under Tipu. By 1797 the Court of Directors had become so concerned at the continued high price of pepper that they ordered the appointment of a special committee to enquire into the reasons for it.[6] But affairs were to become worse. The Cotiote raja rebelled against the Company's authority. No revenue had been collected from his country and the raja had executed three Moplahs by his own authority, contrary to the judicial regulations which the Company had established. On

[1] Home Misc. DLXXXV, 649; and BCP, range 414, LV, 252–5: John Agnew to Bombay, 16 March 1795.
[2] BSPP, range E, IX, 145–52: minute of Sir John Shore, 21 December 1795.
[3] Letters received from Bombay XII: Jonathan Duncan to the Court, letter of 15 January 1796, par. 5.
[4] BCP, range 414, LVIII, 662–5: J. Hutchinson to Bombay, 13 July 1796.
[5] BRP, range 366, XVIII, 120–5: J. Duncan and Stephen Whitehill to A. W. Handley, acting supervisor of Malabar, 1 March 1796.
[6] BCP, range 414, LXV, 269: the Court of Directors to Bombay, 29 October 1797.

2 October 1795 the Bengal government had ordered his arrest, but the raja had taken to the jungle and led his country in rebellion.[1] In this situation Duncan created a new Malabar commission to execute the authority of the supervisor. He appointed to it on 19 May 1796 Thomas Wilkinson the commercial resident at Mahé, Alexander Dow, Augustus William Handley who had taken Stevens's place as supervisor since the latter's suspension, and his own private secretary, Robert Rickards.[2] The membership of the commission changed frequently, but Robert Rickards quickly acquired considerable influence on it. In April 1797 Walter Ewer reported that he led the commissioners, 'a Gentleman of only 7 Years standing in the Service, whose greatest Merit seems to be, that he has found out the weak side of Mr Duncan, whose confidence in him appears to be unbounded'.[3] The first president of the commission was Thomas Wilkinson, a partner in the Bombay agency house of Rivett, Wilkinson and Torin. The three partners of this agency house were in turn to become members of the Malabar commission, and in their persons as in the case of Agnew, Taylor and Stevens before them, one sees the Bombay trading interest guiding the politics of Malabar.

But there was one important difference between the new commissioners and Stevens, Taylor and Agnew. As soon as the former took up their duties they employed the services of Murdock Brown. Brown accompanied Robert Rickards to an interview with the Zamorin who was immediately deprived of the revenue collections of his country.[4] A few days later Brown was also present when Thomas Wilkinson had an interview with the Zamorin's new minister, Ikanda Pannikar. The Minister had half an hour's private conversation with Brown before he made the accusations of extortion against Stevens and Agnew which led to their downfall.[5] Thus the new commission brought Murdock Brown back to prominence and influence and disposed of the power of his enemies.

This new and extraordinary triumph of Brown's needs careful

[1] BSPP, range E, LX, 688–700: minute of Jonathan Duncan, 8 May 1796.
[2] *Ibid.*, 781–2.
[3] Home Misc. CDXXXVIII, 89: W. Ewer to Henry Dundas, 25 April 1797. Duncan confirms this himself. He told Richard Johnson in February 1798 that he had particularly given his confidence to Rickards. See Rylands English MSS, Johnson Papers 190, 11: Duncan to Johnson, 14 February 1798.
[4] BRP, range 366, XIX, 6024.   [5] *Ibid.* 766–9.

investigation. That he and the new commissioners had a common interest in attacking Agnew and Stevens is apparent. Rickards appears to have been particularly zealous in uncovering their activities.[1] Rickards and Brown were both *protégés* of Duncan and it is probable that the confidence which Duncan placed in Rickards had something to do with their mutual association with Brown. Rickards was very friendly with Charles Forbes, and in 1802 at any rate when Rickards was again on the Malabar coast they had commercial dealings together.[2] He was later to become a prominent opponent of the Company's commercial monopoly.[3] His years on the Malabar coast, particularly as the collector of Irvenaad from 1791, must have given him considerable knowledge of Brown. Alexander Dow, too, knew Brown well from the days of the first commission when he had been Farmer's colleague, and Wilkinson as the commercial resident at Mahé must have had a familiar acquaintance with him. Bearing in mind Ewer's report that Brown had influence with the Bombay servants by reason of his association with them in supplying arms and ammunition to Haidar Ali and Tipu,[4] and with the knowledge that Brown had the friendship of David Scott,[5] it seems not unlikely that Wilkinson and his two partners, Rivett and Torin, also had commercial interests in common with him.[6] This supposition is borne out by the records of the Bombay Mayor's Court. Between 1790 and 1793 a case was heard in the court in which Moosa, the prominent Tellicherry merchant, prosecuted Murdock Brown for a debt of Rs 30,750, the price of 500 candies of pepper. Brown maintained that he had not received the pepper from Moosa, whereupon Moosa called on James Rivett as a witness and produced a letter which Brown had written in 1790. In this Brown said that James Rivett had under-

[1] Personal Records XII, 548.

[2] IOL, European MSS D100, f. 15: Charles Forbes to Robert Rickards, 12 December 1802.

[3] R. Rickards, *The present system of our East India government and commerce considered in which are exposed the fallacy, the incompatibility, and the injustice of a political and despotic power possessing a commercial situation also, within the countries subject to its dominion* (London 1813). Alexander Walker was very critical of Rickards and thought he was a party to Stevens's extortion from the Cartenaad raja. WB 182, a.12: Walker to Duncan, 13 January 1808.

[4] See above, p. 78.   [5] See above, p. 55.

[6] Brown advised Wilkinson as the commercial resident at Mahé to reduce the price which the Company offered for pepper; BCP, range 414, LXV, 440: Murdock Brown to the Malabar commissioners, 1 September 1799. A reduction of the Company's price could only mean diminished supplies.

taken to make up any deficiency in the payment for the pepper.[1] Robert Taylor supported Moosa's case[2] and the court found in his favour.[3] The evidence clearly shows that James Rivett, and presumably his partners, were engaged in trade with Murdock Brown, and that this trade brought them into conflict with Robert Taylor, the friend of Agnew and Stevens. Much that would otherwise be obscure in Malabar politics falls into place.

The new commissioners brought views to their task which were firmly set on one course of policy. This was the course which Stevens and his colleagues had pursued before them. In their first pronouncement the commissioners declared that

such have been the pernicious effects of the Rajahs influence & power wherever either has been allowed to be exercised, that we have doubts of the Government of this Province ever being successfully or satisfactorily administered, as long as the shadow of authority remains in the hands of the native chiefs whose habitual inclinations to an arbitrary use thereof, it has been found so difficult to controul...[4]

They proceeded to carry out these ideas in Cotiote where in May the Company's forces had made an unsuccessful attempt to seize the person of the Cotiote or Pyché raja, but had burnt and plundered his house.[5] The raja continued his resistance from the jungle and Colonel Dow declared that military force could not subdue him. On his own initiative Dow allowed the Pyché raja to resume his authority in July 1796, but the other three commissioners condemned the action.[6] Duncan and the supreme government upheld Dow's arrangement, but the commissioners did not at first restore the district and the plundered booty to the raja, and they addressed him in language which Ewer declared was responsible for the warfare that followed.[7]

According to Ewer the commissioners were setting the province in flames because of the insolent contempt with which they treated

---

[1] Bombay Mayor's Court Proceedings, range 418, XVI, 2305–19.
[2] *Ibid.* 2335–6. [3] *Ibid.* 2305.
[4] BRP, range 366, XIX, 568–9: the Malabar commissioners to Bombay, 30 June 1796.
[5] BM Add. MSS 12,582, 44–57.
[6] *Ibid.* Dow was apparently not involved in the corruption; WB 18, d. 4: H. Scott to A. Walker, 31 May 1797.
[7] Home Misc. CDXXXVIII, 89–95: W. Ewer to Henry Dundas, 25 April 1797. The raja replied to the commissioners' letters on 24 December 1796, 'Great or small, from one high station to another, whatever be the Fault, such writing as this I never saw in particular from the Company's Government...'

the rajas.[1] He thought Murdock Brown, 'the Chief Incendiary of the Country', was playing a not inconsiderable part in this. The Cartenaad raja accused Brown of disrespect by writing to him without giving him his proper titles. In Ewer's opinion this was a very serious matter 'as Contempt of the Rajahs, has always been one of the first Seeds of Revolt'.[2] Brown also appears to have had an intimate connexion with the Pyché raja himself and he acted as the intermediary between the raja and the commissioners in April 1797. The raja sent two agents to see Brown at Mahé and it appears that he sought his advice and asked for his intercession.[3] These facts provide curious insights into the interests and purposes of the commissioners and pose the problem of what lay behind Brown's cooperation with them in this aggressive policy towards the rajas.

The mercantile house of Rivett, Wilkinson, and Torin acting with Robert Rickards, provided amidst many changes in the membership of the commission a continuity of policy which led to their clashing seriously with Jonathan Duncan. This policy, as has been seen, was also attempted by James Stevens, another Bombay merchant, and it had as its object the destruction of the power of the rajas. Here in Malabar was a forward school of imperialists bent on removing by force the administrative and judicial authority of the local princes and determined to replace it with English officials and institutions. They were to press this policy against all the advice and wishes of a governor of Bombay who by his training in Bengal should have been most disposed to adopt it. Furthermore, they actively employed and favoured a man whose whole career on the Malabar coast had shown conclusively that he never engaged in anything which did not further his private commercial interests. Here it seems is the private merchant turned imperialist to safeguard his trade. The private trader had two opponents to contend with: the rajas who sought to protect their own privileged commercial position, and those directors and servants of the Company who wanted to supply the Canton and Leadenhall Street treasuries and

---

[1] Home Misc. CDXXXVIII, 111–13: W. Ewer to Henry Dundas, 10 May 1797.

[2] *Ibid.* 165: W. Ewer to Henry Dundas, 17 July 1797. Alexander Walker agreed wholeheartedly with Ewer's views; WB 182, d. 18, 'Malabar, No. 6'.

[3] BSPP, range 380, LXVI, 1073–8: report from Murdock Brown, 20 April 1797: 'the Raja's intention in sending them [the two agents to Mahé] was to hear what I said and advised on the subject'; *ibid.* 1074.

not the private pockets of their employees. The policy which met these two dangers, therefore, combined an attack on the rajas' administrative powers with an insistence on free trade.

This latter interest appears clearly in the policy of Richard Torin who on 31 August 1797 gave it as his 'decided opinion' to the Bombay government 'that it is totally impossible at present, and will be for some years to purchase the Investment from the Pepper Cultivators; my predecessor gave this plan his utmost attention, and experienced the impracticability of it...'[1] This contrasts with the opinion which Jonathan Duncan and James Stuart, the governor and commander-in-chief, delivered in October of the same year, that it was practical for the Company to buy pepper directly from the cultivators at a rate higher than they would receive from the rajas or merchants, but at a price much lower than the Company had to pay to the contractors. They thought that the objection that the Company might be involved in bad debts could be overcome, particularly in the districts where the Company was in charge of the revenue collections, by encouraging the cultivators to deliver their pepper at the market price in lieu of revenue. If these experiments were successful, Duncan and Stuart thought, they could be gradually extended into the other districts to the exclusion of all other competition.[2] Nothing could be more threatening to the interests of the private merchants and they persisted in opposing the policy. It is significant, though, that in January 1799 Richard Torin so far departed from his views as to propose that when peace came the Company might impose an embargo on the exporting of pepper from the province. The reason for his proposal was his fear that 'Ships of all Nations [would] resort to the Coast for Pepper', and he was particularly concerned because there was no indication that the government intended to retain Mahé at the peace, 'a Circumstance those Interested in the welfare of Malabar Province cannot but remark with regret & dread'. More pepper came to Mahé, he pointed out, than could be collected from the whole of the rest of the province.[3] The Bombay merchants feared the competition of their European rivals more than that of the Company.

[1] BCP, range 414, LX, 1032: R. Torin to Bombay, 31 August 1797.
[2] *Ibid.* LXV, 283–4: minute of J. Duncan and J. Stuart, 29 October 1797.
[3] *Ibid.* 422–5: minute of R. Torin, 5 January 1799.

But before there was any real possibility that Mahé would be returned to the French, the political and commercial policy of the commissioners was set on one course and Murdock Brown gave it his support. Brown's keen intelligence and ready opportunism had preserved his fortunes under many masters, and it seems that he decided it was to his interest to cooperate with the commissioners. It is possible that his quarrel with Moosa made it difficult to preserve his independent position in the province. He could whole-heartedly join the commissioners in opposing any advancement of the Company's commercial advantages, and he knew the value of a close alliance with men who intended to master the province. It is significant that in 1797 he began buying land in the vicinity of Mahé which he was to develop into the large plantation on which he grew his own supplies of pepper.[1] In this way he secured his own commercial interests in alliance with the commissioners.[2]

There was much at stake for the Bombay merchants in Cotiote. The country produced about half of the pepper supplies of the whole province[3] and these were threatened by the Pyché raja. In January 1797 Rickards and Wilkinson ordered bodies of men into the district to protect the pepper from plunder.[4] Because of the Pyché's rebellion the price of pepper had risen to extravagant heights.[5] In January the commissioners determined to end the revolt by capturing the raja, and they sent an armed expedition into Cotiote, but it was helpless against the Pyché's mode of jungle warfare, and met with disaster. Ewer reported that it had lost more men than had Cornwallis at the seige of Seringapatam.[6] The forward policy had suffered a check. Furthermore, the disaster determined Duncan to visit the province himself in an attempt to pacify it, and he recalled Rivett and Wilkinson to the presidency to sit on the council.[7] As he left Malabar Rivett recorded a minute in which he protested 'in the most decided terms that...the very existence of the Company's Government in Malabar, or at least its

[1] Home Misc. CDXXXVIII, 165: W. Ewer to Henry Dundas, 17 July 1797.
[2] See above, pp. 101–3.
[3] BCP, range 414, LIX, 416–18: 15 February 1797.
[4] BSPP, range 380, LXV, 83–5: T. Wilkinson and R. Rickards to C. Peile, 22 January 1797.
[5] BCP, range 414, LIX, 416–18: 15 February 1797.
[6] Home Misc. CDXXXVIII, 111–13: W. Ewer to Henry Dundas, 10 May 1797.
[7] BSPP, range 380, LXV, 610: 6 April 1797.

existence on a footing compatible with the interest or honor of the British name, still depends on the effectual subjugation, or the most unconditional Submission, of the Pyché Raja...' and that any negotiation with him could only be seen as a sign of weakness.[1]

The minute began a controversy about the Company's policy in Malabar which split the Bombay government into two camps, and which was taken to the Court of Directors. Duncan's policy was to end the warfare in Cotiote by negotiating with the raja. He was eventually successful in this and pensioned him off, but the administration of the country was handed over to the senior member of the Pyché's family, Rama Varma, and was not taken over by the Company.[2] Duncan's views were what he declared the first commissioners' had been: he trusted 'to Time, and to the united operation of a judicious degree of steady and conciliatory conduct, on the part of those entrusted with the local Management, for the gradual Corroboration and Extension of the Company's authority, in the ultimate exercise of the supreme local Power, within the Province...'[3] Rivett and his colleagues, on the other hand, were bent on 'carrying on the War, both against the Pyché and even eventually against Tippoo' who was known to be helping the insurgent.[4] In minutes to the Court of Directors Rivett and Robert Rickards condemned Duncan's 'unhappy spirit of mistaken moderation' which had allowed the Cotiote raja to show 'a proud neglect of constituted Authority, and an unpardonable requisition of legislative and judicial Power'. It was this retention of power by the rajas which they attacked most violently, and which Rivett declared was persisting in the southern as well as the northern part of the province.[5]

The commissioners' own solution to the problem reveals more than a little of the interests they were working for. In a letter which they sent to the Court of Directors on 1 January 1798 they recommended the proposals of Robert Rickards which were based on his opinion that 'the Authority of these Chieftains had, under the

[1] BSPP, range 380, LXVI, 948–50: minute of J. Rivett, 27 April 1797.
[2] Rylands English MSS, Richard Johnson's Papers 177, 11: 'A short State of what led to, and of the consequences of the Warfare in Cotiote'; an account which Duncan sent to Johnson, 14 February 1798.
[3] BM Add. MSS 13,695, 91: minute of J. Duncan, 18 November 1797, enclosed in Duncan's letter to Wellesley of 10 September 1798.
[4] Rylands English MSS, Richard Johnson's Papers 177, 11.
[5] BSPP, range 380, LXVIII, 891–9: minute of J. Rivett, 15 April 1798.

System of Administration hitherto subsisting in Malabar, encreased to an improper height'.[1] Rickards proposed that the government should station its junior servants in the province to act, with the aid of interpreters and military detachments, as collectors of the revenue. The rajas were to be deprived of that function. He also demanded the abolition of the local courts of justice and their police 'in view to the alleged notorious abuse by the Deroghas, or Native Judges, and Magistrates of the trust reposed in them, more specially in the Southern Districts; and that their limited judicial authorities should be transferred to the European Collectors...'[2] But Rickards did not rest there. He proposed that Mr Murdock Brown should be employed to revise all the revenue assessments in Malabar 'with a view to the equitable Reduction, and general Equalization of the ordinary subsisting Rates'. Rickards urged Brown's appointment on the grounds of his 'entire want of confidence in Native Agents' and promised that Brown's employment would result in increased cultivation and agriculture.[3] Here was imperialism yoked to free trade. Rickards' scheme provided for the coercion of the rajas but the limiting of the Company's power to interfere with the supplies of the private trader. Under Murdock Brown's direction the Company's share of the pepper crop would, no doubt, suffer a considerable decrease.[4]

The dispute between the party of coercion and the party of moderation became bitter and acrimonious. Duncan wrote to Richard Johnson, the resident at Hyderabad, to dispel 'the shafts of Misrepresentation & malevolence, that in all such Contexts intermingle more or less their baneful attacks' and confessed that he was hurt most by the fact that 'Rivett & particularly Rickards were Men, on whom I had bestowed my Confidence', and to whom he had given preferment.[5] Duncan also asked his uncle John Michie to win support for his policy in the Court of Directors.[6] Of the

[1] BM Add. MSS 13,695, 73–88: extract of a letter from the Committee of Government in Malabar to the Court of Directors dated 1 January 1798 and sent by Duncan to Wellesley, 10 September 1798.

[2] *Ibid.*   [3] *Ibid.* 73.

[4] The rest of the committee expressed its doubts whether the rate of taxation was too high and they thought that Murdock Brown must after all rely on native agents to make any new assessments. They therefore turned down this part of the scheme.

[5] Rylands English MSS, Richard Johnson's Papers 190, 11: Duncan to Johnson, 14 February 1798.

[6] Michie Papers, MSS 5881, file 2: Duncan to John Michie, 2 February 1798.

members of the Bombay Council he had the support of William Page and Lieutenant-General Stuart. Stuart in particular protested vigorously against 'the System of force & coercion that some Politicians would recommend' on the grounds that it would only produce a general revolt. He also accused Rivett of very much exaggerating the Company's weakness in Malabar. In Stuart's view it was natural that the rajas should oppose any attempt to dispossess them of their power and the Company should only look to the accomplishment of this end 'by the secret and gradual Agency of time'. The administration of the Bombay government in Malabar, he asserted, had been corrupt and they had no right to expect the rajas and people of the province to look to it for protection.[1] Walter Ewer had earlier expressed very similar views. The province, he told Henry Dundas, could never be civilised and it was ridiculous to think of governing it by courts of law. The Nayars were quite wild and the judges on circuit needed to be attended by an army. The people were just as happy in the places where the rajas had judicial powers as they were under the English courts.[2] In Ewer's opinion 'The wisest & most humane Method wou'd be to give up the Country to the Rajahs on certain Conditions, to allow them to govern as they think proper, by which means we shou'd acquire their Esteem & Affection...'[3]

One of these conditions to Ewer's mind was that the Company should have a monopoly of the pepper trade. His plan was that the Company should return to the system of taking all the pepper which the province produced at a fixed sum instead of taking half the crop for nothing. This, Ewer maintained, would encourage its growth and protect the cultivators from the avarice of the rajas. To make this possible private trade in pepper should be forbidden.[4] The plan, as Ewer recognised, was much against the interests of the pepper merchants, and if it were to be effective reforms were necessary in the customs department to prevent smuggling. This meant the provision of a properly staffed customs service with considerable powers of enforcement, and the equipment of a troop of horse and a fleet of boats to patrol the coast. Only by these

---

[1] BSPP, range 380, LXVIII, 922–6: the minute of Lieutenant-General Stuart, 25 April 1798.

[2] Home Misc. CDXXXVIII, 141–4 and 151–6: W. Ewer to Henry Dundas, 17 July 1797.

[3] *Ibid.* 173.

[4] *Ibid.* 115–18: 10 May 1797; and 181–5: 10 September 1797.

means could the activities of Murdock Brown and Moosa be curtailed.[1]

Two opposing policies were therefore put forward for the government of Malabar in 1798; the one advocated coercion and the establishment of the Company's authority and institutions in the province, but it also provided for the interest of free trade. This was the imperialism of the private merchant. The other policy of the disinterested administrators and army officers opposed the use of force and was content that the people should for some time retain their old rulers and institutions. But at the same time they insisted that private trade should give way before the Company's monopoly. The weakness of this policy lay in its refusal to recognise that a commercial monopoly and the maintenance of the power of the rajas were incompatible. It looked back to the days when the rajas had supplied the Company with pepper because they feared the power of Mysore, and did not take into account the changed conditions on the Malabar coast.

Despite the protests of Duncan and Stuart and the support which they eventually gained from the Court of Directors,[2] it was Rickards's policy which prevailed. In June 1798 the commissioners told the northern superintendent that the object they had much at heart was 'the Establishment of the Company Authority in Cartinaad, by gradually undermining that of the Raja, thro' the means of a Company's Servant permanently stationed there...'[3] and they were concerned at the Cartinaad Raja's opposition to the measure. In September Colonel Dow suggested a plan for totally destroying the remaining influence of the Pyché raja in Cotiote. He thought the Company should take into its employment the headmen of every revenue district and win their support by giving them a stated salary or percentage of the revenue collections. He further sug-

---

[1] Home Misc. CDXXXVIII, 185–7: 10 September 1797. Cf. Bastin, *The Native Policies of Sir Stamford Raffles in Java and Sumatra* 80–1, for the policy which Ewer followed in Sumatra.

[2] Despatches to Bombay XIX, 308–14: 20 March 1799. The Court said, 'It is obvious that too much has been attempted at once, and that we have already experienced considerable inconvenience by an endeavour to introduce too quickly a regular Government into Countries not prepared for such Improvements'. The Court said that the rajas should have been allowed to keep their revenue and judicial powers, until the country was ready for the introduction of the Company's authority.

[3] BRP, range 366, XXII, 1416–7: the Malabar commissioners to the northern superintendent, 26 June 1798.

gested that more military posts should be established there and
that roads should be built to improve the communications.[1] On
29 September the commissioners informed the Bombay government of their decided opinion that the inhabitants of Malabar must
be disarmed.[2] General Hartley, one of the commissioners, demanded the introduction of military law in the province and the
resumption of all the revenue collections from the rajas.[3] Meanwhile, in accordance with Rickards' proposal, Murdock Brown
was engaged in making the revenue assessments of the estate of the
Narangoly Nambyar. His influence with Duncan seems to have
gained him this opportunity,[4] and on 13 July 1798 he used this
experience to recommend a change in the Company's pepper
policy. He gave his fervent opinion that 'unless a very moderate
money revenue is substituted to the present mode of collecting in
kind by annual surveys there is little hope of seeing the quantity
increased much beyond what it has been of late years'. And as
added evidence for his cause he cited the discontent of the inhabitants of Randaterra 'at the present mode of surveying the Pepper
vines and levying the Tax in general'.[5]

But the days of Bombay's authority over Malabar were numbered. In 1797 Lord Mornington was appointed to succeed Sir
John Shore as governor-general, and he began his voyage to
India in November of that year with plans already formed for the
overthrow of Tipu Sultan. In this he had the full support of
Henry Dundas.[6] It was a policy which was decided in England
and there is no evidence that the Bombay presidency played any
material part in it. Since the acquisition of Malabar the Bombay
servants had paid little attention to the power of Mysore; they had
been too preoccupied with their own interests. Mornington's
imperious will made all the decisions and after the fall of Seringapatam on 4 May 1799 Tipu's remaining territory on the Malabar
coast was annexed by the Company. Bombay servants were employed to enquire into the revenues and commerce of Canara, and

[1] BSPP, range 380, LXXII, 3558–60: Dow to the Malabar commissioners,
19 September 1798.
[2] *Ibid.* 3545–7: 29 September 1798.
[3] *Ibid.* LXXIV, 4714–37: minute of General Hartley, 3 October 1798.
[4] Letters received from Bombay XVI: par. 4 of the revenue department, letter of
13 June 1799.
[5] BRP, range 366, XXIII, 1,780–1 and 1,785: Murdock Brown to the Malabar
commissioners, 13 July 1798.
[6] Philips, *The East India Company*, 102–3.

Murdock Brown was not slow to find a place with them.[1] But Mornington soon showed his dissatisfaction with the state of disorder which continued in Malabar, and in August 1799 Duncan was mortified to learn that the governor-general intended to transfer Malabar to the authority of the Madras government.[2] After this measure had been formally announced to the Bombay government in May 1800, Mornington privately wrote to Duncan to warn him of his intention to end the separate existence of the Bombay presidency and to incorporate it completely with the government of Madras.[3] But for the time being, Bombay was to keep control of the Company's commercial concerns on the Malabar coast.

This last decision was firmly supported by the Court of Directors under the chairmanship of David Scott. The Court took pains to point out to the governor-general that Bombay and Surat were 'the Critical places on which principally depends the extensive Trade carried on for eight months in the year. . .from one end of the Malabar Coast to the other, to the Gulphs and from Cape Cormorin to Scindy', and that they provided cargoes for China, Madras, Bengal and Europe.[4] Because of these circumstances the Court declared that:

it appears to us obvious that the management of all the Commercial concerns on these Coasts and all the Boats and Shipping should be continued exclusively to the Bombay Presidency, and that the Commercial Chiefs and Factors should have the superintendance of the same Districts, and be vested with the same Powers, as they formerly possessed, in Order to give them that degree of respectability and consideration in the Eyes of the Natives which is necessary for carrying on the business entrusted to them.[5]

This meant that the Bombay commercial servants in Malabar were to be given the civil control and police power in the possessions they had held in Malabar under Tipu and in the new conquests of Cochin and Mahé. The importance of Bombay's commerce had kept this limited authority for its servants. Moreover, it was

[1] BSPP, range 381, IV, 3856–7: minute of J. Uhthoff, 4 June 1799.
[2] Michie Papers, MSS 5881, file 2: J. Duncan to Jonathan Michie, 21 August 1799.
[3] BM Add. MSS 13,694, 44: Lord Mornington to J. Duncan, 20 June 1800.
[4] BSPP, range 381, XXIV, 3758–65: the Court of Directors to Bengal, 2 December 1800.
[5] *Ibid.*

David Scott who was responsible for preserving the independence of the presidency. 'The transfer which you notice as to have been the intention of Government', he told Duncan on 15 June 1801, 'would certainly have been put in execution had it not been for me, and indeed the Bill was framed for it in Parliament but I completely overset the intention. Indeed it was with great difficulty that I agreed to so much as was transferred, and I doubted then, as I do still, of the propriety of it'.[1]

But the loss of Malabar was a heavy blow. Duncan wrote to all the friends he could in England and to Henry Dundas, begging them to use their influence to transfer him to another post where he would have authority over more than the '2 or 3 trifling Islands not equal to the one hundredth part of what I possessed the Administration of in Benares...'[2] The Bombay servants addressed a protest to the governor-general which infuriated Mornington and he demanded its withdrawal.[3] The presidency had to accept its fate. But although the Bombay servants could not see it at the time the golden days of the Malabar pepper trade had gone for ever. By the beginning of the nineteenth century Malabar was only producing 8 per cent of all the pepper grown in the east whereas Sumatra alone was producing more than 50 per cent.[4] At the same time the Company found that it could not compete in price with the Americans who traded in the ports of northern Sumatra, shipped the pepper at low carrying rates to New England and thence to Europe, where they swamped the market.[5] The price on the London market slumped from $15\frac{5}{16}$d. per pound in September 1801 to $9\frac{11}{16}$d. in September 1803. In September 1805 it was down to $8\frac{3}{4}$d.[6] After 1806 the Berlin and Milan decrees closed the continental markets and the London warehouses were full. No pepper was sold at the Company's March sale that year. The trade never recovered. There was a temporary boom after the peace, but in 1817 the London price was $7\frac{1}{2}$d. per pound and in 1824 it was 5d.[7]

---

[1] Philips (ed.), *The Correspondence of David Scott* II, 310: David Scott to J. Duncan, 15 June 1801.

[2] Michie Papers, MSS 5881, file 2: J. Duncan to Jonathan Michie, 21 August 1799.

[3] BM Add. MSS 13,694, 44: Mornington to J. Duncan, 20 June 1800.

[4] J. Bastin, *The Changing Balance of the Early South-East Asian Pepper Trade* (Kuala Lumpur, 1960), 21.

[5] *Ibid.* 44–7.

[6] Parliamentary Papers, 1812, VI, Appendix to the Fourth Report, 220.

[7] Bastin, *op. cit.*, 48–53.

All profit had gone. This meant a revolutionary change in the centuries-old Malabar economy and it coincided with political upheavals in the province. Although the Madras government abolished the Malabar commission and reorganised the administration of the province it was too late to forestall the effects of the previous years' misgovernment. In 1803 the province rose *en masse* and rebelled in support of the Pyché raja and his adherents. But the rebellion was not so much political as a protest against the heavy revenue assessments and the devaluation of the coinage, the legacy of Bombay's rule. It was not until 1805 that the rebellion was finally put down and the Pyché raja killed.[1] The province was left exhausted and with its economy shattered. Mahé was returned to the French in 1817 for the same reason that the British withdrew from the west coast of Sumatra in 1824: the settlements had lost all commercial significance.

The eight years of Bombay's administration in Malabar throw an interesting light on the designs of British imperialism in western India at the close of the eighteenth century. There was nothing new about the Company's policy; it was the same as that followed by the Portuguese and Dutch since the sixteenth century, and had but one object: a monopoly of the spice trade. The Company failed in their object for two reasons. Like their European rivals before them they were unable to master the country. While Bombay was in charge of the province the rajas retained their military strength and powers of government and they used them to defend their interests as the principal pepper merchants of the country. While Mahé remained a French free port it was impossible to control the rajas' commercial activities. But secondly, the Company failed in its object because many of its most important servants had private trading interests of their own and they pursued a policy which was designed to protect those interests at the expense of the Company. The Company could have saved the situation for itself by paying the market price for the pepper it wanted, and a few enlightened men like Cornwallis recommended this course, but the Court of Directors could not be brought to acquiesce. To this extent the Company retained its old mercantilist aims, and while the province was under Bombay the interests of the Company's pepper trade determined the nature of its revenue settlements.

[1] Logan, *Malabar* I, 528–43.

But there is a new element of imperialism which one sees emerging more clearly in this period: the imperialism of the private trader. It has been shown how the private merchants were bringing pressure to bear on the older interests within the East India Company in an endeavour to open the trade between London, India and Canton, and how through people like David Scott they were gaining power at Leadenhall Street.[1] But in Malabar one sees their influence on the whole administrative policy of the Company. Before Mornington's arrival in India they were pushing ahead with a forward policy of their own. They led the demand for the use of force to destroy the power of the local princes and to establish British officials and institutions in their place. This demand, though, was coupled with an insistence that the Company should leave the pepper trade entirely free and open to private merchants. In this way they were laying the pattern for the policy of succeeding decades. It now remains to be seen whether this pattern of interests emerges in Bombay's relations with Gujarat, and how far the imperialism of the private trader fitted in with the new imperialism of Lord Wellesley.

[1] Philips, *The East India Company, 1784–1834*.

CHAPTER 5

THE SHACKLES OF GUJARAT,
1784–1800

The disasters of the Maratha war did not put an end to the interests of the Bombay servants in Gujarat. The winning and exploiting of the Malabar province provided the chief outlet for the ambitions and energies of many between 1784 and 1799, but the growing cotton trade between Gujarat and China and the Company's piece-good trade from Surat involved the presidency in the politics of the north. The year 1784 was crucial for these commercial interests in Gujarat. The Commutation Act created an unprecedented demand at Canton for the raw cotton of the province which caused the sales to leap from an average of 300,000 tales a year to 2,160,217 tales within three years.[1] The effect was to give Bombay an unrivalled superiority in the trade from India to Canton. Between 1775 and 1800 cotton from Gujarat provided almost half of the total merchandise exported from India to China, and of every ten country ships trading at Canton in the same period six came from Bombay as against two from Madras and two from Bengal.[2] For the Company and the private merchants of Bombay the trade and politics of Gujarat became of ever-increasing importance.

To the Bombay merchants the cotton trade meant the expansion of commerce, shipbuilding and private wealth, but to the Court of Directors it meant the safety and prosperity of their enormously lucrative tea trade from China to England. For although the cotton trade with its profits was almost entirely in the hands of the private merchants,[3] 'the close correspondence between the trends of the Company's export trade and the import curve for raw cotton shows how dependent the Company was on Indian cotton for financing its exports'.[4] The Court of Directors and the Board of Control were not slow to realise this and to explore the possibility that the Company itself might profit by the trade. George Smith

---

[1] Pritchard, *The Crucial Years*, 145.

[2] *Ibid.* 175.

[3] *Ibid.* 393.

[4] *Ibid.* 146.

had given them ample information,[1] and in May 1786 William Wright, the Company's auditor, drew up plans with this object in view. He found that from 1775 to 1784 the Company had imported on its own account only one-eighth of the total amount of raw cotton which its own ships carried from India to Canton, and only one-twenty-second of the whole quantity imported from India. Nevertheless the Company had made $61\frac{1}{3}$ per cent profits on the cotton it had sent, and the auditor considered that the Company's share of the trade should be greatly increased to the benefit of the Canton treasury.[2] The difficulty lay in providing the funds to purchase the cotton at Bombay as the load of debt there made it necessary to draw supplies from Bengal. The auditor was also aware of the severe competition in the trade which the Company would experience from the private merchants, but he trusted in his belief that:

as the Cotton Makers are so immediately under the Management and Controul of the Company at Bombay and Surat, their Authority and Influence might be *duly* exerted so as to have the preference in the purchases or contracts and it may be supposed that by proper attention in the Bombay Servants the Company might obtain the Quantity required at a more easy Rate than at present; which being a great increase of their former usual Demands would probably have the Effect of depriving private Traders of a great part of what they procured when the Company were not able or desirous of taking off a larger Quantity.[3]

The auditor's optimism about the willingness of the Bombay servants to deprive themselves of trade was as misplaced as his belief that the cotton-makers were 'under the Management and Controul of the Company'. For in 1784 the Company's influence in Gujarat was of the slenderest kind and depended almost wholly on their position at Surat. But Surat was primarily a manufacturing city supplying piece-goods for the Company's European investment, and the supplies of raw cotton came from the other ports of Gujarat, particularly Broach.[4] The cession of this important port and district to Sindhia in 1783, so lamented at the time[5], was quickly to be more bitterly felt by the Bombay merchants. The

---

[1] See above, p. 52.
[2] Home Misc. cccxl, 331–40: No. 65 of 'Mr. Dundas's Papers of Accounts', 16 May 1786.
[3] *Ibid.* 335–40.   [4] See above, p. 30.   [5] *Ibid.*

Marathas would not allow the English resident to collect the debts owing to the Company's servants from the time of the English occupation, and contrary to their agreement with the Company to exclude other European nations from trade with Broach, they allowed the Dutch to export piece-goods from the city. The English resident reported in January 1785 that the Dutch had bought goods to the value of Rs 15,000 and he feared that they would re-establish a factory there. In his opinion this might be followed by the French and Portuguese gaining 'free Liberty to trade to Broach, which is a good Mart for their Staples, & the Fountain Head for Cotton & Piece Goods'.[1]

The resident urged the Bombay government to bring pressure to bear on Sindhia to grant an exclusive trade to the English and to establish such privileges for the Company's factory as were necessary to protect trade. He wanted the Company and the English private merchants to pay customs dues no higher than those agreed with the nawab of Broach in 1764, and demanded that the Company's brokers, manufacturers and linguists should be under the protection of the factory and exempt from taxation. A further privilege he sought was that boats with English passes and colours should be allowed to sail unmolested and have their cargoes restored if they were wrecked. The English should be free to pass in and out of the town at will, and the Marathas should force the inhabitants of Broach to pay all their debts.[2]

The Bombay government transmitted these demands to the governor-general, Macpherson, and asked for his mediation with Sindhia.[3] They received some satisfaction when in March James Anderson, the resident with Sindhia, gained the latter's assurance that the Dutch would not be allowed to trade with Broach.[4] But Macpherson determined on more concessions and he ordered Anderson to obtain Sindhia's permission for the annual export of goods by the Company, paying customs duties of $1\frac{1}{2}$ per cent on all articles except cotton.[5] This was the rate which the Company had settled with the nawab of Broach in 1764 and compared very favourably with the duties of $6\frac{1}{2}$ per cent which were levied at

[1] BSCC, range D, LXXII, 17–21: L. S. Cockran to Thomas Day, 17 January 1785.
[2] *Ibid*. 21–3.
[3] *Ibid*. 33–4: Bombay to Bengal, 1 February 1785.
[4] *Ibid*. 104–5: James Anderson to Bombay, 14 March 1785
[5] *Ibid*. 182–5: Bengal to Bombay, 12 May 1785.

Bombay.[1] Macpherson thought that Sindhia would not make this concession to the English private merchants, but he ordered Anderson to negotiate a rate for them not above 6 per cent.[2]

Even while these negotiations were going on the new English resident at Broach, Joseph Hughes, complained to the chief of Surat of the intolerable treatment which he had received from the Maratha officers since taking up his appointment. His servants had been molested and he protested that:

By being treated continually with such unmerited Insolence without ever being able to get the least redress, My situation here is rendered utterly insupportable & while I am supposed to be treated with the respect & Civility due from the Servants of a power in strict amity with the Honble Company I have on the contrary never yet met with anything but insult & Contempt.[3]

Despite this unpromising state of affairs the Bombay government hoped that Sindhia could be brought to agree to their exporting an unlimited amount of goods at the rate of 1½ per cent duty, but Anderson declared this to be impossible and finally got the Bombay board to stipulate for 800 candies of cotton and piece-goods to the value of Rs 1,50,000.[4] On 9 January 1786 the Company signed a treaty with Sindhia which provided for most of these demands and allowed the Company to exercise jurisdiction over all its servants, English and Indian, at its factory.[5] Yet three months later the resident at Broach reported that the insults against him continued and that he had on one occasion been refused admittance into the town for several hours. He expressed his conviction that the treaty would not be fulfilled and reported another breach of its terms in the Marathas' seizure of the cargo of a boat with an English pass which had been wrecked off the Broach bar.[6]

These incidents did not promise much for the future of the English trade with Broach, and at Surat also the Marathas were causing trouble which threatened to disrupt the Company's trade. Since the Maratha conquest of Gujarat the gaikwar and the

---

[1] PRO 30/11/7, f. 296: 'Observations on the English possessions in India privately communicated to Henry Dundas', 20 September 1785.
[2] CSCB, range D, LXXII, 183: Bengal to Bombay, 12 May 1785.
[3] *Ibid.* 282–4: Joseph Hughes to Surat, 8 September 1785.
[4] Home Misc. DCV, 255–6.
[5] BSPP, range D, LXXIII, 137: 9 January 1786.
[6] *Ibid.* 342–4: Joseph Hughes to the chief of Surat, 10 April 1786.

peshwa had levied chauth on the revenues of Surat. They collected every year a set sum of Rs 42,000, and their collectors, the two chautheas, levied a further Rs 11,000. In addition they took a third part of the dues collected in the nawab's two custom houses, the phoorza and the kooskie, and a third part of the revenue from fines imposed in the nawab's court or adowlat.[1] By an agreement with the Marathas the function of the chautheas was confined to the mere receipt of their share of the revenues, but as Charles Malet later said, 'the moderate Exercise of Power is by no means the Characteristick of the Mahrattas',[2] and in 1786 the ageing and infirm nawab complained of the exactions and innovations of a new chauthea. According to the nawab he had increased the usual number of sepoys under his command to between two hundred and three hundred, had armed them with English muskets, and stationed them outside the houses of the nawab's subjects to enforce his demands, and, as it seemed to the nawab, to usurp power in the city.[3] The English chief tried to smooth out the disputes, but Malet suspected that the new chauthea's conduct might be the result of the intrigues of some of the nawab's relations who hoped through the influence of the peshwa to gain power for themselves in Surat on the nawab's death. Malet recognised the danger to the English interest and urged that the nawab's military force should be put on a respectable footing[4] and that he should be made to pay for it instead of relying completely on the Company for his support.[5]

A further indication of trouble from the north came in February of the same year when the Bombay council agreed to lend guns and ammunition to the raja of Bhaunagar. This was to enable him to reduce a fort which was in the possession of the Kolis, whom the council observed, 'have ever been Hostile to the Company and now are constantly making depredations on our trade by taking our Boats and distressing our Merchants, & which sometimes have obliged the Company to fit out Expeditions against them at no

[1] BSPP, range D, LXXIII, 126: the nawab of Surat to the committee appointed to investigate the disputes between him and the chauthea, 4 February 1786.
[2] Home Misc. CCCXXXIII, 84–5: C. W. Malet to Cornwallis, 28 March 1789.
[3] BSPP, range D, LXXIII, 126–8: the nawab of Surat to the Surat committee, 4 February 1786.
[4] *Poona Residency Correspondence* II, ed. Sardesai, 6: Malet to Cornwallis, 5 April 1786.
[5] BSPP, range D, LXXIII, 322–4: Malet to Bombay, 7 April 1786.

inconsiderable Expence...' They were therefore pleased that the raja should relieve them of some of the trouble.[1]

It was from a Gujarat suffering from these disturbances and in which the Company had such little power that the Court of Directors demanded increased investments. In April 1786 they ordered as large a supply of piece-goods as the state of the Bombay treasury would allow with the aim of restoring their finances after the war.[2] Two months later they ordered the Bombay government to provide cargoes of raw cotton for five ships, the whole amounting to about 33,000 bales, and paid for by bullion shipped from England.[3] On 8 November the Court addressed the Bombay government in the terms suggested by their auditor, setting out their new policy of profiting by the cotton trade to Canton, and their hopes of obtaining cotton at a price lower than that paid by the private merchants. They threatened their Bombay servants with serious consequences if their orders did not result in cargoes arriving at Canton with profits of 65 per cent.[4] In the same letter the Court expressed its severe displeasure at the continued failure of the Bombay government to send adequate investments of Surat piece-goods to England where they were very much in demand by Bristol and Liverpool merchants for the slave trade to Africa.[5] So serious was the failure that the Company had to satisfy the Africa merchants by permitting the import of Indian piece-goods from foreign markets.

The Bombay government heeded the seriousness of the Court's orders[6] but the chief of Surat pointed out the difficulties of obeying them. The demand for cotton had forced the price so high that the contractors would only sell it to the high bids of the private merchants.[7] In response the government decided to take advantage of the treaty made with Sindhia in September 1785 and to export 1,600 bales of cotton from Broach.[8] This was done, but in May

---

[1] *Ibid.* 188: 27 February 1786.
[2] Despatches to Bombay VIII, 277: 7 April 1786. Philips, *The East India Company*, 46–7.
[3] BSPP, range D, LXXIV, 35–6: the Court to Bombay, 2 June 1786.
[4] Despatches to Bombay IX, 37–9: 8 November 1786.
[5] *Ibid.* 41–4. The Eden free-trade treaty with France signed in September 1786 also led to an increased export of piece-goods to Europe; Pritchard, *The Crucial Years*, 219.
[6] Letters received from Bombay VIII, 493–5: 27 January 1787.
[7] BSPP, range D, LXXIV, 54: Surat to Bombay, 30 January 1787.
[8] *Ibid.* 96–7: Bombay to Surat, 7 February 1787.

1787 a committee appointed to examine the cotton found it to be 'of so bad a Quality & so full of Seeds, Dirt, and Leaves, that We think it totally unfit to be accepted on account of the Honble Company...'[1] It was not only the Company's cotton which was in this bad state. On 11 May the chief cotton merchants, Daniel Seton, on behalf of himself and Miguel de Lima é Souza, David Scott and Company, John Forbes, Patrick Crawford Bruce, John Snare and six Parsis, sent a letter to the Bombay government protesting vigorously against the adulteration of the cotton which they sent to China from the northern ports. The Hong merchants at Canton, they said, had complained in 1785 of this adulteration which was practised by the Broach and Surat contractors, but since then it had grown out of hand. Broach and Jambusar cotton, they reported, had always been worse than that from Bhaunagar and Cutch, although for several years the quantity of dirt and leaves mixed with it had not exceeded 5 to 7 seers in each bale. But in 1786 the average had been from 50 to 60 seers and at the time of their protest it amounted to from a quarter to a third of the total weight of each bale.[2] Hardly a bale of a very large crop, they claimed, was merchantable and the situation was ruinous to them. Even if there were only $5\frac{1}{2}$ maunds of seed in each candy they stood to lose 4 lacs and Rs 5,000 on the crop of 30,000 bales, besides the confidence of the Hong merchants. The Chinese, they told the government, were probably on the point of converting all their own cotton fields into rice grounds because the cotton imported from India was cheaper and superior to their own, but as they would assume that the merchants were responsible for the cotton frauds, they might reverse their policy to the great loss of the private merchants and the Company.[3] One of the speediest ways of correcting the abuse, the merchants urged the government, was to appoint a committee of merchants to sample the cotton and to reduce the contract price in proportion to the quantity of seed found in each bale.[4]

[1] BCP, range 414, XLVII, 61: 8 May 1787.
[2] *Ibid.* 65–68: Cotton merchants to the Bombay government, 11 May 1787.
[3] *Ibid.* 67. In 1790 James Drummond told Henry Dundas from Canton, 'The immense quantity of cotton come to Market this Season as well as its inferior quality has given a very considerable check to this Trade...' and he went on to repeat the arguments of the Bombay merchants; NLS, Melville MSS 1069, f. 54v: James Drummond to Henry Dundas, Canton, 14 January 1790.
[4] *Ibid.* 68.

The situation was a most unpromising one for the commercial hopes of the Company and the private merchants. They had no control over the ports whence the cotton was shipped with the exception of Surat, and there the disputes between the nawab and the chauthea flared up into affrays which interrupted trade. On 30 May Malet reported to Bombay that a violent dispute had broken out between the Company's chief and the nawab on one side and the chauthea on the other, which led to the nawab's plundering the chauthea, and the latter's leaving the town and blockading it from the outside.[1] Everything pointed to the continuance of these brawls and the interruption of trade between Surat and the surrounding country.[2]

It was therefore no mere chance which led Malet to send to Cornwallis on 26 June 1787 a copy of a letter from the Bombay government on the subject of the Marathas' wish to recover Salsette. This was an object which was very close to Nana Farnavis's heart, and he had broached the subject to Malet and offered a cession of territory in Gujarat in return for its restoration.[3] The Bombay government referred the question to the governor-general and the Court of Directors but their letter to Malet left no doubt of their wishes. 'In our Opinions the restitution of Broach with its districts and Collection of the Chout at Surat, both Peshwa and Guicawar are the only objects which Merit the attention of this Government as an equivalent for the Renunciation of Salsette.'[4] The Bengal government was sufficiently interested to ask Bombay for their arguments in favour of this course.[5] In reply, the Bombay government observed that circumstances had altered considerably since the Court of Directors had urged them to acquire Salsette from the Marathas, and especially since the Court had announced its 'views with particular earnestness to the extension of the Cotton Trade to China which would be furthered most essentially were Broach ceded...as part of the purchase of Salsette'. If the rest of the purchase price were made up by the cession of the Maratha chauth of Surat, which would free the city from

---

[1] BSPP, range D, LXXIV, 240–5: Malet to Bombay, 30 May 1787.
[2] Home Misc. CCCXXXIII, 84–7: Malet to Cornwallis, 28 March 1789.
[3] *Poona Residency Correspondence* II, ed. Sardesai, 119–20: Bombay to Malet, 26 June 1787.
[4] PRO 30/11/18, f. 443–443v: copy of a letter from the Bombay government to Charles Malet, 26 June 1787, sent by Malet to Cornwallis.
[5] Letters received from Bombay VIII, 627: 20 November 1787.

the chauthea's interference and exactions, the balance of advantages, according to Bombay, would be on the Company's side.[1]

These proposals received powerful support from Charles Malet. On 15 January 1788 he wrote to Cornwallis from Poona pointing out the few advantages which the Company gained from the possession of Salsette. 'Should, therefore the Exchange of this Island ever become a Matter of Discussion,' he continued,

the assistance of additional property in the rich and commercial Province of Guzerat may not be unworthy the Attention of Your Lordship in Council. The whole of the Trade of the most productive Part of that Country centres on the Cities of Surat, Broach, and Cambay, on the three great Rivers Tappi, Nerbudda and Myhe, and by a proper arrangement of influx in those Cities, I conceive as great a share of the Cotton Trade as might be found requisite might be secured for the China Market whence would arise a very improved fund for supplying the investment from thence to Europe and the mother Country be greatly relieved from the Drain of its specie for the supply of that Market.[2]

To Malet the growth of the China trade was dependent on the taking of territory in India. His ideas were not casually formed or idly thrown out. In September of the same year he repeated them more forcibly to Cornwallis. Salsette, he declared, should only be given up in return for

the Establishment of a Commercial Interest in the rich and fertile Province of Guzerat. In that case the acquisition of the Towns of Surat, Broach Cambay on the three great rivers Tappy, Nirbudda, and Myhe would necessarily throw the whole Trade of the Province into our hands, by which Means, exclusive of the present Investments of the Company, consisting, I believe principally of Piece Goods for the African Market, the Company might command the important Raw Produce of Cotton, Indigo, and Tobacco...[3]

This was a new note in the politics of the Bombay presidency. The first expansionist adventures of the Bombay servants in Gujarat and not a little of their activity in Malabar had been characterised by many shady private interests masquerading as the public good and without any clear-sighted policy or even competent plans to direct them. The direction and influence had come

[1] Letters received from Bombay VIII, 628–30: 20 November 1787.
[2] PRO 30/11/22, ff. 251v–252v: Malet to Cornwallis, Poona, 15 January 1788.
[3] PRO 30/11/26, ff. 451–2: Malet to Cornwallis, 30 September 1788.

from astute opportunists such as Murdock Brown. But with Charles Malet a new vision was born, and it was one which influenced Cornwallis and his successors in Calcutta, and Henry Dundas and the Court of Directors in London. In Malet's outstanding mind and energy, his clarity of vision and devotion to an ideal of a British empire in India, one sees the forerunner of the young men who helped to build Wellesley's empire. Indeed there was not a little of Wellesley in him. Walter Ewer said of him that he was 'fit for the highest Station in India', adding, 'he has a good deal of Asiatick State about him, is very fond of shew and I should imagine may be easily gained with Titles, or gaudy honors'.[1]

But Malet's imperialism was not the vision of a 'Sultanised Englishman',[2] nor did it spring from any desire to advance himself. It was a hard-headed and tenaciously held policy to increase the trade and power of the English nation in India. To Malet the two went together: trade created power, and power was necessary to increase trade. It was a policy which was familiar to the Bombay presidency and Malet was only extraordinary in the force and clarity of mind with which he pursued it. For him the names Surat, Broach, Cambay, the Mahi, Narbada and Tapti, had long been significant. In 1780, as a young man of twenty-eight, he wrote, 'Surat, Broach and Cambay form the shackles of Gujrat...',[3] and he passed his years as the Company's resident at Cambay from 1774 to 1785 in endeavouring with single-minded determination to persuade his superiors that Cambay was the last link in a chain which the English could lock round Gujarat.[4] His own commercial concerns[5] and unrivalled knowledge of Gujarat enabled him to see the economic possibilities of the area and he condemned the blundering and self-seeking which characterised Bombay's first attempts to make conquests in the north. The policy he put forward in 1788 was already formed in 1780. In that year he wrote to R. H. Boddam that Bombay should have secured from the

[1] Home Misc. CDXXXVIII, 22–3: W. Ewer to Henry Dundas, 30 November 1796.
[2] *The Memoires of Sir James Mackintosh*, ed. Mackintosh, I, 212: Mackintosh declared 'every Englishman who resides here very long, has, I fear, his mind either emasculated by submission, or corrupted by despotic power. Mr Duncan may represent *one genus*, the Braminised Englishman; Lord W[ellesley] is undisputably at the head of the other, the *Sultanised* Englishman.'
[3] *The Poona Residency Correspondence*, 'Selections from Sir C. W. Malet's letter book 1780–84', ed. Sinh, letter 32, p. 57: Malet to General Goddard, 15 October 1780.
[4] *Ibid.* letters 1, 7, 8, 15, 44, 62, etc.   [5] See above, p. 26.

Marathas the northern part of Gujarat bounded by the river Mahi in the east, Marwod to the north, and the sea to the south and west. 'The produce of its soil is various, rich and abundant', he declared, 'amongst which the present precarious state of our American and West Indies possessions entitle indigo, tobacco and cotton to particular notice. Its manufactures are numerous and excellent, its commerce extensive, and its sea-ports convenient, its inhabitants are a fine race of people...'[1]

But Malet's emphasis was not on securing mere commercial privileges in the way that the Company had when they first founded their factories in Gujarat. His eyes were set on annexation. The Company must rule the cities which provided their trade. This was a new and daringly aggressive policy to propound for the Company in western India where Bombay and Surat were tiny islands of English power in the midst of the Maratha armies. But Malet had had an unrivalled opportunity to observe the effects of Maratha rule in Gujarat and to see at first hand the devastation and impoverishment which they and a nawab of Cambay could wreak in a once-prosperous city.[2] In his eyes the Marathas were the destroyers not only of wealth and commerce but of the arts and culture of the province.[3] And the faithlessness, the debauchery and corruption of the Mohammedan nawab of Cambay convinced him that only English rule could relieve the city and its inhabitants from their misery.[4] The pursuit of commerce developed in him the sense of an imperial mission, which would unite commercial advantages to the Company with the promise of justice and peace to the people whom he sought to rule.[5] They, 'relieved from vexatious demands and oppressive impositions, on the contrary experiencing the happiness of a firm and steady government would feel themselves interested in defending and supporting our power'.[6] Once adopted, this policy offered almost limitless prospects. 'Nor in the capture of Cambay', he wrote in 1782,

[1] *The Poona Residency Correspondence*, 'Selections from Sir C. W. Malet's letter-book, 1780–84', ed. Sinh, letter 27, pp. 45–6: Malet to R. H. Boddam, 12 August 1780.

[2] See pp. 28–9.

[3] Home Misc. CCCXXXIII, 87–90: Malet to Cornwallis, 28 March 1789.

[4] 'Selections from Sir C. W. Malet's letter-book, 1780–84', ed. Sinh, letter 15: Malet to R. H. Boddam, 8 April 1780; and letter 48, p. 87: Malet to W. Hornby, 24 July 1781.   [5] See pp. 28–9.

[6] 'Selections from Sir C. W. Malet's letter-book, 1780–84', ed. Sinh, letter 27: Malet to R. H. Boddam, 12 August 1780.

would the Company's advantages rest on it alone, claims from hence arise on that capital and most desirable sea port Gogo, which by giving us a footing in the western Peninsula opens a new prospect inviting the exercise of our arms, our policy and that great line of liberal justice which, by reducing to order a country plundered by a thousand petty predatory chieftains is as easy to execute, as worthy the attention of a great and generous people, and the more readily to be adopted when consistent with their interest, their honour and perhaps necessary to the re-establishment of their affairs.[1]

The defeat of the Bombay army in Gujarat and the responsibilities of his position as the resident at Poona suppressed some of this youthful optimism in Malet's letters to Cornwallis, although his policy remained the same. But it did not meet with much enthusiasm from the governor-general. Cornwallis's policy of reform and retrenchment put any idea of extending the possessions of the Bombay presidency out of the question,[2] and he instructed Malet in February 1787 to inform the peshwa that the Company was completely satisfied with the possessions it had and would not engage in a war to increase them.[3] But at the same time he ordered Malet to find out possible ways of increasing trade between the Maratha country and the Company's territory.[4] Furthermore, in September 1788 he instructed the resident to negotiate at Poona for the cession of the Surat chauth because he wanted to end the disputes and trouble it occasioned, and he suggested that Malet should offer Fort Victoria in exchange.[5] But on no account would Cornwallis consider taking territory in Gujarat in exchange for Salsette. He told Malet firmly in October 1788 that such a policy would only lead to altercations with the Marathas and that the sole extension of territory which the Company wanted was the province of Cuttack to link Bengal with Madras.[6] Indeed it was at this time that Cornwallis was deciding that the Company gained nothing from its possessions on the west coast, which led him to propose the abolition of the Bombay presidency.[7] With this plan in mind Cornwallis asked Malet on 19 September 1788 for information on the value of Surat and Fort Victoria to the Company, and on 5 May 1789 he asked the Bombay government for particulars of the

---

[1] *Ibid.* letter 62: Malet to W. Hornby, 22 February 1782.   [2] See p. 48.
[3] *Poona Residency Correspondence* II, ed. Sardesai, 9: Cornwallis to Malet, 26 February 1787.
[4] *Ibid.*   [5] PRO 30/11/162, f. 101: Cornwallis to Malet, 19 September 1788.
[6] *Ibid.* f. 107v: Cornwallis to Malet, 22 October 1788.   [7] See pp. 46–7.

commercial and political advantages of these settlements.[1] By 8 August following he was convinced that the Company gained no advantages from these dependencies of Bombay,[2] and there followed the crisis in the existence of the presidency when its survival rested on the decision of Henry Dundas.[3]

At the critical time between May and June 1790 when Dundas was collecting all the information he could find on Bombay and its interests before deciding on its future, the copies of Malet's correspondence with Cornwallis had an important influence on him.[4] Dundas was brought to see Bombay, Surat and the whole province of Gujarat with fresh eyes. For the first time he appears to have understood the importance of the province in his cherished scheme of supplying the needs of the Canton treasury from India.[5] The persistence with which Malet hammered again and again at this point had its reward. Forbidden by Cornwallis to negotiate at Poona for territory on the western coast, Malet had to press for the cession of Cuttack, but he did not allow Cornwallis to forget Gujarat. When the peshwa's minister offered Broach, Cambay and Gogah in return for Salsette in November 1788, although in fact none of these places was in the peshwa's gift, Malet reminded the governor-general that

were We inclined to adopt Views of putting Bombay in a situation to defray its own expences by Territory or Commerce those offers would probably merit attention since next to Bengal there is no Country in India, in point of Produce or Situation, that presents so great and tempting advantages, while in Climate, Fertility, and Beauty, it is scarce equaled by any Country in the World.[6]

What Dundas read convinced him that Surat was of key importance to the trade of India with the Persian and Arabian Gulfs and with China, and that it must be retained and improved.[7] Dundas

---

[1] BSPP, range E, I, 306–8: Bengal to Bombay, 5 May 1789.
[2] PRO 30/11/150, f. 134v: Cornwallis to Dundas, 8 August 1789.
[3] See above, p. 47.   [4] See above, p. 49.   [5] *Ibid.*
[6] PRO 30/11/27, f. 414v: Malet to Cornwallis, 7 December 1788.
[7] See above, p. 49.

In August 1788 Dundas wrote to Pitt about proposals to restore the Dutch to their former commercial privileges in India, particularly at Broach. It was then Dundas's opinion that 'Broach is a Material Possession for us in India in so far as it is connected with the Ideas presently in agitation relative to the furnishing of this Country with the Raw Material of Cotton from India, and nothing can ever be admitted to interfere with that System'; PRO 30/8/157, ff. 49–50v: Henry Dundas to Pitt, 13 August 1788.

agreed with Cornwallis that Cuttack was an important object to negotiate for, but he maintained that if it were not to be obtained in exchange for Salsette he could not see 'any solid reason why an increase of Revenue, either from the Guzerat or Broach Country, would not be a very desireable addition to all the other advantages resulting from the free and unrestrained possession of the City and Government of Surat'.[1] In November of the same year Dundas re-asserted his ideas in reply to Cornwallis's criticisms. He brushed aside arguments that the Bombay government would be corrupted if it ruled Gujarat, and tried to convince Cornwallis by pointing out the necessity of increasing Bombay's revenue to support its military establishment. 'I mention Guzerat', he continued, 'in preference to all others, because of the convenience of its situation, and the Commercial Advantages I am satisfied are to be obtained by it, abounding as it, and its Neighbourhood does, with Cotton; and bounded, as it is, by the Gulphs of Cambay and of Sinde'.[2]

But Dundas's concern with Surat went beyond the mere retention of the Company's position there. His awareness of the importance of Surat's trading relations[3] led him to stress the need for reform in the city, a need which he was convinced of by reading Malet's letters and the correspondence of the Bombay government with Cornwallis.[4] Dundas was led to conclude from this that 'the whole Government and Revenue of the City of Surat ought to be in our Possession if we are at all to retain possession of that Subordinate; which, for the reasons I have already given, I feel it very essential for our Interest that we should...', and at the same time he thought the Company should strive to obtain the Maratha chauth. This was important if the Company were to have power to regulate the city's trade and customs so as to promote the prosperity of Surat and its surrounding districts.[5]

This question of the government of Surat was brought particularly before Dundas's notice by events which showed that the prosperity of the city and the Company's trade was endangered by misgovernment. In November 1788 the Bombay government complained to the chief of Surat of the debasement of the nawab's

[1] PRO 30/11/116, f. 88–88v: Henry Dundas to Cornwallis, 4 June 1790.
[2] *Ibid.* ff. 118–9: Henry Dundas to Cornwallis, 10 November 1790.
[3] *Ibid.* f. 86: Henry Dundas to Cornwallis, 4 June 1790.
[4] *Ibid.* f. 86v.
[5] *Ibid.* ff. 86v–88: Henry Dundas to Cornwallis, 4 June 1790.

currency, which, they said, was responsible for the disappearance of the good Bombay coinage.[1] The chief was able to satisfy them on this point, but in December 1788 Bombay received the news of a serious riot at Surat in which the Muslim population attacked the Parsis and inflicted much suffering on them. The most disturbing feature of the riot was that two officers of the nawab were responsible for inciting the Muslims to attack and plunder the Parsis instead of acting according to their duty to restore order. The chief insisted that the Bombay government must take steps to appoint a naib who would be independent of the nawab and have power sufficient to remedy the evils of his government. Such a step, the chief declared, was essential, 'as the glaring misconduct of the Nabob's officers who hold offices of trust, & the total neglect of the Police, so very necessary in a large City & its suburbs, have long since attracted out attention, & called loud for amendment...'[2] In March 1789 Malet pointed out to Cornwallis the evils of the perpetual disputes and violent clashes between the nawab and the chauthea and also the dangerous state into which the defences of the city had fallen because the nawab refused to spend money on their upkeep. The burden fell entirely on the Company who supported the garrison of the castle and the fleet at a considerable expense.[3]

In July of the same year Malet found cause again to 'lament the mixed and undefined state of the Government of Surat' in yet further cases of oppression by the chauthea and disputes with the nawab.[4] It was therefore not surprising that when the Bombay government wrote to the governor-general explaining the importance of Surat to the Company they should end by proposing that he should negotiate at Delhi for the reversion of the entire government of the city to the Company on the death of the ageing nawab. The result, according to Bombay, would be an increase in the Company's revenue, 'their Commerce extended & great abuses and disorders which frequently now prevail & which it is difficult to remedy entirely would be effectually prevented'.[5]

Soon after this proposal was made, the nawab of Surat died on 11 March 1790, and Bombay repeated its demand to control the

[1] BSPP, range D, LXXV, 359: Bombay to Surat, 28 November 1788.
[2] *Ibid.* 380–1: Surat to Bombay, 5 December 1788.
[3] Home Misc. CCCXXXIII, 71–97: Malet to Cornwallis, 28 March 1789.
[4] BSPP, range E, I, 366–9: Malet to Bombay, 22 July 1789.
[5] *Ibid.* 462–4: Bombay to Bengal, 27 October 1789.

entire government of the city.[1] But Cornwallis would not consider their request in the circumstances of the war against Tipu Sultan in which he needed the help of the Marathas and was fearful of exciting their jealousy.[2] He recommended that the nawab's eldest son should succeed his father. The Bombay government had to accept the decision. But it did not neglect the opportunity to impress reforms on the new ruler. The Company's chief pointed out necessary improvements in the administration of justice and strongly urged a reduction of taxes on the necessities of life in the city.[3] The opportunity, though, of taking over the government of Surat in the way urged by Dundas, Malet and the Bombay government was allowed to pass by. But the war against Mysore put an end to Cornwallis's ideas of abandoning the western coast, and he replied to Dundas's letters on Gujarat in a different vein from his earlier attacks. 'We do not differ in our estimation of the value of Guzerat', he wrote on 3 September 1791, 'but I am well convinced that unless the power of the Peshwa's Government should fall to pieces by an internal convulsion we can never obtain possession of it but by a Maratta war, which is a price that I believe neither of us at present are inclined to pay for it.'[4]

After this exchange between Dundas and Cornwallis the problems of peacemaking and the settlement of Malabar occupied the governor-general and the Bombay government at the expense of Gujarat. But the Court of Directors on their part were paying increased attention to the province, as their interest in the cotton trade to China grew. In April 1789 they wrote to Bombay deploring the practice by which the Company's ships, which were capable of carrying from 1,500 to 2,000 bales of cotton, carried at the most 800 bales for the Company and the rest for private merchants.[5] The Court ordered its servants at Bombay to send as much cotton as possible to Canton on the Company's account,[6] and the directors criticised the way in which their orders for cotton in 1786 were carried out. The Broach contractor had failed to supply the

[1] *Ibid.* II, 58: Bombay to Bengal, 19 March 1790.
[2] Home Misc. DCVII, 527–8; and BSPP, range E, III, 132–3: Cornwallis to Bombay, 24 May 1790.
[3] BSPP, range E, III, 146–7: Surat to Bombay, 5 July 1790.
[4] PRO 30/11/151, f. 82–82v: Cornwallis to H. Dundas, 3 September 1791 (printed by Ross in *The Correspondence of Cornwallis* II, 112).
[5] BCP, range 414, XLIX, 280–94: the Court to Bombay, 22 April 1789.   [6] *Ibid.*

quantity asked for and there had been from 30 to 40 lb. of seed in each 100 lb. parcel. Bombay was alarmed at the obvious seriousness with which the directors pursued their plans. They remarked that if the directors intended to take any further share in the trade it would be 'the means of raising the price of that Article to the Merchants as well as to themselves'.[1] But the Court continued to order cotton, and in April 1790 sent sixty chests of dollars for the sole purchase of that article.[2] The directors also increased their demands for piece-goods. In 1790 they extended their orders to include those produced at Cambay,[3] and in May 1791 they ordered four lacs-worth of piece-goods from Surat, most of which were destined for the African slave trade.[4] Again in 1792 they repeated in strong terms their demand that the Surat investment should be completed.[5]

The directors' new spirit of enterprise, competing with the demands of the private merchants, brought out afresh the problems of commercial dealings with the Marathas. Resident succeeded resident at Broach but their complaints of Maratha oppressions and of insults to the English factory continued. In August 1790, Nathan Crow wrote a bitter paper of complaint against the licentious and insulting behaviour of the durbar and Sindhia's soldiers towards him, for which he could get no redress and which prevented him from carrying on business.[6] The Bombay government sought redress through the resident with Sindhia,[7] but the Maratha chief accused Crow of interfering in the government of the town. Crow was concerned above all to assert the right of the factory to protect its employees and agents:

The Power of protection is the Grand provision in the treaty which gives strength and Influence to the Factory, without it there would be no security to its Dependants, and everyone would fly from any transactions for the Company through fear of the displeasure of the Mahratta Govt., which has regularly from the first Establishment of the Factory discouraged and intimidated all those who have embraced its service... Unless the Power of Protection be firmly asserted, the British Flag must hang with disgrace and every intent of the Factory frustrated.[8]

---

[1] BCP, range 414, XLIX, 323: Bombay to the Court, 20 November 1789.
[2] Despatches to Bombay XI, 439: 21 April 1790. [3]*Ibid.* 427.
[4] *Ibid.* XII, 461–2: 4 May 1791. [5] *Ibid.* XIII, 89–94: 14 March 1792.
[6] BSPP, range E, III, 267–79: N. Crow to Surat, 20 August 1790.
[7] *Ibid.* 282: 10 September 1790.
[8] *Ibid.* V, 284: N. Crow to Surat, 31 March 1792.

Crow's words were given extra force when one of the Company's sepoys guarding the factory was murdered, an event which brought forth a strong protest from Cornwallis, and a demand for immediate reparation and the removal of the agent who ruled Broach for Sindhia.[1]

Nathan Crow's emphasis that the Company must assert its power at Broach if it wished to protect its trade found support at Surat, where the chief, John Griffith, faced the problem of carrying out the directors' orders for an increased investment of piece-goods. Besides the obstacles created by the Maratha chautheas and the oppressions of the nawab of Cambay, which made the provision of an investment there very difficult, the Company faced strong competition in purchasing goods at Surat from the French, Dutch and Portuguese.[2] These European competitors bought large quantities of piece-goods of an inferior quality for the African slave trade, but they were prepared to pay more for them than the Company gave for the high-quality fabrics which it bought for the European market.[3] Their competition was therefore formidable and the mutual jealousy of the several classes of weavers made the Company's task of completing its investment more difficult. Furthermore, Surat supplied a large part of Hindustan with piece-goods and exported from nine to ten lacs' worth annually to the Gulfs of Persia and Arabia.[4] This demand made it impossible for the Company to bring any economic pressure to bear on the weavers. Griffith asserted that the Company would have to give them higher prices in order to compete with the foreigners,[5] but in his opinion this policy would not succeed by itself. He was convinced that the indolence of the weavers made them dislike the strict performance of engagements and thought it 'absolutely necessary to insist on a preference being given to this Company's concerns—and that the necessary Number of Weavers be compelled to work for the Company's which, from their Political Character here, and the relation in which they stand towards other powers, I am of opinion they have a right to expect'.[6]

At Surat and Broach the Company's officials were pressing for

---

[1] *Poona Residency Correspondence* II, ed. Sardesai, 245: Cornwallis to Major Palmer, 9 August 1792.
[2] BCP, range 414, LII, 144–5: J. Griffith to Bombay, 14 April 1792.
[3] *Ibid.* 145–6: minute of J. Griffith, 14 April 1792.
[4] *Ibid.* 146.   [5] *Ibid.* 147.
[6] *Ibid.*

the use of power to protect the Company's commercial interests. Charles Malet, too, was ever on the watch for opportunities of advancing these concerns. Early in 1793 the disputed succession in Gujarat following the death of Fateh Singh Gaikwar threatened to result in disturbances and invasion. Sindhia and the peshwa supported different claimants, and one of these, Manaji Gaikwar, sought the aid of the Company against a threatened invasion of Gujarat by Sindhia.[1] Malet was intent on preserving the independence of Gujarat, and suggested that the English should act as intermediaries between the claimants. He was also quick to see the opportunity of gaining commercial benefits from the situation. 'I have a strong persuasion', he told the Bombay government, 'that the cotton might be benefited by certain Arrangements with the Guicawar Government.'[2] Again when Mahadji Sindhia died on 12 February 1794 and was succeded by Dowlat Rao, a boy of fourteen, Malet urged the governor-general to seize the opportunity of negotiating for the restoration of Broach to the Company in return for political support.[3] He continued to press for the transfer of the gaikwar's collection of chauth in Surat from the gaikwar's officer to the nawab, in order to relieve the city from some of the disputes and disturbances attendant on its collection.[4] But Malet met in Sir John Shore the same reluctance to interfere in Maratha affairs, the same fear of rousing Maratha jealousy, which had governed Cornwallis's policy towards Gujarat.[5]

Malet was not a man to be easily deterred or to lose sight of the objectives he had early set himself. His career as the resident at Cambay had moulded his mind and created ambitions which all his involvement in the wide field of Maratha intrigue and politics did not change. Cambay gave him the opportunity of urging his views on Shore. Malet heard from Raoba, the minister of Govind Rao, the new gaikwar, that the peshwa's ministers were intriguing to overturn the weak government of the nawab of Cambay and to seize the city and its district. Malet immediately wrote to Shore to say that if the government of Cambay were too weak to defend itself the Company should annex the place rather than allow its

[1] BSPP, range E, VI, 152–8: Malet to Bombay, 21 May 1793.
[2] *Ibid.* 157–8: Malet to Bombay, 21 May 1793.
[3] *Poona Residency Correspondence* II, ed. Sardesai, 320 and 324: Malet to Sir John Shore, 12 February 1794 and 17 February 1794.
[4] *Ibid.* 320–1: Shore to Malet, 17 February 1794.
[5] *Ibid.*

'annihilation by the Marrattas'.[1] The reasons he gave were forceful and familiar:

From its admirable commercial situation, its possession by the Company would indubitably be productive of infinitely more extensive benefits to that rich part of Guzerat of which it is the port and to the Commercial interests of the western side of India in general, than by the Marrattas, whose Govert. is palpably hostile to commerce as is strikingly exemplified in the comparison of the present state of Broach with what it was under our Govert. It is worthy of notice, Honble Sir, that the sea-ports of Surat, Broach and Cambay on the rivers Tappi, Nurbadda, and Myhe, command the most valuable part of the commerce of the rich and trading province of Guzerat; the first we possess, the second we did possess, and the third is in a state that in a manner invites and long has invited our possession, having for many years preserved its independence by the credit of our support.[2]

Malet's assertions were sufficiently convincing for the governor-general to ask for further particulars on the importance of Cambay's trade and the force needed for its protection.[3] In June 1794 Robert Holford, the resident at Cambay, replied with a glowing account of the commercial importance which the city could attain if it were annexed by the Company.[4] At that time the place exported only Rs 30,000 worth of piece-goods for the European market because only a few manufacturers, and those compelled by need, remained under a government 'existing on the plunder and oppression of its Subjects, to a degree that has really annihilated both commerce and industry'. If the Company protected the lives and property of the people of Cambay, Holford declared, the city could increase its manufactures to any extent desired, particularly those wanted for the African market. The weavers who had left the town would return to it, and the Company could profit from the city's particularly favourable position for procuring raw materials at low prices. The Company could then command the manufactures of the whole place. Ninety villages were dependent on Cambay, and Holford estimated that it would need two battalions of sepoys and some artillery for its defence. He also pointed out that if the Company established its power there it could command the whole of that part

[1] *Ibid*. 330–1: Malet to Shore, 28 February 1794.
[2] *Ibid*.
[3] BSPP, range E, VII, 367: Malet to Bombay, 10 May 1794.
[4] *Ibid*. 452–5: R. Holford to Bombay, 22 June 1794.

of the coast. From Cambay the Company could destroy the pirates and robbers who preyed on its trade and shipping.[1]

This latter point was by no means an unimportant one to the trading interests of Bombay. Complaints of piracy and the seizure of boats laden with cotton and piece-goods by either Maratha fleets or the piratical tribes which went under the name of Kolis and infested the Gulf of Cambay, were but too frequent occurrences.[2] In 1793 their depredations became so serious that the Bombay government resolved to send cruisers and troops in an attempt to destroy the pirates' boats in their ports,[3] a course which was authorised by the governor-general,[4] and was carried out in the following year.

But the supreme government did not consider that Cambay provided a better base for attacking the pirates than Bombay, and as it emerged that the nawab of Cambay paid chauth to the Marathas, and that the acquisition of the city by the Company would be looked on with jealousy by the peshwa, the Bengal government discouraged the idea of negotiating with the nawab for its cession. Nor would the governor-general consider any schemes for recovering Broach from the Marathas, and he was content to advise Malet to find fair means of frustrating the Maratha plans to seize the city.[5] Malet pursued his schemes alone. He suggested in July 1794 to the Bengal government that they should offer to give a village in Benares to the peshwa's minister, Nana Farnavis, in return for the chauth of Cambay and Surat, but he himself recognised that the Marathas were unlikely of their own accord to give up such fruitful sources of power and influence.[6]

But Malet was to find support from another direction. On 17 June 1793 Bombay learnt that England and France were at war. Eight days later the Court of Directors wrote to their servants at Bombay explaining that it was their most earnest desire to seize the opportunity of the probable annihilation of French commerce in India and the decrease of that of other nations, to capture the European market for piece-goods. To this end they ordered

[1] BSPP, range E, VII, 455: R. Holford to Bombay, 22 June 1794.
[2] See for example *ibid.* I, 189–90: Malet to Bombay, 14 April 1789.
[3] *Ibid.* VI, 502: 6 November 1793.
[4] *Ibid.* VII, 5–6: 6 December 1793.
[5] Home Misc. DCV, 433–5.
[6] *Poona Residency Correspondence* II, ed. Sardesai, 366: Malet to Bengal, 19 July 1794.

Bombay to survey the manufacturing districts of Gujarat and to collect all the information which would help them to increase the supply of Surat piece-goods. They wanted to know the number of looms employed, the ease or difficulty of production, the burden of taxes borne by the manufacturers, and whether they obtained fair prices for their work or were oppressed by the contractors.[1] On 21 May 1794 they repeated their demand for more Surat goods. These were commanding a rising price in Europe and were finding fresh markets in the West-Indian islands conquered from France.[2]

These demands brought the position of Cambay back to prominence. It was not possible to carry out enquiries in the Maratha manufacturing districts, and the committee appointed to the task could get information only from Surat, Broach and Cambay. In March 1795, W. G. Farmer, then chief of Surat, made a report on Cambay in which he repeated all that Holford had said of the commercial prospects of the place if the Company could protect its inhabitants. He emphasised the advantage of all its manufactures going exclusively to the Company, and sounded the nawab on the question of the Company's protecting the weavers. Farmer was of the opinion that if the Company threatened to desert the city entirely, the nawab would allow them to protect the manufacturers.[3] The Bombay government welcomed the attempts to attract weavers back to the city, but was timid on the question of protection for fear of the Marathas' reaction.[4] But Holford made it plain that nothing less than the full protection of the Company would induce weavers to return to Cambay, as they had bitter experience of the previous promises of the nawab and his utter disregard for them.[5]

The course of trade was moving the Company to increase its pressure on the government of the country. In April 1795 the Court of Directors gave orders that everything should be done to remove the competition of foreign Europeans from the piece-good trade of Surat.[6] To this end they decreed that the Company should buy up not only the high-quality goods usually exported by them, but also those of a lower quality supplied to foreigners. The

---

[1] BCP, range 414, LIII, 313: the Court to Bombay, 25 June 1793.
[2] Despatches to Bombay XIV, 422–4: 21 May 1794; Philips, *The East India Company*, 79 and 105.
[3] BCP, range 414, LV, 200–3: minute of W. G. Farmer, 15 March 1795.
[4] *Ibid.* 204. [5] *Ibid.* 462–5: R. Holford to W. G. Farmer, 4 June 1795.
[6] Despatches to Bombay XV, 288–300: 28 April 1795.

directors were intent on monopolising the European market. They realised that if this were to be done it was first necessary to reform the contract system at Surat. Under this system the Company made arrangements with a contractor who procured the goods for them from a large number of small merchants. These had not the means to pay a penalty if they failed in their engagements, and indeed it was far more profitable for them to sell their goods to the higher bids of the Company's rivals. The Court insisted that the Company should find means of securing a preference in the trade which, they declared, was theirs of right.[1] This meant the intervention of the Company's power.

Events soon showed that if trade were to flourish this course was becoming a matter of urgency. On 6 August 1795 rioting broke out again in Surat. Muslim mobs attacked the Hindus and plundered property worth three or four lacs. Ten days after the outbreak the shops remained closed and trade and manufactures were at a standstill. The nawab declared that he could not control a mob which felt its religion to be in danger, and he would not give the Hindu money-lenders and shopkeepers any assurance that the rioting would not break out again.[2] The effect on trade was serious. A great number of the weavers were Muslims, but they relied on the Hindu moneylenders for advances of cash with which to purchase their materials. Moreover, since those weavers who were Hindus were afraid to work, the Muslim spinners who supplied them with thread lost their employment.[3] The provision of goods for the Company was at a standstill and the moneylenders were unable to continue their loans. It emerged that the riot had begun when Muslims accused the Hindus of molesting one of their priests, although the man had been caught in the act of burgling one of the Hindu merchants' homes. The nawab and his officers had done nothing to prevent a mob from assembling and looting the Hindu shops, and it was reported that they had even given the mob every assistance. The Hindus demanded assurances from the Company that some system would be adopted to give them and their property full protection, and they threatened to leave the town unless this were done.[4] It was obvious that some sweeping

[1] Despatches to Bombay xv, 288–300: 28 April 1795.
[2] BSPP, range E, VIII, 241–3: Surat to Bombay, 16 August 1795.
[3] *Ibid.* 247: Surat merchants to W. G. Farmer, 13 August 1795.
[4] *Ibid.* 254–9: Surat to Bombay, 8 August 1795.

changes were necessary at Surat.[1] The Bombay government sent accounts of the riot to the governor-general and pointed out that the force which the Company maintained in the city was insufficient to keep law and order and to protect the inhabitants.[2]

The repercussions of the riot continued for some time. In December 1795 the Company's contractor reported that the delivery of piece-goods had fallen considerably short of the Company's orders. He blamed the riot, and reported that it had been followed by a strike lasting for several days among the Muslim weavers.[3] He made further complaints of the 'frequent, indeed almost incessant, Disputes and cessations from work, of the Cottree Cast, who manufacture the principal part of the Surat Goods. . .', and complained that his orders for goods from Cambay had not been carried out. At Cambay he had no direct control over the investment but was forced to rely on agents to procure the goods for they alone could protect the weavers from the oppressions of the government.[4] This report forced the Surat commercial board to think seriously about the situation. The directors had ordered them to review the whole system of contracting with merchants for the investment, and on 21 December J. H. Cherry drew up a minute on the subject. He asserted that it was impossible to provide an investment without using contractors as the Company could not control the thousands of workmen by any other means. The weavers lived not only in Surat and its suburbs but throughout the surrounding Maratha country, and none were under the Company's authority. Unless these men became the subjects of the Company and could be organised in aurangs as in Bengal, the system of employing contractors and sub-contractors was the only possible one.[5] In Cherry's opinion the Company could only

---

[1] *Ibid.* 243–4. Surat said about the refusal of the nawab to give any assurances to the shroffs and brokers: 'and very particularly, the great Disappointment which may accrue to the Company by the stoppage of the Investment at a Season when the best Goods are made and that if those Assurances are in some shape given on the part of the Company, which the Nabob wholly declines to give, and the currency of Business, now altogether impeded, thereby restored, it will give you, Honble Sir, very just and fair Ground for the Establishment of any System you may deem most expedient, for the future Security of the City, whether agreeable or not to the Nabob. . .'

[2] *Ibid.* 260–1: Bombay to Bengal, 26 August 1795.

[3] BCP, range 414, LVI, 1033–5: Bomanjee Muncherjee to the Surat chief and council, 16 December 1795.

[4] *Ibid.*

[5] *Ibid.* LVII, 50: minute of J. H. Cherry, 21 December 1795.

monopolise the piece-good trade by buying goods of all qualities all the year round, and by making it the interest of the weavers to work for the Company. To do this, he declared, it would be necessary to exempt them entirely from the payment of loom taxes and the numerous oppressive taxes on raw materials which were levied by the nawab. He also recommended that the Company's commercial resident should have the power of mediating in the weavers' disputes 'and when co-ercion or punishment may be requisite to bring the same before the President of the Board as Chief of the Place'. The tendency of these proposals was unmistakable. Cherry did not fail to recognise it. 'This will however naturally excite Jealousy and opposition, as will the Company's investing the greatest part of the Foreign Goods, and materially interfere with the Nabobs revenues by lessening the Phoorza Customs, but it must rest with Government to determine how far such obstacles to the Company's wishes are to be submitted to...'[1]

That some such changes were necessary was made doubly apparent when the committee appointed to investigate the manufacturing towns made its report on 23 December. They had been unable to get passes from the Marathas to report on the conditions at Broach, Cambay and in the rest of Gujarat, and could give information only on Surat.[2] But they were able to show the heavy burdens under which the manufacture of piece-goods in that city laboured. At the beginning of the process they found that the cleaning of the raw cotton was done by the poorest people of the town who bought it in small quantities and paid for it slowly, a method which raised the price by 20 per cent.[3] About 1,250 candies of cotton were brought into Surat annually. The nawab levied a tax of Rs 10 a candy on it,[4] and the same amount on the 4,000 maunds of cotton yarn which were brought in from the surrounding country. In addition the 500 or so cotton dealers of Surat paid an annual levy to the nawab. There were also taxes on indigo, and the nawab collected 18½ per cent of the value of the finished cloth. By the time that the piece-goods were in the hands of the Company these several taxes had raised their cost considerably. Furthermore, the committee found that the weavers were discouraged from increasing their production by the organisation of the trade. The dealers who supplied the Company's contractor with the

[1] BCP, range 414, LVII, 52–4: minute of J. H. Cherry, 21 December 1795.
[2] *Ibid.* 14–42: 23 December 1795.   [3] *Ibid.* 18.   [4] *Ibid.* 23.

152

finished goods provided the weavers with all the raw materials and advanced money to them for their food and necessities. The weavers complained to the Company that the dealers used this system to pay them less for their work than was their due.[1] In the opinion of the committee the Company would increase their investment if the weavers were able to buy their own raw materials and sell their finished piece-goods directly to the Company.

It fell to Jonathan Duncan on his arrival as governor at Bombay to consider this report and its proposals. In February 1796 he gave his opinion that where the Company had some influence, in Surat and the surrounding villages, the commercial resident should make contracts directly with the weavers and so attach them to the Company's interest by giving them the full price for their work. But this was not possible in the Maratha districts, and the Company had to rely on intermediate agents, knowing that if they attempted to give the weavers greater financial rewards, these would only be wrung from them by the Maratha government.[2] On 9 February Duncan nominated Daniel Seton as the provisional chief of Surat, and gave as the reason for his choice Seton's promise to cooperate with the commercial resident in providing the large investment of piece-goods ordered by the directors. He also thought that Seton would show energy in promoting the reforms at Surat which Duncan declared would be necessary in the following year, and that he would succeed in getting the nawab's consent 'to let all the Weavers employed for the Company within the Limits of Surat remain under the special protection of the Commercial Resident, as well perhaps as to procure an abolition or Mitigation of the Taxes now paid by them'.[3]

This policy of promoting the Company's commercial interests led to further clashes with the Marathas in Surat. The Marathas shared the receipts of the nawab's customs houses, the phoorza for exports by sea and the kooskie for exports by land. But the Company had its own customs house at Surat, the latty, and at the beginning of 1796 it reduced the rates there from $6\frac{1}{2}$ to $2\frac{1}{2}$ per cent to encourage trade. There had always been complaints from the merchants that the Maratha chautheas used physical violence to force them to export through the phoorza and not the

---

[1] *Ibid.* 24–42.
[2] *Ibid.* 224–5: minute of J. Duncan, 8 February 1796.
[3] Home Misc. CCCXXXIII, 345–8: minute of J. Duncan, 9 February 1796.

latty, so that the chautheas could increase their revenues,[1] but at the reduction of the Company's customs the Marathas threatened to recoup their losses by exactions and obstructions on the trade by land to and from Surat.[2]

In May Daniel Seton, the new chief, brought up again the question of negotiating with the Marathas for the commutation of their chauth of Surat, and he gave his opinion to Duncan that the gaikwar might be prevailed upon to agree. Before this Seton had already taken steps to increase the Company's power in the city. In April he prevailed on the nawab, after an arduous negotiation, to withdraw for one year the taxes he levied on the Company's piece-goods.[3] The Bombay government hoped that the nawab would be brought to relinquish the tax permanently, and rejoiced at the prospect of the advantage over its competitors which the Company would gain from the concession.[4] In July they won this further object, and the nawab relinquished the tax for ever.[5] In May the commercial resident announced his plan for monopolising, as nearly as possible, all the piece-goods produced in Surat for the European market.[6] The following September a further step forward was made when Duncan wrote to the nawab of Cambay and gained his approval for the Company's extending its protection to an increased number of weavers at Cambay. This success gave hopes of a greater increase of the investment from there.

But the Company's commercial plans were to find no easy fulfilment, and it was drawn more and more to use its power of intervention. In 1796 a vessel arrived at Surat from Lisbon furnished with several lacs of capital with which to buy piece-goods. The chief and council at Surat feared the effects of this competition on their own investment and they instructed the nawab to prohibit the sale of piece-goods without his express consent. The Bombay government cancelled this order on the grounds of the difficulties it would create with the Portuguese, but also because it would defeat the Company's object of encouraging the manufacture of piece-goods at Surat. But Bombay was alarmed to discover that the Portuguese company which sent this ship was proposing to de-

---

[1] See for example BRP, range 366, XVIII, 55–60: A. Ramsay to Bombay, 16 January 1796.
[2] *Ibid.* 41–3: Bombay to Bengal, 21 January 1796.
[3] BCP, range 414, LVII, 473–7: Surat to Bombay, 27 April 1796.
[4] *Ibid.* 477: 6 May 1796.   [5] *Ibid.* LVIII, 625: 6 July 1796.
[6] *Ibid.* LVII, 504: minute of J. H. Cherry, 8 May 1796.

velop a regular trade between Surat and Lisbon and had appointed a consul-general and a resident at Surat. The government feared that this trade would 'very materially obstruct and prejudice the Company's annual investments of that article...',[1] and sought advice from Bengal. At Surat the commercial resident applied methods of his own to defeat the Portuguese competition. He stationed sepoys in the streets and over the looms to deter the Portuguese from buying up the piece-goods on which the Company had advanced money.[2] But it was not long before he too advocated sterner measures and the direct intervention of the Company to secure the investment. For besides the competition from the Portuguese he was struggling with the class of manufacturers called the Ketteries, 'a disaffected obstinate, and dissolute set of people, who never work but when compelled by absolute want...' who had the exclusive privilege of manufacturing a certain type of cloth wanted by the Company.[3] Moreover, he found all the Surat weavers only too ready to break their engagements and to sell their goods to foreigners, and was 'continually compelled to court or artfully force the Inclination of every class of Artizans employed and combat by stratagems and management alone...' their schemes of self-interest.

In London the directors considered the riot of August 1795 and sent orders in February 1797 that the Bombay government should immediately consider sending further troops to Surat to preserve the city's internal peace and order. The nawab, they laid down, should pay for the troops out of his public revenues.[4] But Bombay was thinking of a further way of asserting the Company's power: the introduction of a court of adowlat into the city.[5] Through this court they could exercise the judicial authority which was then the prerogative of the nawab. And judicial authority could enormously strengthen their commercial position. It was necessary not only to check further outbreaks of violence, but so that the whole system of providing the investment could be brought under the Company's direct control. The committee of enquiry had

[1] BSPP, range E, XI, 1517–21: Bombay to Bengal, 3 October 1796.
[2] BCP, range 414, LVIII, 880–7: 22 October 1796. The Portuguese complained bitterly against these measures; Surat Factory Records, LXXVI, 1797, *passim*.
[3] BCP, range 414, LIX, 383–92: minute of J. H. Cherry, 4 March 1797. See also above, p. 151.
[4] Despatches to Bombay XVII, 123–8: 17 February 1797.
[5] BSPP, range 380, LXVI, 1332–3: 21 July 1797.

revealed the exactions which the contractors practised on the weavers,[1] and which reduced the latter 'to a state of shameless necessity & indifference' and forced them to maintain themselves 'by encroachments on the thread, colour & Workmanship which constitute the quality'. In the eyes of the commercial resident the dealers were also responsible for cheating the Company in the quantity of goods they supplied, and of even inciting the weavers to strike for the purposes of their own disputes.[2] The Surat board had come to place their hopes in the Company's making contracts directly with the weavers. This, they thought, would ensure a fair price for their work and so increase the quality and quantity of the goods. But this system could only be made to work if the commercial resident possessed

the fullest and most unequivocal support of Government, and even if necessary the aid of the Nabob's authority procured thro' the medium of the President of the Board. His law is summary and his punishment prompt & severe; one instance of application to him followed by punishment if merited, would probably render a second unnecessary for a length of time . . .[3]

But the Company could not easily command the nawab's authority. They were not entitled to any general judicial authority by the Moghul's concessions, and they could count on the strongest opposition from the nawab and the Marathas who together shared the proceeds of the court of justice.[4] Whenever the nawab's position was threatened he incited the Marathas to advance their own claims in order to thwart the Company,[5] and this policy was to be expected in the case of the adowlat. Any reform which the Company wanted to make in Surat, concluded the officials there, appeared to 'hinge upon the last, or Marratta Chout; the removal of which would soon pave a Way rendering the others easy'.[6] In July 1797 the Bombay government discussed again in detail the desirability of removing the chauth and the means of doing it. They referred to 'the vexatious Interference of the Chouteah in every Branch of the interior administration of the City', and the 'constant and serious disputes' which 'frequently produced the approach of large bodies of troops & the obstruction of all intercourse between

[1] See above, pp. 152–3.   [2] BCP, range 414, LX, 1113–16: 18 October 1797.
[3] *Ibid.* 1119.   [4] BSPP, range 380, LXVI, 1332–43: 21 July 1797.
[5] *Ibid.* LXVII, 1650–8: Surat to Bombay, 25 August 1797.
[6] *Ibid.*

the City & Country to the great Inconvenience & Injury of the trade of the City, the repetition of which is frequently threatened & always to be apprehended'.[1] They recognised the continuing efforts of the resident at Poona to remove the chauth by proposing cessions of territory, but as these efforts had failed they asked for further suggestions to accomplish this end.[2]

Far-reaching proposals came from Surat. In August the committee which had been appointed to consider the best ways of achieving reform put forward a scheme which offered not only Fort Victoria, but the castle and fleet revenues, and the remote jaghirs of the nawab to the Marathas in exchange for both shares of the chauth, the peshwa's and the gaikwar's, and the Chorasi pargana.[3] This plan, the committee pointed out, would apparently limit the Company's influence to the neighbourhood of Surat, by ceding the nawab's jaghirs, but as the nawab and the Company's influence in this territory was, in their opinion, more apparent than real, an exchange for the Chorasi pargana would be of greater advantage to the Company. For the pargana encircled Surat to the extent of twelve miles and could provide the city with all necessary supplies of food and 'as much Cotton as the Company usually invest of the first Staple—nay even to the extent of 5,000 Bales', while 'the Manufactures for the Europe Investment might likewise be considerably promoted by Acquisition of the territory'.[4]

These plans for increasing the Company's power and territory were made quite independently of the war then being waged between England and France. At Surat the Company's commercial interests and not the French menace were the mainspring of action. Nevertheless, Bombay did not escape entirely from the French alarm. In February 1796 the settlement heard that two French frigates and a corvette had been sighted off Diu, the Portuguese possession, and there was some fear that they had captured the place.[5] But the Portuguese repulsed them and they sailed westwards towards the Indus.[6] This sign of French interest

[1] *Ibid.* LXVI, 1332–43: 21 July 1797.
[2] *Ibid.* J. Uhthoff had raised the question in March to the governor-general; *Poona Residency Correspondence* VI, ed. Sardesai, 16–17: Uhthoff to the governor-general, 31 March 1797.
[3] BSPP, range 380, LXVII, 1650–8: Surat to Bombay, 25 August 1797.
[4] *Ibid.*
[5] BSPP, range E, IX, 249: 16 February 1796.
[6] Rylands English MSS, Melville Papers 670, 22: extract of a letter from Alexander Adamson to J. Bruce, February 1796.

in that quarter created some alarm. Charles Malet feared that the French would acquire a base on the coast whence they could attack the Company's trade and even form connexions with the petty chiefs of Gujarat.[1] In August of the same year Bombay received the news that a French and Dutch squadron had sailed for India, and although their fears were later quieted,[2] Malet wrote to the Court of Directors in October 1797 suggesting the expediency of acquiring Diu from the Portuguese. He pointed out its commanding position over the whole western coast of India and of the Arabian and Persian Gulfs, and its importance to the Company as a base from which to attack the northern pirates.[3] Alexander Adamson also used the occasion to emphasise the importance of having the Gulf of Cambay and the mouths of the Indus river surveyed.[4]

But the Company had acquired an interest in that region apart from their concern with the possible plans of the French. In May 1793, John Bruce, Henry Dundas's secretary, who had just published his historical work on the government of British India in which he discussed the possibilities of extending British trade in the east,[5] wrote to Alexander Adamson at Bombay on the recommendation of David Scott.[6] Bruce asked Adamson to provide information for Dundas on the west coast of India and the countries bordering the Gulfs of Arabia and Persia and the river Indus. A year later Bruce wrote to Henry Dundas's nephew, Philip, expanding his request for information, and asking whether political changes had happened in the countries bordering on the Indus, which might give the Company new markets for their goods. This would be practical if the anarchy which had led to the closing of the Company's factory at Tatta in 1755 had been quelled.[7] John Griffith was able to tell Bruce that Sind produced piece-goods, cotton, indigo and horses.[8] Adamson also sent Bruce a

---

[1] BSPP, range E, IX, 299–300: Malet to Bombay, 17 February 1796.
[2] *Ibid.* X, 1,222: 6 August 1796 and 1,480, 13 September 1796.
[3] Home Misc. LX, 213–21: extract of a letter from Malet to the chairman of the Company, 28 October 1797.
[4] Rylands English MSS, Melville Papers 670, 22: extract of a letter from Alexander Adamson to J. Bruce, February 1796.
[5] Bruce, *Historical View of Plans for the Government of British India*, etc., 560.
[6] Home Misc. CDLVIe, 1–3: J. Bruce to A. Adamson, 16 May 1793.
[7] *Ibid.* 63: J. Bruce to Philip Dundas, 27 May 1794.
[8] *Ibid.* CDLVIb. 639: J. Griffith to A. Adamson, Surat, 17 February 1794, forwarded by Philip Dundas to Bruce.

letter from Captain Reynolds, who was attempting a survey of the area thinking his enquiries might open fresh sources of trade by means of the Indus from Tatta to Multaun and Kandahar.[1] These enquiries awakened considerable interest among Bombay merchants such as Adamson, and in July 1797 the Bombay government suggested to the Court of Directors that they might re-open a factory at Tatta.[2] This, they declared, would give employment to a senior civil servant, open the prospect of a market for their staples and enable the Company to keep a watch on the activities of Zeman Shah. At the same time they suggested the advantages of appointing agents in Cutch and north-west Gujarat to provide 'useful commercial Knowledge' and to supply horses from those parts for the use of the Company's army.[3]

The coast of north-west Gujarat also attracted their attention for the reason given by Charles Malet when he recommended the acquisition of Diu. The activities of the pirates who dominated the coast were not easily suppressed by naval expeditions. The fleet which had sailed from Surat on 6 October 1794 to attack the Kolis had succeeded in destroying a large number of their boats,[4] but the pirates had quickly replaced their losses and continued their depredations. In March 1797 the Bombay government recorded its opinion that the piracy could only be stopped if the Company seized and determined to hold one or more of their sea-ports between the Gulfs of Cutch and Cambay. The Company could annex this territory, they pointed out, without interfering with the Marathas whose power did not extend so far along the coast, and the acquisition could be the means of supporting a naval squadron to control the pirates. Similar measures, they added, were also necessary on the coast south of Bombay which was the scene of the piratical activities of the Bhonsla and the Malwan raja.[5] The Bombay merchants had suffered heavily from the latter,[6]

[1] *Ibid.* CDLVIe, 185–6: A. Adamson to J. Bruce, 17 April 1795.
[2] BSPP, range 380, LXVI, 1352–4: 21 July 1797.
[3] *Ibid.* This early interest in Sind is ignored by R. A. Huttenback in his article, 'The French Threat to India and British Relations with Sind, 1799–1809', in *The English Historical Review* LXXVI (1961), 590–2.
[4] IOL, European Photostats XII, the letters of George Barnes, f. 40: 1 January 1795.
[5] BSPP, range 380, LXV, 448: 14 March 1797; and Letters received from Bombay XV, par. 2 of the letter of 31 July 1797 in the political department.
[6] BSPP, range E, I, 435–6: petition of Bombay merchants to the government of Bombay, 6 October 1789; and *ibid.* VI, 43–7: 16 February 1793.

and the governor-general recognised in October 1796 that the Company would have to seize the forts and part of the coastal territory belonging to this chief in order to safeguard the presidency's trade. But Shore insisted that this action must await a more favourable turn in the politics of India.[1]

It is clear from this evidence that the growth and protection of trade, far more than the supposed menace of French imperialism, directed the eyes of the Company at this time towards the acquisition of territory on the Gujarat and Konkan coasts. The rising demand for raw cotton and piece-goods was bringing pressure to bear on a society which was not capable of adapting itself to fulfil the need. In Surat the whole economic and political organisation was holding back the growth of trade, and misgovernment and disorder, of which piracy was but one feature, extended throughout the province. The piece-good trade was mainly of interest to the Company, but both the Company and the private merchants increasingly demanded and competed for greater supplies of raw cotton. In November 1796 the Court of Directors ordered Bombay to send 15,000 bales of cotton to China to remedy the finances of the Company at Canton,[2] and the Company's supercargoes there urgently repeated the demand.[3] But these orders, according to the private merchants, gave the northern cotton dealers a pretext for demanding exorbitant prices, and they asked the government to help to lower the price by rejecting tenders for cotton which were above Rs 110 a candy.[4] One reason for the rising price of cotton in Gujarat was the conduct of Sindhia's agent at Broach. In February 1797 the Bombay merchants complained to the government that their agents had been frustrated in their efforts to buy cotton by a certain man, Poorbhodass, who 'uniting in his own Person the power of Government and Speculations in Trade makes the former subservient to the latter, and is thereby enabled to get the whole of the cotton produced in those districts into his own hands for which he asks a most exhorbitant Price far exceeding the utmost given in former years'.[5] Joshua Uhthoff, Malet's

---

[1] BSPP, range E, XI, 1702–6: Bengal to Bombay, 3 October 1796.
[2] BM Add. MSS 12,582, 38–40: the Court to Bombay, 3 October 1796.
[3] BCP, range 414, LIX, 49–50: Canton to Bombay, 13 November 1796.
[4] *Ibid.* 264–5: Forbes, Smith & Co. to the Bombay government, 22 February 1797.
[5] *Ibid.* 238–9: cotton merchants to the Bombay government, 20 February 1797.

successor at Poona, represented these grievances to Sindhia, but he warned the Bombay government that as they had no power to stop Poorbhodass from trading in cotton, and 'as the institutions and conduct of the Marattas are rather inimical, than friendly, to the encouragement of commerce; the merchants under your protection cannot implicitly depend upon effectual relief. . .'[1] At the same time the practice increased of adulterating the cotton by moistening it or adding salt to it, which besides reducing its value, led to a number of fires breaking out on the ships to China. The Bombay Insurance Society urgently sought the government's intervention with the Marathas on this question[2] and Uhthoff pressed Sindhia to forbid the practice.[3]

At Surat this commercial pressure was bringing the Company's affairs to a crisis. In January 1798 two large Portuguese ships lay at the Surat bar waiting to receive the piece-goods which the energies and ready money of their agents had succeeded in collecting. The Portuguese could afford to make a large investment, as the Bombay government realised, since the peace which had been established between Portugal and France would allow them to monopolise the European market for piece-goods unless the Bombay government could deprive them of their supplies.[4] On 8 January the members of the Surat commercial board reported that they had been forced to use the nawab's authority to compel the Ketterie weavers to fulfil their engagements, as the contractors declared that they could do nothing without the intervention of government.[5] But they were soon to find that the powers of government which could be called on at Surat were not instruments fit for the Company's use. The Surat board investigated the nawab's courts of justice and found them to be uniformly corrupt and venal.[6] They were evaded at will by the Maratha chautheas and the foreign European traders, who often imprisoned people connected with their business without any form of trial. Furthermore, there were numerous other evils which obstructed commerce

---

[1] BSPP, range 380, LXV, 755–6: J. Uhthoff to Bombay, 3 April 1797. The price of cotton at Broach was raised to Rs 130–140 a candy. See BCP, range 414, LIX, 763: Duncan to the Court of Directors.

[2] BCP, range 414, LX, 1194: the Insurance Society to the Bombay government, 21 December 1797.

[3] BSPP, range 380, LXVIII, 281–3: J. Uhthoff to Bombay, 6 February 1798.

[4] BCP, range 414, LXI, 15: the Surat board's minute, 1 January 1798.

[5] *Ibid.* 33–41: Surat to Bombay, 8 January 1798.

[6] BSPP, range 380, LXXI, 2871–3: Surat to Bombay, January 1798.

in the city: the 'very general neglect of Agreements...producing a total want of Confidence between Man & Man'; the lending of money at exorbitant interest rates; 'bankruptcy wholly unattended to, and not unfrequently a premeditated Scheme to defraud Creditors... or Bankrupt as well as Creditor fall a sacrifice to the rapacity of the Government, which under a pretended interference for the public good, leaves little for either party...'[1]

In February the supreme government reviewed all the reports on Surat which it had received from Bombay, and announced its conclusion that it was 'desirable that the Influence & actual power of the Company in Surat, should be encreased, rather than diminished; & that a Systematic Administration should be established there, under the nominal Authority of the Nabob but under the real controul of the Company'.[2] But the difficulty lay in carrying out this policy. Bengal agreed with Bombay that the first step must be to secure the surrender of the Maratha chauth. The supreme government agreed with the Surat committee's plan to obtain the Chorasi pargana, and instructed Bombay to negotiate with the nawab for the establishment of a force at Surat 'adequate to the preservation of the internal Peace & Tranquillity of the City' to prevent any further rioting. The Company, declared Bengal, was bound to take such measures for the good government of the city but the nawab must be made to pay his proper share.[3] The day before these instructions were sent to Bombay Uhthoff wrote to Sir John Shore from Poona reporting the peshwa's request to be supplied with arms. The proposal, Uhthoff realised, might involve the Company with Sindhia and the nizam, but if the Company wanted the Chorasi pargana, the removal of the two Maratha chautheas from Surat and 'Commercial Privileges, or, at least, freedom of Trade in the Marhatta Country, particularly in the Piece Goods & Cotton of Guzerat', they could probably only obtain them by falling in with the peshwa's demand.[4]

There was nothing which could be done in time to make the Surat investment for that year a success. In March the chief wrote to the Maratha officials in the manufacturing districts and asked them to stop the weavers from breaking their engagements

[1] BSPP, range 380, LXXI, 2873–81: Surat to Bombay, January 1798.
[2] *Ibid.* 2459–61: Bengal to Bombay, 20 February 1798.
[3] *Ibid.* 2461: Bengal to Bombay, 20 February 1798.
[4] *Poona Residency Correspondence* VI, ed. Sardesai, 130–1: J. Uhthoff to Sir John Shore, 19 February 1798.

with the Company,[1] but in May the resident at Broach reported that the Portuguese had gained the assistance of Poorbhodass, to whom Sindhia had mortgaged Broach, and were purchasing cloths from a large number of weavers there, despite the treaty which excluded foreign Europeans from trade with the city.[2] On 12 May the Surat commercial board reported to Bombay that there was a deficiency in the investment of goods worth Rs 46,529. For this they blamed the high price of cotton and thread, the competition of the Portuguese, and the obstinate refusal of the Ketterie weavers to work, a refusal which not even the exercise of the nawab's authority could alter.[3]

In September this circumstance, and the arrival of the Court's letter of February 1797,[4] brought the question of Surat to a head in the Bombay council. It was the same council which debated the role of British power in Malabar:[5] Duncan, Stuart, Rivett and Page. On that issue it had been bitterly divided between the policy of Rivett, representing the pushing imperialism of the private trader, and the cautious administrative outlook of Duncan and Stuart. These divisions were only partially reconciled. Again it was Rivett who pressed for action. In a minute of 21 September he declared that the state of justice and finance at Surat demanded immediate reform, not by the Moghul power which perpetuated the abuses, but by the English government which had the right and power to intervene.[6] In his view the Company must establish 'a more prompt, impartial, efficient, and œconomical administration of Justice' and reform the taxes which so oppressed the people. But the first essential, he stressed, was the surrender of the Maratha chauth.[7] Stuart pointed out that nothing could be accomplished unless the Company increased its military establishment at Surat and disbanded the nawab's forces, as any reforms would have to be forced upon the nawab.[8] He thought this was doubly necessary as the French were upon the Red Sea, but Rivett would not have the issues clouded by these considerations. Surat, he asserted, would be the last place which the French would attack as they would cut

[1] BCP, range 414, LXI, 316–17: minute of D. Seton, 30 March 1798.
[2] *Ibid.* 428: the resident at Broach to Surat, 4 May 1798.
[3] *Ibid.* 405–8: Surat to Bombay, 12 May 1798.
[4] See above, p. 155.   [5] See above, pp. 119–21.
[6] BSPP, range 380, LXXI, 2949–54: minute of J. Rivett, 21 September 1798.
[7] *Ibid.* 2954.
[8] *Ibid.* LXXII, 3152–5: minute of Lieutenant-General Stuart, 28 September 1798.

themselves off there from all support.[1] But opposition came from Duncan. He put forward legalistic objections to coercing the nawab. The Company, he felt, was not entitled to insist on the nawab's obedience, and he thought it best that reform should wait until the nawab's death.[2] But, because of the strong views of his colleagues, Duncan decided to refer the whole question again to the supreme government which had come under Wellesley's vigorous direction.[3] This he did in a report dated 6 November in which he traced the whole question back to the riot at Surat in 1795.[4]

But the Bombay council did not let the matter rest there. They began negotiating with the nawab of Surat for a subsidy to finance the increase of the Company's military establishment in the city,[5] and in December 1798 the chief proposed new regulations to prevent the abuse of fraudulent bankruptcies, a measure which would intrude on the nawab's judicial power.[6] On 15 January 1799 matters were altered by the arrival at Bombay of the news of the nawab's death,[7] which was quickly followed on 4 February by the death of his infant son and heir.[8] The event for which the Bombay servants had been waiting had arrived. Duncan instructed Seton not to acknowledge the next heir, Nassooreddin, the late nawab's brother, until he agreed to pay the English a subsidy for their troops, to admit them to judicial power, and to unite his customs houses with the Company's under their single control.[9] Duncan took this step, after prodding from his council, but without the instructions of the governor-general.[10] Wellesley was then at Madras directing the war against Tipu, and he had not read Duncan's report on Surat, but told him to 'decide without further reference any parts of the question which may press for determination'.[11]

---

[1] BSPP, range 380, LXXII, 3160–1: minute of J. Rivett, 28 September 1798.
[2] *Ibid.* 3741–4: minute of J. Duncan, 26 October 1798.   [3] *Ibid.* 3745.
[4] *Ibid.* 3891–940: Duncan to Wellesley, 6 November 1798.
[5] *Ibid.* LXXIV, 4569–70: Surat to Bombay, 28 November 1798.
[6] *Ibid.* range 381, I, 1065–87: minute of the chief of Surat, 13 December 1798.
[7] *Ibid.* range 380, LXXV, 259: Surat to Bombay, 8 January 1799.
[8] *Ibid.* 601.
[9] *Ibid.* range 381, III, 2337–8: Duncan to Seton, 9 February 1799.
[10] Duncan told Henry Dundas that it was 'more in consideration to the views of my Colleagues, than to my own sense of the entire reasonableness of our Claim...' that led him to increase his demands from the nawab shortly before the latter's death; Harvard Melville MSS, IOL microfilm reel 649: J. Duncan to H. Dundas, 6 May 1799.
[11] BM Add. MSS 13,693, f. 17v: Wellesley to Duncan, Madras, 5 February 1799.

Throughout the following twelve months the settlement of the government of Surat engrossed the energies and attention of the Bombay government. When the final step was taken and the nawab was removed from power, it marked the beginning of the expansion of British power in Gujarat and along the north-west coast. One by one 'the shackles of Gujarat' fell under the Company's control. Because the crucial decisions were made during the governor-generalship of Wellesley, one of the greatest periods of expansion in the history of British India, this thrust to the north-west has been included generally in accounts of Wellesley's political ambitions, his desire to exclude the French from the west coast or to curb the power of the Marathas.[1] It is therefore important to establish the responsibility for the annexation and the motives behind it, not only to explain this critical phase in the expansion of the Bombay presidency, but to investigate more carefully what has passed under the name of Wellesley's imperialism.

To see the events leading to the annexation of Surat in their setting it is necessary first to look at the other areas where Bombay was considering territorial encroachments. It has been asserted that the interest of the English in Sind under the governor-generalship of Wellesley shows the extent to which the expansionist policy pursued by the Company in this quarter was impelled by the French threat to India.[2] But although this political interpretation explains Wellesley's interest, it leaves out of account the part played by the Bombay presidency, and particularly their commercial interest in Sind in the 1790s.[3] In October 1798 Wellesley's first concern was undoubtedly with the threat of invasion from Zeman Shah and possible French intrigues with that prince, and he suggested that the people of Sind might be encouraged to rebel against him.[4] In Wellesley's eyes the prospect of re-establishing the Company's factory at Tatta was desirable not so much for commercial as for political reasons.[5] Nevertheless

---

[1] Even P. E. Roberts in his *India under Wellesley* claimed that the governor-general's political ambitions decided the fate of Surat, and that in ordering the deposition of the nawab he overrode the protests of Duncan. See Roberts, *op. cit.* (London, 1929), 115.

[2] Huttenback, 'The French Threat to India and British Relations with Sind, 1799–1809', *The English Historical Review* LXXVI (1961), 590.

[3] See above, pp. 158–9.

[4] BM Add. MSS 13,693, ff. 8v and 11: Wellesley to Duncan, 8 October, 1798 and 24 October 1798.

[5] *Ibid.* f. 25: Wellesley to Duncan, 7 April 1799.

the Bombay presidency continued to show a keen interest in the commercial prospects of the area,[1] and Duncan insisted to Wellesley that the factory had commercial as well as political objects.[2] Nathan Crow, whom Duncan appointed as the Company's resident in Sind, wrote lengthy reports on the possibility of increasing the Company's commerce with the area,[3] and the Bombay government instructed him to explore the market for British staples and Indian products. Bombay hoped that Tatta would provide piece-goods to supplement the Surat investment and in December 1799 declared that, if the cloth from Tatta were cheaper than that made at Surat, Crow might expect the orders for it to prove extensive. This would be especially so if a peace in Europe brought renewed foreign competition for the Surat cloths. In the event both the political and commercial objects of the Company were frustrated by the jealousy of the merchants of Sind and the fears of the prince.[4] Crow was expelled from the country, but he did not leave without suggesting to Duncan that the Company had an opportunity of seizing Karachi[5] which he had earlier represented as a place of considerable trade.[6] The expulsion of the Company from Sind meant the failure of Wellesley's political objects in seeking an alliance with the prince, and Crow declared that the advantage of 'getting Currachee into our own Possession, Compared with the most Sanguine expectations to be entertained from this Government form in my humble opinion, a most important calculation...'[7]

Thus, although the Company's activity in Sind in 1799 and 1800 was the direct result of Wellesley's political schemes, it was also inspired by the expanding commercial concerns of the Bombay presidency. The evidence of Bombay's interest in the area earlier in the decade leaves little doubt that the Company would have attempted to re-establish its connexions there in the interests of commerce even if there had been no threat from Zeman Shah and the French. For the expanding trade of the

[1] BM Add. MSS 13,695, ff. 303–8: A. Ramsay to J. Duncan, Surat, 12 November 1798.
[2] *Ibid.* 13,696, ff. 135–6: Duncan to Wellesley, 27 April 1799.
[3] BCP, range 414, LXIV, 949–51: N. Crow to Bombay, 30 September 1799; and BM Add. MSS 13,699, f. 141: Crow to Duncan, 25 November 1799.
[4] Home Misc. CCCXXXIII, 487–500: N. Crow to Duncan, 26 August 1800.
[5] *Ibid.* 500.
[6] BM. Add. MSS 13,698, f. 222: N. Crow to Duncan, 3 October 1799.
[7] Home Misc. CCCXXXIII, 500: Crow to Duncan, 26 August 1800.

presidency was bringing more and more of the north-west coast within its concern. In March 1798 Daniel Seton reported that two agents had arrived at Surat from the small port of Rattalow which was a few miles further up the coast from Bhaunagar. Their mission was to offer the port to the Company in return for protection. The place, according to Seton, was 'an extensive District with an excellent River & Bunder, highly beneficial for Trade from its situation... The Country produces all kinds of Grain and Cotton'.[1] But it suffered from the fact that the Company's convoy did not sail further than Bhaunagar and the merchants of Rattalow had to take their goods by land to that port at great expense. Seton thought the proposals were commercially advantageous and directed enquiries to be made. It was found that the peshwa claimed tribute from the place, and because of this the Bombay government would not make a decision without taking into account all the political considerations. Duncan asked Palmer, the resident at Poona, to negotiate the matter with the peshwa.[2] Palmer could get only promises of answers from the jealous durbar and the agents returned to Rattalow unsatisfied.[3] But the place could not be forgotten. The increasing demand for cotton both by the Company and private merchants made Bhaunagar and its surrounding country of the first importance to Bombay, and by July 1798 this demand for cotton was also bringing Cutch and Porbander within the orbit of the Company.[4]

Furthermore, the continued depredations of the northern pirates on the cotton trade renewed the question of annexing their ports. This was not a simple matter, as the pirates were protected by most of the rulers of the coast including Bhaunagar, Gogah, Junagar and Porbander, and these chiefs paid tribute to the Marathas.[5] Bombay submitted the question to the governor-general, but the merchants were losing patience. In March 1800 the most important Bombay firms petitioned the government on learning that the whole of the Broach fleet, carrying a cargo worth about Rs 130,000, had been captured by the northern pirates.[6] Unless the Company

[1] BSPP, range 381, XXXIII, 3129–32: D. Seton to Duncan, 16 March 1798.
[2] *Ibid.* 3132–4: Duncan to Palmer, 31 March 1798.
[3] *Ibid.* 3134–6: Duncan to Palmer, 15 April 1798.
[4] *Ibid.* range 380, LXX, 2067: J. H. Cherry to Bombay, 11 July 1798.
[5] *Ibid.* range 381, V, 4371–5: Surat to Bombay, 26 July 1799.
[6] *Ibid.* IX, 1003–5: Bombay merchants to the Bombay government, 12 March 1800.

acted vigorously, declared the merchants, the consequences would be ruinous to the trade of Bombay and therefore to the Canton treasury. The pirates south of Bombay were no less troublesome, and in March 1800 Joshua Uhthoff suggested that the Company should give the Malwan raja the protection he asked for against the peshwa, in return for the cession of his territory between the Ghauts and the sea. This, Uhthoff declared, would be the means of destroying the Malwan pirates and of checking the activities of the other piratical bands between Goa and Bombay.[1]

At the time, then, when affairs at Surat were approaching a crisis the Bombay government was maturing a policy of territorial expansion. This was the direct consequence of commercial developments: an expanding trade thwarted by misgovernment and disorder. The life of the Bombay settlement was trade, and all the forces of the presidency were driving the government towards a policy which would allow trade to grow. This was not a creation of Wellesley's imperious mind. Indeed in 1799 Wellesley was thinking in terms of disbanding the presidency rather than of expanding it. On 7 June 1799 he told Henry Dundas, 'Malabar has been miserably mismanaged by the People of Bombay, who are unquestionably the least qualified of any description of the Servants of the Company in India to administer important concerns of Revenu & Govt.', and he suggested the presidency should be reduced to the status of a commercial factory and military station.[2] It did not occur to Wellesley at this time to seek cessions of territory from the peshwa in the subsidiary treaty he was trying to impose on him, and he only considered this course in July 1799 because the peshwa himself suggested it.[3] Nor was there much alarm from the French after the defeat of Tipu Sultan and Nelson's victory of the Nile. The only pressure came from Bombay itself and the time was propitious. On the death of Nana Farnavis the Maratha confederacy fell apart as Sindhia and the peshwa vied for supreme power. As in 1775, Maratha divisions provided the opportunity for territorial gains in Gujarat, and in Wellesley the Bombay presidency was fortunate in having a governor-general whose political ambitions could be made to accommodate

[1] BSPP, range 381, x, 1477–9: J. Uhthoff to Bengal, 14 March 1800.
[2] BM Add. MSS 13,457, ff. 39–40: Wellesley to Henry Dundas, 7 June 1799.
[3] *Poona Residency Correspondence* VI, ed. Sardesai, 474–5: the secretary of the governor-general to W. Palmer, Fort St George, 20 July 1799.

their demands. Wellesley wanted to direct the policy of the Maratha confederacy and the subsidiary treaty was the means to this end. Whether the subsidy was paid by cessions of land or in money was of little concern to him except insofar as the Bombay government convinced him one method was better than the other.[1]

It was Jonathan Duncan and his colleagues who took the responsibility for Bombay's first steps towards expansion in Gujarat. They had the orders of the Court of Directors to guide them given in the Court's letter of 17 February 1797 which arrived in September 1798. These proposed that the nawab should subsidise a force at Surat adequate to preserve law and order and to prevent a repetition of the riots of 1795.[2] But Duncan and his colleagues went beyond this and demanded the establishment of the Company's judicial power in the city[3] and the satisfaction of what Seton called 'one of the Company's grand views at Surat...the providing the investment'.[4] Indeed Duncan showed a remarkable tenacity and vigour over Surat from the middle of 1799 which was in marked contrast not only to the attitude he took in September 1798 but to his whole policy in Malabar when he opposed the aggressive outlook of Rivett and Rickards.[5] The Court's orders gave him some of the confidence he needed to act, but he also had personal motives for wishing to gain the Court's esteem. In March 1799 he learnt that the man to whom he had entrusted his fortune in Benares had embezzled the greatest part of it, an amount which Duncan later declared to be £30,000.[6] Duncan saw that his only hope of recovering his finances lay in his remaining for as long as possible as the governor of Bombay, and he asked his uncle to use his influence to stop the Court from appointing a successor.[7] Within a few months the financial blow was followed by another which was even more shattering to his self-esteem. In August 1799 he learnt of Wellesley's plan to remove Malabar from the authority of the Bombay presidency, and he contemplated with bitterness the

[1] *Ibid.*
[2] BSPP, range 380, LXXI, 2858: 21 September 1798.
[3] *Ibid.* range 381, III, 2337–8: Duncan to D. Seton, 9 February 1799.
[4] *Ibid.* XIV, 4056–9: D. Seton to J. Duncan, 18 August 1799.
[5] See above, pp. 119–21.
[6] Michie Papers, MSS 5881, file 2: J. Duncan to Jonathan Michie, 19 July 1800.
[7] *Ibid.* 31 March 1799 and 12 June 1800, when he writes from Surat, 'I am still detained here, by the Company's Business, which is however in a fair Way of being fully concluded to the public Advantage & my own Credit'.

'2 or 3 trifling Islands' he was left to rule.[1] The prospect could only make him more eager to extend the authority of his presidency, and in this the pressure of the whole establishment was behind him.[2]

But Duncan found a difficult opponent in Nassooreddin at Surat. From April 1799 onwards Seton argued with, threatened, and cajoled him to agree to Duncan's demands, but Nassooreddin refused to discharge his sepoys, to allow the Company an adowlat, or to offer more than a lac of rupees as a subsidy.[3] Neither side would bend and Duncan pressed the governor-general for instructions.[4] In this situation the Portuguese returned with redoubled vigour to purchase piece-goods, and the Company's contractors appealed to the Surat board for help. The delivery of piece-goods to the Company, they declared, had almost stopped, as the Portuguese paid Rs 80 for the most inferior goods whereas the Company paid only Rs 74 for cloth of the highest quality. 'Unless', they insisted, 'it is in the power of the Board to enforce the performance of engagement with us by which we are to fulfill those we have entered into with the Company, we see no possibility of the Investment being provided...nothing now but the interference of Government can enable us to deliver the Goods we have pledged ourselves to provide...'[5]

The governor-general had responded to Duncan's letters so far as to bring up the question of the Surat chauth again at Poona.[6] He included it in his proposals for a subsidiary treaty with the peshwa suggesting that it should be commuted in part payment of the proposed subsidy.[7] But the peshwa would not agree to the point and Palmer had to abandon it.[8] It was not until 10 March 1800 that Wellesley at last replied to Duncan's repeated requests for instructions. The reply came in the form that the Bombay

---

[1] See above, pp. 124–5.
[2] See J. Taylor, *Letters on India* (London, 1800), 11–13, for Bombay's reaction to the transfer of Malabar to Madras. See also *The Correspondence of David Scott*, ed. Philips, II, 313: Scott to Rivett, 16 June 1801. 'The revolution at Surat has been very apropos though it does no [sic] make up for your loss of Malabar.'
[3] BSPP, range 381, III, 2340–3 and 2374–5: Seton to Duncan, 1 April 1799.
[4] Home Misc. CDLXX, 89–90: Duncan to Wellesley, 13 February 1800.
[5] BCP, range 414, LXV, 131–2: the contractors to the Surat board, 10 January 1800.
[6] BSPP, range 381, V, 4006–7: W. Palmer to Bombay, 18 July 1799.
[7] *Poona Residency Correspondence* VI, ed. Sardesai, 470: Palmer to Wellesley, 26 July 1799.
[8] *Ibid.* 479: Palmer to Wellesley, 10 August 1799.

presidency had hoped for. Wellesley agreed with them and the Court of Directors that the mismanagement and corruption of the nawab's government in the administration of justice, police and external defence, called for the Company to take upon itself 'the entire Civil and Military Government of the City'. As the power of the Moghul emperor was extinct it was the duty of the Company 'to protect the Persons and properties of the Inhabitants of that City...' and to provide a 'just, wise, and efficient administration'.[1] The nawab must be pensioned off, his sepoys disbanded, and new judicial regulations established by the Company. The interference of the chautheas was to end, although until the Marathas relinquished the chauth the payment of their revenues had to continue. Finally, Wellesley authorised Bombay to negotiate with the gaikwar for the cession of his chauth and promised to recommence negotiations with the peshwa.[2] The governor-general imparted vigour and authority in his directions, but no new policy. This piece of Wellesley's imperialism was made by the Bombay government, encouraged by the Court of Directors, and awaited only the opportune moment for its fulfilment.

Duncan set sail for Surat shortly after receiving the governor-general's letter and he arrived there on 2 May.[3] But it was not until 15 May that he was able to proclaim the establishment of the Company's government in the city. Nassooreddin proved obstinate to the last and in negotiating with him Duncan relied heavily on the assistance and mediation of a Bombay cotton merchant, Miguel de Lima é Souza.[4] De Souza was one of the Company's subjects at Bombay, although he was a Portuguese. He appears, at least for some time, to have acted in partnership in the cotton trade with Daniel Seton,[5] and he was also a partner in the firm of Tate and Adamson.[6] Although Bombay stressed officially that its policy towards Surat was governed by the Company's commercial interests, in particular the piece-good investment, in fact it was as important to the private merchants that the English should control the city. Surat was still the commercial capital of Gujarat, and the cooperation of its bankers and money-lenders was essential to the well-being of the cotton trade. Disturbances in

[1] BSPP, range 381, XIV, 4131–6: Bengal to Bombay, 10 March 1800.
[2] *Ibid.* 4136–47. [3] Home Misc. CDLXXII, 227.
[4] BSPP, range 381, XIV, 4022–3, 4160–1 and 4200–4. [5] See above, p. 134.
[6] Furber, *John Company at Work*, 249.

Surat could affect the money-market[1] and therefore the whole organisation of the trade. Also the practice of adulterating the cotton was carried on to a considerable extent at Surat as the cotton was brought to its quays from the smaller ports of Gujarat. De Souza obviously had considerable influence in the territory round Bombay because he had been employed in 1795 and 1796 to negotiate with the Malwan raja.[2] His employment by Duncan at Surat marked his rising influence with the governor and the growing interest of the private merchant in the politics of Gujarat.

The annexation of Surat, however, was primarily intended to serve the Company's interests and within five days of the proclamation of the Company's rule it was made clear what these interests were. On 20 May Duncan created the office of judge and magistrate to administer civil, criminal and police powers in the city. At the same time he published a body of regulations which the court was to uphold. The most prominent and the most detailed of them concerned the provision of the Company's investment.[3] There were twenty-two rules 'for the better management of the provision of the Company's Investments at Surat in preventing Manufacturers or other persons in their Employ from embezzling the Money advanced to them or disposing of the Goods, otherwise than in due pursuance of their engagements...' They were also to ensure justice and freedom from oppression for the manufacturers. The latter cause was provided for by regulations which forbade the Company's officials to compel the weavers to work for them unless they were under engagements or indebted to the Company. The weavers were free to prosecute the commercial resident in the adowlat if they had complaints against him. But the other rules were all designed to strengthen the Company's commercial position. The weavers who worked for the Company were to give engagements not to work for or to give their cloths to anyone else. Any weavers or dyers who used inferior materials would forfeit double the value of the defective article, and any weaver found guilty of selling cloths to others while working for the Company would forfeit the cost of them. The commercial resident was empowered to place peons over weavers who did not deliver their

[1] See above, p. 150.
[2] BSPP, range E, X, 1164–73: correspondence between the Malwan raja and de Souza, 12 April 1795–10 February 1796.
[3] *Ibid.* range 381, XIV, 4435–48: 20 May 1800.

cloths on time, and the weavers or merchants who failed in their engagements could be fined up to 35 per cent of the price of every cloth which they did not deliver. In addition, anyone procuring cloths from weavers while knowing them to be the Company's, or anyone deterring weavers from making engagements with the Company could be fined as the court saw fit, while anyone who defrauded the Company of money intended for the investment would be liable to forfeit four times the sum involved. All these regulations applied to contractors, manufacturers and cotton dealers alike.[1]

But the high prices given by the Portuguese defeated even these regulations. The processes of the adowlat were too slow and cumbrous to be any real restraint on the weavers, and Cherry reported to Bombay in 1801 that,

since Commerce which though always exposed to obstruction will not admit of Controul, but ever find its own level, in the interest of the Trader, the untoward Speculations of the Portuguese while they continue profitable, cannot fail to retard the Company benefiting by the practical effects otherwise to be expected from the excellent theory on which that change [of government] has been established...'[2]

It was Malabar all over again. The Company had used its power to protect its trade, only to see that trade then slip through its fingers lured by the higher prices of the Portuguese.[3] Duncan's reaction was first to insist on the greater use of force,[4] and then to suggest that the commercial resident should make contracts directly with the weavers with as little intermediate agency as possible.[5] But Cherry declared that the Company could only get the investment it wanted by paying higher prices to the weavers. The demand for raw cotton was so great that the price had risen from Rs 110 to 115 a candy in 1795 to Rs 140 to 150 six years later,[6] and was contributing to the rising cost of the piece-goods. But these prices were more than the London market would pay. On 15 May 1801 the Court of Directors reported that the Surat investment had proved unprofit-

---

[1] BSPP, range 381, XIV, 4435–48: 20 May 1800.
[2] BCP, range 414, LXVII, 364: Cherry to Bombay, 19 February 1801.
[3] The Portuguese could sell piece-goods at Lisbon for prices from 33 to 107 per cent higher than those given at London; *ibid*. 56: H. Fawcett to Bombay, 14 January 1801.
[4] *Ibid*. LXVI, 1347–51: Bombay to Surat, 24 December 1800.
[5] *Ibid*. LXVII, 411–28: minute of Jonathan Duncan, 9 April 1801.
[6] *Ibid*. 363–73: J. H. Cherry to Bombay, 19 February 1801.

able at their sales and ordered its reduction.[1] The Company had either to find means of reducing the price of cotton or look beyond the piece-good trade for its profits. Both courses took it outside the gates of Surat into 'the rich and commercial Province of Guzerat'.[2]

The annexation of Surat marks the climax of the Company's vigorous efforts to restore and expand its trade. The outbreak of war in Europe in 1793 led to a greatly increased demand for Indian piece-goods which the directors urgently wished to supply.[3] This brought a new pressure to bear on the Company's old establishment at Surat which had long suffered from the evils of divided government and which proved incapable of adapting itself to fresh needs. The misgovernment and disorder of Surat and the limitations of the Company's authority in the face of foreign competition hampered the expansion of trade, and Charles Malet and the Bombay government convinced Dundas that the Company must annex the city if its trade were to develop.[4] The measure only awaited the right political circumstances which came with the defeat of Tipu Sultan and the disintegration of the Maratha confederacy. The annexation was in no way part of a grand imperial design to defeat the aims of the French or to add indiscriminately to the territory of the Bombay presidency, although the Bombay servants had their own private reasons for urging on the measure. As in Malabar private merchants like James Rivett and Miguel de Lima é Souza supported the annexation but as the measure largely favoured the Company's piece-good trade the private merchants did not play such a conspicuous part. The outstanding figure in this period of the Company's relations with Gujarat was Charles Malet. He alone saw clearly and consistently what policy he wanted the Company to pursue on the north-west coast. Malet's imperialism was concerned with the extension of British commerce, but it had a clarity of design and loftiness of vision which Wellesley could not add to. In 1800 Surat, the first of Malet's 'shackles of Gujarat', was under the full control of the Company, and the Bombay presidency was maturing a policy of further annexation. It remains to be seen whether this followed Malet's or Wellesley's design.

[1] BSPP, range 381, xxv, 5146: the Court to Bengal, 15 May 1801.
[2] See above, p. 136. [3] Philips, *The East India Company*, 105.
[4] See above, pp. 140–1.

CHAPTER 6

THE THRUST TO THE NORTH,
1800–03

It was either in Jonathan Duncan's nature or part of his policy to avoid taking the final responsibility for the decisions of the Bombay government. In 1812 Robert Rickards described the

practice common to the Governor in matters involving any responsibility. As President of the Council he gave his vote last; and whenever he had secret, yet partial scruples, after the majority had decided a measure generally according to his wishes, he would endeavour to shelter himself against possible censure, in respect to particular parts, by a half record of his doubts, without openly expressing them in the first instance, for the equal and candid consideration of the other members...[1]

He had followed this course in September 1798 when the Bombay government discussed the future of Surat,[2] and in May 1799 he justified the enlarged demands on the nawab by telling Henry Dundas that his council had forced him to make them.[3] And in accordance with this policy he was at pains to point out in his letters and minutes that his pursuit of further territory in Gujarat after the annexation of Surat was at the command of the governor-general.[4] But Wellesley had only endorsed in his instructions a policy which the civil servants of Surat and Bombay had created. They wanted the Company to acquire the Chorasi pargana because it would give Surat a territory which could supply the city with provisions, piece-goods and raw cotton for export without any interference from Maratha power.[5] It was also the Bombay civil servants who kept up the pressure for the cession of the gaikwar's and peshwa's chauth. Moreover, it was Duncan who on 30 May 1800 wrote to Robert Holford and asked him whether the nawab of

[1] Parliamentary Papers, 1812–13, X, 178.
[2] See above, pp. 163–4.
[3] Harvard Melville MSS, IOL microfilm reel 649: Duncan to Henry Dundas, 6 May 1799.
[4] BSPP, range 381, XIV, 4241–2: Duncan to Wellesley, 29 May 1800.
[5] See above, p. 157.

Cambay might be prevailed upon to cede the city and its district to the Company.[1]

All this suggests either that Duncan was held captive by his council, or that he was bent on expanding the presidency's territory in Gujarat while anxious not to incur the disapproval of his superiors and determined to keep his office. It appears that from the end of 1799 the latter explanation is the true one. On 12 June 1800 he told his uncle, Jonathan Michie, that affairs at Surat were almost settled 'to the public advantage and my own credit', and he added, 'I have further views to their [the Company's] Good in this Quarter when I hope in a few days to accomplish, by getting them some Country around it'.[2] It seems that Duncan thought that his schemes of expansion would meet favour with the Court of Directors and enhance his reputation. But if he had personal motives behind his policy there was also the active support if not strong pressure of his council and other influential members of the Bombay establishment to direct his actions. The whole body of civil servants must have joined him in wishing to make up for the loss of Malabar by taking territory elsewhere. But the annexations when they came were not made indiscriminately. Behind Duncan, working with him and influencing him, were men with decided interests in Gujarat.

Before General Stuart left Bombay for England in January 1800 he wrote a lengthy paper on the Company's interests in Gujarat which he later delivered to Henry Dundas.[3] It was to be expected that as the retiring commander-in-chief of Bombay much of his concern would be with the strategic significance of Gujarat to the Company. But Stuart was very emphatic that military strategy should be guided by commercial interests. 'The true utility of our establishments in India', he wrote, 'arises from the commerce they produce, the sailors they maintain, the numbers of people to whom they afforded food or labour, the commodities by this means exported or imported, with the industry and the spirit of adventure thence created.' The empire which the Company had won should be supported by 'a just combination of military strength with objects relating to trade'. In his scheme the Company could gain

[1] Home Misc. CDLXXIII, 191–2: Duncan to Holford, Surat 30 May 1800.
[2] Michie Papers, MSS 5881, file 2: J. Duncan to Jonathan Michie, 12 June 1800.
[3] Owen (ed.), *The Despatches etc. of the Marquess Wellesley*, 567: a paper by General Stuart dated 31 January 1800 and submitted to Henry Dundas in July 1800.

these two objects by annexing the coasts of India. This strategy would 'secure to us everywhere the commerce' and allow the fleet to defend the empire. Stuart considered that the western coast of India was neglected, that its commercial wealth was undervalued and that the coast was open to French attacks. He picked out Gujarat as particularly deserving attention because of its

military and commercial advantages of the first importance. It is a small Country, but it is the richest in India. From it almost all the Cotton is brought which is exported from Bombay to China and Europe. The produce of the sales at Canton in this article of the private trade alone amounts to nearly a Million a year...It would secure to us the best manufacture of piece goods, and the Command of the cotton market, the most valuable staple of India.[1]

On the military side he pointed out the advantage of taking the whole or part of the province to shut the French out of western India, to provide a bulwark against Zeman Shah and to suppress the pirates who haunted its coast and did so much to prevent the expansion of trade.

The views which Stuart put forward in this paper, and the language in which he expressed them appear to have been inspired by his protégé and confidant, Captain Alexander Walker, who was then a member of the Malabar commission.[2] Walker was a conspicuously able officer in the Company's army. He had arrived as a cadet at Bombay in 1780 and had fought in the first war against Tipu Sultan. He had volunteered as one of the hostages who were handed over to Tipu during the peace negotiations of 1784, and he had suffered for his bravery.[3] He fought in the second campaign against Tipu and was later appointed General Stuart's military secretary. In 1797 he accompanied Stuart to Malabar when he joined the Malabar commission. During this time he gained considerable knowledge of politics and administration, and a contempt for corrupt government. Stuart had the highest opinion of Walker and recommended him to Duncan as 'open-handed and Honourable'.[4] The relationship between the two men was one of close friendship and mutual respect. Stuart encouraged his secretary to write reports on the affairs of the presidency which he sent to Dundas. One of these, on Malabar, earned Wellesley's

---

[1] *Ibid.* 568.   [2] WB 181, d.16: Walker to Duncan, Calicut, 10 August 1800.
[3] *Ibid.* d.18.   [4] WB 186, a.1: Stuart to Duncan, 16 February 1800.

congratulations and he expressed his high opinion of Walker's 'talents, integrity, knowledge and general Character', and hoped that when Stuart left India Walker could be persuaded to join his own entourage.[1] But Walker's ambition in 1800 was to stay in Bombay and ultimately to succeed to Stuart's position as commander-in-chief.[2] Yet ambition did not rule his life. He told his friend Dr Helenus Scott that since his mother was comfortably provided for he would be content to return to England in the same 'middling state of society' which was his when he left. He could, he said, use a great deal of money, but he could also manage well without it.[3]

Walker's ability and integrity contrasted strongly with the shady careers of the majority of the Bombay establishment, and in 1799 he attracted the attention of Duncan who appointed him as the third member of the Malabar commission. In this capacity Walker received from Duncan several friendly and confidential letters, but he confessed to Scott that he was nevertheless mystified by certain aspects of Duncan's behaviour towards him.[4] Both Walker and Scott were aware of a certain deviousness in their governor's conduct which they found difficult to explain.[5] But this did not deter Walker from compiling ruthlessly honest reports in which he exposed all that he knew of the corruption and venality of Bombay's administration in Malabar. In a report intended for Dundas, Walker called for drastic reforms of the Bombay establishment. Its numbers, he insisted, should be cut by a third, and the directors should be stopped from sending out unneeded recruits. Promotion should be by merit and not by seniority. The civil servants should be far better educated and should be given decent salaries.

Much of this must have made uncomfortable reading for Duncan, but Walker's schemes did not stop at internal reforms. He had strong views on the presidency's external policy which were summed up in Stuart's paper and which Walker repeated in August 1800 in a private letter to Duncan.[6] The Company should aim to acquire territory on the coast of Gujarat. This would secure Bombay's lucrative commerce, could be easily defended by the fleet, and would also serve to exclude the French if they should

[1] WB 182, d.18: Wellesley to Stuart, 12 January 1800.
[2] WB 181, d.16: Walker to Stuart, August 1800.
[3] *Ibid.* Walker to H. Scott, June 1800.   [4] *Ibid.*
[5] WB 180, a.5: H. Scott to Walker, undated (?1805).
[6] WB 181, d.16: Walker to Duncan, 10 August 1800.

develop ambitions in that quarter. Walker was influenced in his views by the opinion of his friend, Helenus Scott, who was a surgeon on the Bombay establishment.[1] Scott was a friend of Malet's and he was also on good terms with David Scott.[2] But it is scarcely necessary to trace the source of Walker's ideas because they were almost certainly common to the whole Bombay establishment in 1800. Walker and Stuart were probably only extraordinary in that their ideas were not guided by self-interest.

But in 1800 it was the men with private commercial interests who were in a powerful position to control the policy of the government. If James Rivett did not personally trade in cotton he had close ties of friendship with the men who did. Of the chief cotton merchants, Charles Forbes, P. C. Bruce, Henry Fawcett and Alexander Adamson, only Forbes had no official position, while Fawcett had particular influence as accountant-general. But the influence of these men did not rest solely on their long-established position in the settlement. All of them, but particularly Rivett and Adamson, were closely connected with David Scott, the chairman of the Company. Adamson had been Scott's partner in trade and even when Scott was forced by the Court of Directors to trade in the name of his son the association remained very close.[3] For Rivett, Scott had a personal friendship which made him declare in March 1800 that even if Bombay were reduced to a mere military settlement, 'At all events my friend you may rest assured that I will be attentive to the suggestion in your letters as it refers to you, as also that while I have any influence *you* never shall be out of my view.'[4] Rivett and Adamson were closely linked by interest and friendship.[5] To this circle could be added the name of de Souza, the partner of Tate and Adamson.

These powerful connexions would have been less important if Jonathan Duncan had been a strong reforming governor of the stamp of Cornwallis. But in 1800 Duncan's natural timidity in the face of authority was made far worse by his peculiarly vulnerable position. He was desperately anxious to remain as governor of Bombay in order to repair his fortune and keep some of his self

---

[1] WB 181, d.4: H. Scott to Walker, 16 July 1799.
[2] *Ibid.*: H. Scott to Walker, 21 September 1795.
[3] Philips (ed.), *The Correspondence of David Scott* I, 33–4: Scott to Adamson, 22 April 1795.
[4] *Ibid.* II, 240–1: Scott to Rivett, 20 March 1800.
[5] *Ibid.* II, 313: Scott to Rivett, 16 June 1801.

respect. He took the separation of Malabar from the presidency as a personal attack on his honour and abilities and confessed in October 1800 'the mortifying reflections that I cannot at present altogether stifle'.[1] A greater fear for his future came when the governor-general informed Duncan in June 1800 that he intended to end the separate existence of the Bombay presidency and to incorporate it with the government of Madras.[2] In this crisis only one man could save Duncan and his presidency, and he was David Scott. In October 1800 Duncan wrote to Scott that he relied on his good offices to safeguard the future of the presidency and its governor.[3] From 1800 until 1803 Duncan consistently relied on Scott for support and encouragement in the face of snubs from his superiors, criticism of his policy, and the petty rubs and disagreements which Duncan's over-anxious mind magnified into grand attacks on his authority.[4] In June 1802 Duncan again expressed his fear that the presidency would be dissolved 'in which case', he told Scott, 'I shall hope to be favoured with your advice as to my future proceedings. My fortune will not then... be above $2\frac{1}{2}$ lakhs of rupees at the very utmost, a sum too small to think of coming home with, if I can with honour remain a few more years in India.'[5] In November of the same year Duncan expressed his hope to Scott that the latter would use his good offices with Castlereagh, who had succeeded Dartmouth at the Board of Control, to make the new president not less 'friendly disposed to me than you had induced the late President of that Board to become'.[6] And in July 1803 Duncan wrote in a flurry of gratitude to Scott on learning that the latter had overcome an attempt to remove him from Bombay. It emerges very clearly from this letter how much Duncan's personal ambition and concern for his fortune governed his attitudes. He told Scott that since he had acquired territory worth twenty-four lacs of rupees to rule, a mere nomination to the supreme council would not compensate for his losing the governorship of Bombay. He would only consent to it if

---

[1] Philips (ed.), *The Correspondence of David Scott* II, 292: Duncan to Scott, 17 October 1800.

[2] See above, p. 124.

[3] Philips (ed.), *The Correspondence of David Scott* II, 291–2: Duncan to Scott, 17 October 1800.

[4] See for example *ibid.* II, 359: Duncan to Scott, 19 October 1801; and 388: Duncan to Scott, 4 February 1802.

[5] *Ibid.* II, 399: Duncan to Scott, 29 June 1802.

[6] *Ibid.* II, 409–10: Duncan to Scott, 26 November 1802.

he were put after Barlow in the succession to the governor-generalship. Since his fortune had reached three lacs it was sufficient 'to decline any pecuniary considerations of office that can be construed into degradation', and 'although hardly perhaps sufficient to enable me to figure as a baronet concerning which I feel therefore no particular anxiety; neither shall I feel it burdensome if without solicitation it be conferred on me'.[1]

Although Scott found Duncan's voluminous correspondence, constant appeals for support, and complaints of being misused, somewhat tiresome, and often expressed his irritation,[2] yet he used his influence to keep Duncan at Bombay. It was Scott who fought Wellesley's proposal to dissolve the presidency, and he was also responsible for keeping the Bombay commercial residencies in Malabar.[3] Although he boasted that his own private interest did not influence his policies,[4] it is clear that he did not forget the interests of his old friends and the agency house of David Scott Junior and Company. It seems likely that there was more than kindness behind his treatment of Duncan. Duncan was useful to him. His government had respectability but he was pliant enough to do what Scott wanted. Duncan was made aware that the price of Scott's support was his alliance with the Bombay trading interest. This was made obvious to him in the early part of 1800. Alexander Adamson had hoped, through Scott's influence, to succeed to the office of customs master, but by an oversight J. H. Cherry was appointed to succeed instead. In a private letter which Scott ordered Adamson to destroy, he promised the latter that by way of compensation the two offices of the marine should be combined into one and bestowed on him.[5] Although Scott pushed the measure through the Court of Directors one of his opponents raised objections and claimed that Duncan had knowledge of Adamson's malpractices, which included private trade in marine stores and clandestine trade. Thereupon Scott wrote to Duncan and asked him to send a letter to England, preferably to Charles Grant, clearing Adamson of these charges and declaring him to be 'a very upright man and a meritorious servant'.[6] This followed a letter written in

[1] *Ibid.* II, 421–2: Duncan to Scott, 3 July 1803.
[2] See above, p. 26.   [3] See above, p. 125.
[4] Philips (ed.), *The Correspondence of David Scott* II, 350: Scott to Adamson, 25 September 1801.
[5] *Ibid.* II, 255: Scott to Adamson, 24 April 1800.
[6] *Ibid.* II, 270–2: Scott to Duncan, June 1800.

April in which Scott told Duncan, 'I am sorry to learn that you don't look upon Mr. Rivett or Mr. Adamson as friendly to you. Their correspondence with me speaks them very friendly, and I hope you will find them so at last'.[1] The same letter also dealt with the transfer of Malabar and Scott's promise of support. 'Give yourself no uneasiness as to changes of country on your own account, as you may rest assured I shall never lose sight of either your pecuniary emolument or the credit of your situation.'[2]

The implications of this correspondence in 1800 were obvious. If Duncan wished to remain as the governor of Bombay he had to give up the moderate and independent line, the gropings towards a fair and just policy, which he had attempted in Malabar, and to throw in his lot with Rivett and Adamson and their friends. The man whom Cornwallis had sent to reform Bombay had to turn a blind eye on illicit practices and fall in with a policy of territorial expansion pursued for interested motives. It says much for Duncan's innate honesty that although he hastened to reply to Scott and to claim that he held Adamson in high esteem, he had to confess that he had seen a receipt which showed that Adamson had been trading in copper which was classed as marine stores.[3] But Duncan's conscience permitted him to do his best to fall in with Scott's request, and in March 1801 he wrote to Scott pointing out that he had done

as much in favour of that gentlemen (who is now as well as Mr. Carnac, late Rivett, on very good terms with me) as the circumstances of his own degree of contravention of the true spirit and even letter of the primary regulations for his office admitted of; and the best proof of this is that Mr. A. has expressed to me his grateful sense of our joint minute respecting him which both he and Mr. Carnac are fully convinced was saying and doing as much as we could possibly venture on...'[4]

Duncan had fallen in with the private-trading imperialists. From 1800 onwards with the divisions over Malabar healed they turned their united attention towards Gujarat.

There was much to concern the cotton merchants in Gujarat in 1800. In the first months of the year J. H. Cherry, the commercial

---

[1] Philips (ed.), *The Correspondence of David Scott* II, 252: Scott to Duncan, 17 April 1800.   [2] *Ibid.* 253.   [3] *Ibid.* II, 290–2: Duncan to Scott, 17 October, 1800.
[4] *Ibid.* II, 301: Duncan to Scott, 26 March 1801. Rivett added Carnac to his name when he received a legacy from General Carnac in 1801 (*Ibid.* II, 313: Scott to Rivett, 16 June 1801).

resident at Surat, attempted to obey the order of the Court of Directors and to purchase for the first time on the Company's account a large investment of raw cotton from Bhaunagar, Jambusar and Broach, for the China market. But he discovered that the price of cotton was rising fast and in April he wrote to Bombay giving an alarming account of the difficulties which oppressed the cotton trade. If any profit was to be made it was essential that the cotton should be cleaned and delivered to the ports of Gujarat at the right time to be shipped to Bombay before the setting in of the south-western monsoon. The difference between great profits or losses hung on its prompt delivery. But in 1800 Cherry found that the Maratha government was delaying for as long as possible before allowing the cotton to be cleaned, and this put the Bombay merchants at the mercy of the cotton dealers. Furthermore he discovered afresh what the Bombay merchants had long complained of, that there was no means of redress against the frauds and malpractices of the dealers:

the obstruction most alarming and serious [he wrote to the government] is that which arises from the total Want of Protection in which those who invest cotton stand, in every part of the Country,—no part thereof being within reach of the Control, or I may say Influence of our Government, unless publicly exerted on the part of the Company; which until all my engagements are made cannot, in the present instance be done without enhancing the Prices demanded still more. From this perplexing Cause, the most alarming Dangers threaten any Purchaser—Obliged, in the first Outset, to advance the greatest part of the money to Persons who excepting their Cotton are possessed of no property, he finds the Delivery invariably delayed—first, as before mentioned, by the Marhattah Sirkar, and next by the Dealers themselves as long as possible; and then has Cotton tendered to him in the most adulterated State, full of Seed, Leaf, and Dirt; and in general wet with Water, in order to add to the Weight...'

Yet the purchaser could not refuse it as the demand was too great and a less scrupulous merchant would buy it. 'This practice', continued Cherry, 'so destructive of all Confidence in Trade is this Year, carried to such a Pitch, and resorted to, with so much security from all Punishment, or fear of it, that it is become necessary to accede to a stipulated Proportion of Water, and Seed, before an engagement can be made for a single Bale...'[1]

[1] Surat Factory Records LXXX, 244–6: J. H. Cherry to Bombay, 7 April 1800.

Cherry's account was given greater force when the chief of Surat forwarded a protest to Bombay from seven Parsi merchants who acted as cotton agents in Gujarat for the Bombay trading houses. They complained bitterly that they had no protection for their trade and advanced immense sums of money only to receive 'Dirt and water instead of Cotton'. They demanded that the Bombay government should use all its influence with the peshwa and the gaikwar 'to put a stop to such iniquitous Proceedings so subversive of all Confidence in Trade, and distructive to the important Commerce of Bombay...'[1] The government asked the resident at Poona to use his influence with the peshwa, and Duncan declared to the Court of Directors on 28 April that one intention of his journey to Surat was to remove the obstacles which threatened the cotton trade.[2]

But at least one cotton merchant was not content with whatever measures the government could take, and was considering private means of securing his supplies from Gujarat. Miguel de Lima é Souza, whose 'ready & zealous Assistance' during the negotiations at Surat was cited by Duncan, had been a merchant at Bombay from 1775.[3] Like Murdock Brown, it seems that de Souza's talents and experience early won the confidence of Duncan on the latter's taking up his post as the governor of Bombay. His Portuguese connexions gave him influence at Goa and Duncan used him in all his negotiations with the governor of that colony. In 1789 de Souza entered into partnership with P. C. Bruce, Fawcett and Company, to build a ship at the Portuguese port of Damaun.[4] He must have traded with Malabar because in 1789 he had Rs 20,000 in the Company's treasury at Tellicherry.[5] In 1795 he obtained the consent of the raja of Colapore, the piratical Malwan raja, to trade in his territory without paying customs charges, and the connexion developed so that de Souza took upon himself the task of negotiating between the raja and the Bombay government on the question of the Bombay merchants' claims against the Malwan pirates.[6] De Souza's experience of the cotton trade of Gujarat, for some of the time as the partner of Daniel Seton and of Tate and Adamson,

[1] BRP, range 366, XXVI, 437–41: Surat merchants to the chief of Surat, 11 April 1800.
[2] Letters Received from Bombay XVII, paragraph 3 of the letter of 28 April 1800.
[3] BRP, range 366, IL, 700: de Souza to Bombay, 12 March 1806.
[4] BPC, range 342, XIII, 186–9.   [5] *Ibid.* XI, 571.
[6] BSPP, range E, 1164–6 and 1168–73: April 1795–July 1796.

apparently gained him the friendship of the bakshi of Surat and considerable influence with the nawab, and he acted as Duncan's right-hand man throughout the difficult negotiations. His knowledge of the language and his extensive trading connexions gave him advantages which no Bombay civil servant possessed and it seems likely that Duncan accepted his services with relief. After the annexation of Surat he achieved an even higher place in Duncan's confidence, and thenceforward was intimately involved in Bombay's activities in Gujarat. But in 1800 he indicated what his private interests in that quarter were. While he was helping Duncan in the Surat negotiations he sent his agent to Broach to enquire into the possibilities of farming that great cotton-producing pargana from Sindhia.[1] De Souza, for one, had the clear idea that his cotton trade depended on the control of territory in Gujarat.

But the reconciliation of Duncan with Rivett and his friends, the determination of the whole Bombay establishment to find compensation in Gujarat for the loss of Malabar, and the threatened state of the cotton trade, determined the Bombay government to pursue a forward policy in Gujarat. This meant intervening in Maratha politics. The governor-general's approval of the scheme to obtain the Chorasi pargana and the Surat chauth gave Bombay its excuse. In October 1800 Duncan told Wellesley that the death of Govind Rao Gaikwar and the probable disputed succession among his sons provided the opportunity for winning these objects.[2] In July he had urged that the Company should annex Cambay for commercial reasons,[3] and in December he proposed to Wellesley that Bombay should capture the island of Beyt. The pirates of Okhamandal had seized shipping in November 1800 which had inflicted losses of from one-and-a-half to two lacs of rupees on the merchants of Surat, and the chief of Surat had asked permission to send a naval expedition against the pirates' bases at Goomtee, Beyt and Dwarka.[4] In December a naval force sailed up the north-west coast of Gujarat and reported that Beyt was the principal stronghold of the pirates. It was a heavily fortified island, and possessed at least forty cruisers, some of considerable size. The commander of the expedition declared that the only

[1] BRP, range 366, XLV, 143–8: W. Steadman to Major Walker, 9 March 1804.
[2] BM Add. MSS 13,700, f. 163: Duncan to Wellesley, 4 October 1800.
[3] Home Misc. CDLXXIII, 160–2: Duncan to Wellesley, 9 July 1800.
[4] BSPP, range 381, XVI, 6164: D. Seton to Bombay, 6 November 1800.

effective method of dealing with the freebooters was to capture Beyt and some of the country round it which, he reported, was fertile and produced grain, oil and cotton abundantly.[1] Duncan urged this course on the governor-general. He pointed out that the island owned a famous temple which annually attracted large numbers of pilgrims and yielded revenues which were capable of maintaining a British establishment.[2]

Okhamandal and the Chorasi pargana were old objects of Bombay's ambition. But new ones presented themselves. From Cambay Robert Holford brought up again the subject of the port of Rattalow, which had first come before the government in 1798.[3] The chief of Rattalow visited Holford in January 1801 and appealed to the Company to protect his territory from the oppressions of the raja of Bhaunagar. The raja was determined to prevent the Company from intervening as he feared that Rattalow might quickly supersede his own port and take the trade of the coast from his hands. Holford recommended forcefully that the Company should give Rattalow the protection it asked for on the grounds of its being 'so eligibly situated for the carrying on a traffic with the many surrounding states and to afford us an opportunity of improving our knowledge...of the Catawar...' He asserted that if the Company gained a footing in Kathiawar it could export grain for itself and avoid paying the exorbitant duties which the raja of Bhaunagar exacted. An English factory at Rattalow would attract a body of merchants from the neighbouring areas, particularly from Bhaunagar where the merchants suffered from the tyrannical acts of the raja. Within a few years, he thought, much of the trade which was then carried on at Ahmadabad, Baroda, Cambay, Broach, Bhaunagar and Gogah, could be attracted to Rattalow.[4]

Whereas the first proposals to extend the Company's protection to Rattalow had come at a time when Bombay had little interest in Bhaunagar and its neighbourhood, the place had assumed considerable importance to Bombay's commercial concerns when Holford sent in his proposals. The Company's determination to send cotton to China on its own account further increased the competition and demand which was drawing cotton to Bombay

[1] BSPP, range 381, XVII, 6899–903: W. Selby to Bombay, 16 December 1800.
[2] *Ibid.* XVII, 6916–18: minute of J. Duncan, 26 December 1800.
[3] See above, p. 167.
[4] BSPP, range 381, XXXI, 2781–4: R. Holford to Bombay, 8 January 1801.

even from distant Cutch. The experiences of the cotton merchants at Broach and Baroda in the past season seemed likely to be repeated in 1801, and Cherry reported that the Maratha officials were monopolising the cotton of their parganas so that they could force the price even higher.[1] Between October 1800 and January 1801 Bhaunagar had provided by far the greatest part of the Company's purchases, 5,929 bales, as against 2,806 from Broach and 1,198 from Jambusar, and at a lower price.[2] But in April 1801 Cherry reported with concern that the price of cotton at Bhaunagar had risen from Rs 90 and 95 a candy to Rs 115.[3] This was still preferable to the Broach produce for which the price was Rs 130.[4] Therefore the proposals concerning Rattalow were more interesting to Bombay in 1801 and Holford persisted in urging them on the government. In May he repeated the advantages which the Company could gain from acquiring Rattalow but he added further ideas which he said had been put to him by the chief of Dhandhuka. These were that the English should obtain the districts of Ranpur, Dhandhuka and Gogah from the gaikwar and the peshwa. By these acquisitions, he asserted, the Company would relieve the inhabitants from the oppression of the Marathas and benefit from the increased manufactures and trade of the districts.[5]

Nothing was done immediately in answer to Holford's proposals as the Bombay government was preoccupied with the Chorasi pargana and the Surat chauth. As Duncan had predicted the disputes in the gaikwar family gave him the opportunity to press his demands, and his repeated requests to the governor-general for permission to act grew more impatient. By supporting Anand Rao's claims to the succession he hoped, he told Wellesley, to 'make a Beginning...to the acquisition of a reasonable Extent of Territory in that Quarter, such as I am advised from Europe that Ministry have it very much in their View to acquire'.[6] By this last thought, it seems, he hoped to galvanise Wellesley into replying to his proposal. But the big trading firms of Bombay—Bruce, Fawcett and Company, Alexander Adamson, and Forbes, Smith and Company—had interests of their own in the districts which Holford

---

[1] BCP, range 414, LXVIII, 1037–40: J. H. Cherry to James Carnac, 11 April 1801.
[2] *Ibid.* LXVII, 64–6: Cherry to Bombay, 18 January 1801.
[3] *Ibid.* LXVIII, 1041: Cherry to J. Carnac: 13 April 1801.
[4] *Ibid.* 1044–56: Cherry to Carnac, 16–23 April 1801.
[5] BSPP, range 381, XXXI, 2793–4: Holford to J. H. Lovett, 6 May 1801.
[6] BM Add. MSS 13,701, f. 99: Duncan to Wellesley, 30 May 1801.

had brought to the attention of the government. In October 1801 they complained that American ships were competing in the cotton trade at Gogah and that they were using that port to ship cotton to America and from there to Europe.[1]

The soaring price and widespread adulteration of the cotton had brought the trade into such a serious state that the merchants and the government were forced to take drastic action. In 1795 the price of a candy of cotton at Broach was Rs 80; in 1801 it was Rs 190.[2] The supercargoes at Canton complained of the bad quality of the cotton and attributed the low price it had fetched in China in 1800 to its adulterated state.[3] Since it was useless to complain to the Maratha officers the merchants and the Bombay government united in December 1801 to make 'a joint and regulated purchase of Cotton' with the object of reducing its price and restoring its quality.[4] Forbes, Smith and Company, Bruce, Fawcett and Company, Alexander Adamson and three Parsis joined with the government in the agreement. Adamson, Fawcett, and Charles Forbes formed the committee which was to manage the concern and the government appointed J. H. Cherry as the president.[5] The merchants and the government agreed to buy the cotton jointly, and to divide it between them. The Company's share was no larger than that assigned to each firm. The commercial resident at Surat and his assistants were given the task of inspecting and controlling the boats which came from the north and west to unload cotton at the port. It was hoped that they would be able to check some of the adulteration and pilfering. The committee appointed local agents to do the same work at Broach, Bhaunagar, and Mandvi in Cutch.

The agreement was a conclusive proof of the alliance between the government and the cotton merchants. Not only had the latter succeeded in limiting the Company's share of the trade but they were able to make use of the Company's power at Surat and elsewhere to control the cotton dealers. James Rivett thought the agreement so important that when he learnt in February 1802 that the Court of Directors intended to withdraw from the cotton

---

[1] BCP, range 414, LXIX, 1313–406: Bombay merchants to the government, 7 October 1801.
[2] *Ibid.* LXVIII, 946–8: G. Prendergast to Bombay, 30 June 1801.
[3] *Ibid.* LXVII, 659–61: the cotton committee to Bombay, 30 May 1801.
[4] *Ibid.* LXXIII, 699–701: Bombay to Bengal, 8 December 1801.
[5] *Ibid.* 702–4.

market that season for lack of money, Rivett proposed that the merchants should lend money to the government for an investment. He feared that if the Company withdrew from the agreement 'the Copartnership wanting its best, and perhaps its only effectual Cement, would thereafter dissolve, and the trade be again burthened with those Exactions and subject to those impositions which have affected its credit and may be said already to have threatened its Annihilation'.[1] In March the cotton committee asked the Bombay government to draw up regulations which could be enforced within the Company's territory. Their object was to get the cotton into the hands of the merchants as speedily as possible and by these means to make its adulteration more difficult.

But the problem could only be tackled effectively if the Company extended its power in Gujarat. The Maratha officials were more often than not parties to the trickery of the dealers and at Broach, Sindhia's official monopolised the cotton. Therefore it is not surprising that in the very month when the cotton agreement was signed the Bombay government decided to take action in Gujarat without waiting longer for the governor-general's instructions.[2] In return for supporting Anand Rao and his minister Raoba in the disputed gaikwar succession Bombay received on 26 December the deed of surrender of the Chorasi pargana and the gaikwari share of the Surat chauth. The government sent a military expedition under Major Alexander Walker to support Anand Rao against his rebellious Arab soldiery and the disloyal factions in his family. The measure, Bombay declared to the Court of Directors, was 'actuated by a desire of promoting what appeared to us, to be His Excellency the Governor General's views in respect to Surat, and also towards the Guykwar State; and as the Scene has latterly Expanded of ensuring to the Honble Company the Political and Commercial advantages which must obviously result from our obtaining a predominant influence in the Guzerat...'[3] To Wellesley the Bombay government justified its action with different reasons, asserting its determination to prevent Sindhia from using the gaikwar's troubles in order to interfere in Gujarat.[4] Duncan

---

[1] BCP, range 414, LXXIII, 713: minute of J. Rivett-Carnac, 19 February 1802.
[2] BSPP, range 381, XXVII, 6618–21: Bombay to Bengal, 27 December 1801.
[3] Letters Received from Bombay XVIII, par. 13 of the letter to the secret committee, 4 January 1802.
[4] BSPP, range 381, XXIX, 179 (unnumbered page facing 178v): Bombay to Bengal, 7 January 1802.

himself went to Surat to supervise the final arrangements whence
he wrote to his uncle Jonathan Michie that if he were not thwarted
in his plans by Lord Wellesley he had no doubt that he would gain

ample Credit, as well as considerable Advantage to the Public, by the
successful prosecution of my Plan, which now promises very fairly in
every respect...I shall endeavour to do the Company's business before
I return, if Lord Wellesley will let me & if he do not, the Court of
Directors or rather the Bd of Controul, may judge, where the fault
lies...at all Events, I am now embarked in what I deem a creditable
undertaking & must abide the Consequences...[1]

The Board of Control, under the influence of Mr David Scott,
could be content that it had turned Duncan, Cornwallis's sound
administrator, into a champion of a forward policy more determined than Wellesley.

At last Bombay had acquired the gaikwar's share of the long-
sought for Surat chauth as well as the Chorasi pargana which the
government assured the Court of Directors, 'has ever been thought
would prove, from its situation and products, an acquisition of the
greatest importance to our local interests in that Quarter...'[2]
Duncan and James Rivett, their bitter disagreement over Malabar
healed, jointly signed the letter to the Court of Directors. They
used every argument to justify their policy. The Court, they
hoped, would approve their

making the Guickwar's present Offers, the Channel of extending our
possessions and Influence into a Country we are in fact bound to defend, and which is also connected by the most intimate ties with the
Trade and prosperity of this place, besides which, we have some reason
to believe that your Honble Court will be satisfied with any adviseable
Exertion, such as we hope, the present may be deemed, that shall have
for its object, not only the obtaining of a suitable circumjacent Territory
for your City of Surat, and freeing it at the same time from the burthen
of the Choute, but shall likewise further tend to establish in your behalf,
a degree of Influence, in almost the only part of the Coast of India, that
now lies open to the Intrigues or Invasion of our Enemies, the French,
or hereafter of your other European rivals.[3]

[1] Michie Papers, MSS 5881, file 2: Duncan to Jonathan Michie, Surat, 5
February 1802.
[2] Rylands English MSS, Melville Papers 696, 128: Bombay to the Court,
enclosed in Duncan's letter to Henry Dundas, 5 February 1802.
[3] *Ibid.*

Whatever were the true views of Duncan and Rivett on the French menace—and in 1798 Rivett had declared that the French would never choose to attack Surat[1]—their joint letter to the directors shows the strength of their new alliance. The war of minutes which had followed their divisions over Malabar was at an end. The hesitation which Duncan had shown over the annexation of Surat, the declaration that his council had forced him to act, these did not appear in 1802. He and Rivett and the private-trading interest were one. The expansionist policy which this alliance promoted soon showed the source of its inspiration. At the end of January 1802 George Brown, the new commercial resident at Surat, asked for 'the exertions of the Strong Arm of Government' against those who were responsible for adulterating the cotton. In response Duncan ordered Major Walker who commanded the Bombay troops in Gujarat to procure orders from Raoba, the gaikwar's minister, which were to be sent to every village. These were to forbid any adulteration of the cotton on pain of severe punishment.[2] The difference between this and former requests was that Walker was in a position to force the gaikwar to cooperate and through the use of British troops to see that the gaikwar's orders were obeyed.

But it was not only Rivett who directed the Bombay government's policy in the interests of private trade. Miguel de Souza had a personal influence with Duncan which had nothing to do with any pressure from Leadenhall Street. It seems that Duncan placed his confidence in de Souza, as he had in Murdock Brown, because the merchant had that superior knowledge of the country and the people which was attractive to a man who had made his career in the revenue line and was ignorant of trade. In 1801 Robert Holford had vainly urged the governor to act on the proposals of the landowners of Rattalow. But in December of that year an agent from Rattalow got in touch with Miguel de Souza who was then at Bombay. The agent declared that he was aware of the 'great confidence everybody, and particularly the Governor' placed in de Souza, and asked him to use his influence on behalf of Rattalow.[3] He described the advantages of the port with its safe anchorage, the cotton, grain and oil which the surrounding

[1] See above, pp. 163–4.
[2] BSPP, range 381, XXIX, 602–3: Duncan to A. Walker, 1 February 1802.
[3] *Ibid.* XXXII, 2736–43: the Rattalow agent to de Souza, 5 December 1801.

country produced, and the five cart roads which converged on it from different directions. He repeated the landowners' offer to cede the country to the English in return for a half-share of the revenues and the Company's protection against the raja of Bhaunagar.[1] It is significant that when de Souza showed interest in these proposals he was able to get Duncan's permission to act. With the governor's support he set off on a personal tour of inspection, travelling round the Gulf of Cambay to see the port. In March 1802 he sent back his report to Duncan and enthusiastically recommended that the Company should accept the offer of Rattalow and its district.[2] He asserted that the raja of Bhaunagar's claim to the place was groundless, and that the raja, despite his protestations of friendship towards the Company, had 'taken every step in his power to prevent the English getting a footing in this extensive Country as well as the Knowledge of the people and Trade thereof'. The raja's oppression had turned the whole area into wasteland except for the village of Dholera where there were three hundred houses still standing. But de Souza declared that the soil was fertile and there was plenty of good water. He was enthusiastic about the port of Rattalow which he claimed provided shelter in the worst weather and the convenience of being able to load the cotton boats without using lighters. He thought that if the Company hoisted its flag at Rattalow not only would the place attract the merchants and trade of the surrounding country, but the girasias or landowners of the neighbouring villages would follow suit and cede their country to the English. The Company would gain considerably from the customs and eventually from the land revenue and they would have the means of 'getting a true Knowledge of the Cattiwar and other Countries and introducing our Trade there as also into Limree, Warwan and the interior parts of those extensive Countries without going through Baunagure'. The English flag and a garrison of one hundred sepoys, he thought, would be sufficient to protect the place, but the Company would have to pay tribute for it to the gaikwar, who farmed the revenues from the peshwa. De Souza's final proposal was that he should undertake the management of the whole scheme himself,

since I have begun with it I shall undertake it, and exert my utmost

[1] BSPP, range 381, XXXII, 2739–40 (misplaced in the volume between 2752–3): the Rattalow agent to de Souza, 5 December 1801.
[2] *Ibid.* XXXII, 2724–7: de Souza to Duncan, 18 March 1802.

endeavours to bring all my views respecting the acquirements of that extensive Country to bear in a short time, in hopes that the Company will defray my expence and when I have completed the object to their satisfaction that they shall then reward me or my family in case of my death according to my merit.[1]

Whereas de Souza had failed in his bid to farm the Broach pargana the same strategy gave promise of greater success at Rattalow and Dholera.

De Souza's enthusiastic report on Rattalow reached the Bombay government at a time when affairs in Gujarat were holding out heady prospects of advancement. The gaikwar and his ambitious minister Raoba were helpless captives in Baroda facing insurrection and the uncontrolled power of their Arab soldiers. They were completely dependent for their rescue on the detachment of British troops which Duncan had sent to their aid. The troubles of the country ran deep. Disorder was everywhere, the government was overwhelmed by debt and the country was mortgaged to moneylenders, who indeed, with the Arab soldiers, ran the country.[2] In this desperate position Raoba proposed that his master should subsidise an English force whose first task would be to defend the frontier against the incursions of the rebel Malhar Rao. In return he offered cessions of territory to the Company and indicated that these might be taken on the sea-coast. In Major Walker's view this last proposal was to 'enhance his offer and as a bribe to comply with his wishes'.[3]

The Bombay government was in a difficult position. Gujarat lay open to their ambitions, but the negotiation of a treaty of subsidiary alliance with a member of the Maratha confederacy without Lord Wellesley's assent was a step which demanded considerable daring and resolve. Despite Duncan's appeals no word had come from the governor-general himself and Duncan had to be content with the advice of the resident at Poona. But such was the spirit of the new Duncan, the ally of Rivett and Adamson, Fawcett and de Souza, that on 15 March 1802 he drew up a treaty of alliance with the gaikwar which provided for the permanent subsidy of 2,000 of the Company's troops and artillery, to be paid for in money or cessions of territory. The treaty also confirmed the cession to the Company of the Chorasi pargana and the gaikwar's share of the

---

[1] BSPP, range 381, XXXII, 2734: de Souza to Duncan, 18 March 1802.
[2] *Ibid.* XXX, 855–6: A. Walker to Bombay, 13 February 1802.   [3] *Ibid.* 848–9.

Surat chauth.[1] On the following day Duncan explained his policy to Wellesley. The subsidiary alliance, he declared, was only an interim measure. Raoba and his master wanted the English to expel the rebel Malhar Rao from Gujarat by force, and by adopting this policy Duncan saw the promise of further acquisitions of territory for the Company. But, he told Wellesley, as he was uncertain how far such extensions of territory coincided with the governor-general's views he intended to preserve Malhar Rao from destruction and keep the means of bringing pressure to bear on the gaikwar's government in the future.[2]

The strain was showing on Duncan. He could get no reply from Wellesley, and he would have to justify his policy to the directors. It was dreadful, wrote an observer, to see him 'hunting after shadows' when he had 'realities within his grasp'.[3] By May Duncan had overcome his timidity and the Bombay government took the decision to crush Malhar Rao and to make a permanent agreement with the gaikwar. The latter ceded a further pargana to the Company.[4] On 3 May Malhar Rao surrendered to the British troops,[5] and on 17 May Duncan was telling Wellesley that if he would agree to the Company's troops joining the gaikwar's for the purpose of collecting tribute, Bombay's authority 'might gradually be extended to, and possession even taken of such part of the western line of Coast from Diu to Dwarka, as your Lordship might be pleased to sanction; either distinctly from, or in concurrence with the suggestions to that effect contained in my separate official address... under date the 11 of November last'.[6] On 9 May Duncan had urged Close, the resident at Poona, to persuade the peshwa to entrust his Gujarat interests to the Company, and he had repeated Raoba's suggestion that should the Company under any circumstances be 'in the way of receiving landed assignments from the Paishwa, they should be taken from Guzerat, in which, including his share of the Surat Attaveesy and Jamboosear, and the Talooka of Ahmedabad, the Paishwa's Revenue may be estimated at 25

---

[1] BSPP, range 381, XXXI, 1649–52: treaty between the Company and Anand Rao Gaikwar, 15 March 1802.
[2] *Ibid.* XXX, 1237: Duncan to Wellesley, 16 March 1802.
[3] WB 186, a.1: E. Trissell to Walker, 7 April 1802.
[4] Home Misc. CDLXXIX, 97–100: Duncan to Wellesley, 12 May 1802.
[5] BSPP, range 381, XXXI, 2062–7: Bombay to the Court of Directors, 13 May 1802.
[6] *Ibid.* 2117–19: Duncan to Wellesley, 17 May 1802.

lacs p. Annum...'[1] Bombay knew as firmly as Lord Wellesley what they wanted from the peshwa.

The thrust for territory in Gujarat had begun, and Duncan had urged on Wellesley his policy of annexing the coastal districts. He explained his views by referring Wellesley to other proposals which he had sent to Calcutta on 11 November 1801. These, too, concerned expansion along the Gujarat coast. They came from a former minister of the nawab of Junagar, which was a considerable state in Kathiawar. The minister, Calianbay, had fallen out with his master, taken possession of a fort near Porbander, and from there wrote to Bombay suggesting that the Company should annex the territory of Junagar which stretched for about 150 miles along the coast between Bhaunagar and Porbander.[2] Calianbay had described in detail the fertility of the country, its crops of sugar, indigo and cotton, and its piece-good manufactures, which he said could equal those made at Surat and be bought at prices 15 or 20 per cent lower. But the inhabitants, he declared, were so oppressed by their ruler that three-quarters of the country was waste and the landowners were in revolt against the nawab. He promised that they would join him in putting the country under the rule of the Company. Duncan sent the memorial to Wellesley and pointed out that if the Company annexed the territory they would be able to curtail the activities of the northern pirates of whom the nawab of Junagar was one of the chief protectors. But he went on to add

besides which, it may be an object of Consideration, how far sound policy may require our possessing a predominant influence on that Coast, with a view of shutting out the French from making Settlements on it to our prejudice; since it is only there, and along the more eastern line of the Coast of Guzerat proper, between Cambay and Surat, that any opening appears to be left to them; and if your Excellency please to avail yourself of the favorable opportunity now offered for our obtaining a permanent influence in the Guicawar's Country, the last of these objects may, I think, be effectually secured, and a good foundation, at the same time, laid towards the Gradual Attainment of the other.[3]

Duncan had hunted out his shadows. The French menace was a useful argument for the building of the British empire in India. But in this case, Wellesley, the great imperialist, saw no reason to

[1] *Ibid.* 2072–4: Duncan to Close, 9 May 1802.
[2] Home Misc. CDLXXVIII, 267–74: memorial on Junagar, 31 October 1801.
[3] *Ibid.* 250–2: Duncan to Wellesley, 11 November 1801.

reply to Duncan's proposals, and even the momentous negotiations for a subsidiary alliance with the Gaikwar did not draw forth an opinion from the governor-general until 20 June 1802 when he belatedly gave his approval to Bombay's proceedings after complaining that he had had no time until then to read Duncan's voluminous dispatches.[1] In London Castlereagh was even less ready to accept arguments of general policy for Bombay's activities in Gujarat. He asked for Henry Dundas's advice on the transactions with the gaikwar and expressed his own doubts.

We profess to interfere to support the Guicowar succession in pursuance of our Treaty, but it is impossible not to see that the Cessions in the Vicinity of Surat have never been lost sight of. Had we supported Anund Row in the first instance on condition of his paying us our Military Expences, & had we in discharge of those Expences negociated for the Cession in question, our interposition would have been liable to less suspicion; but as it now stands explained, extension of Territory is too visible on the face of the transaction. This District may be of some convenience, but cannot be of any great importance to the Company— It is flying at too small game; & it is the more inconvenient at this moment, as, coupled with the transactions in Oude & in the Carnatic, it bears the features of a systematic purpose of extending our Territories in defiance of the recorded sense of Parliament.[2]

Castlereagh's shrewd mind had penetrated deeply. It seems that Bombay's impatience to secure cessions of territory in Gujarat led its government to seize on a possible French menace as the best way of overcoming Lord Wellesley's indifference. It is certain that when Duncan wrote to Wellesley in May 1802 it was not the French menace which inspired his policy of expansion in Gujarat. The decision which the government took between March and May to crush Malhar Row and to make a permanent agreement with the gaikwar, and Duncan's concern to get the peshwa to place his Gujarat interests in the Company's hands, sprang from far different interests. In March the Bombay government received de Souza's report on Rattalow and Dholera.[3] But de Souza did more than urge the government to protect these two villages. It had occurred to him when he visited them that 'as these Villages formed part of the Purgunnahs of Dandooka and Ranpore, that I should not be

[1] BSPP, range 381, XXXIII, 2922–6: Wellesley to Bombay, 20 June 1802.
[2] Home Misc. DIV, 3–4: Castlereagh to Henry Dundas, 11 September 1802.
[3] See above, pp. 192–3.

able to bring my views respecting that place completely to bear, nor to Establish our Trade and enable to introduce it into Cattiwar and Tallawar without having some controul over those Purgun-nahs'.[1] He wrote to the governor privately to convince him of the need to obtain these parganas, and Duncan was sufficiently impressed to write to Colonel Palmer at Poona and ask if the peshwa would farm them out to the Company.[2] The peshwa had not yet sought the Company's help and it seemed unlikely that he would agree to the proposal. But in the meantime de Souza used his influence at Baroda to secure Raoba's promise that he should farm the parganas from the gaikwar who had the temporary management of them.[3] One cannot know whether de Souza secured this promise in return for persuading Duncan to act against Malhar Rao, but the two events certainly occurred at the same time. It is obvious that in May 1802 Duncan was very much influenced by de Souza's ideas, and he asked for his opinion on the proposals which Robert Holford had first put forward the previous May about obtaining Gogah as well as Ranpur and Dhandhuka from the peshwa. De Souza replied on 23 May that he was doubtful about Gogah

as for my part from the little Knowledge I have had of the Country and the Trade thereof I would not have anything to do with the Port and District of Gogo for tho it is the best Sea Port on this side of the Country still if we make a Settlement at Rattalow it will from its situation draw almost all the Trade of Gogo, whence the Revenue of the place by Customs will fall considerably therefore I should be contented with two Districts only Ranpoor and Dandooca because by having them we shall have a great Command over the Country and the Gates of Cattiwar and other Countries be open to us...[4]

It seems therefore that it was de Souza's plans and the prospects which they held out to the Bombay trading interest which inspired the government's policy between March and May 1802. Indeed, between February and the end of May de Souza had shown himself to be a man of action not content with mere plans for expanding trade in Gujarat and Kathiawar. He was determined to develop Rattalow into a great port and to draw the trade of the surrounding country to its warehouses and to him as its supreme manager and

[1] BRP, range 366, IL, 671–3: de Souza to Bombay, 13 September 1805.
[2] *Ibid.*
[3] *Ibid.*
[4] BSPP, range 381, XXXI, 2805–7: de Souza to Duncan, 23 May 1802.

merchant. He had begun by buying wheat and cotton and sending it from Rattalow to Bombay. He had written to his friends at Surat and Damaun to make the place known and they had brought their ships to the port. He had attracted labourers to the village and employed them to plough the land. The success of his measures was soon apparent for merchants asked permission to build houses and shops there and the raja of Limri began negotiating for the Company's friendship. On 3 June de Souza sent a grant in the name of the gaikwar and the peshwa to Duncan which consented to the Company's acquisition of Rattalow and the surrounding country. At the same time he reported that agents had arrived at Rattalow from one of the Kathiawar chiefs to offer their master's services to him and the Company.[1] De Souza's commercial strategy was beginning to work. By September he could report to Duncan that fifty vessels had visited the port, and that many merchants, particularly those at Ahmadabad, had ordered their agents at Bombay to send all their goods directly to Rattalow instead of to Broach, Jambusar and Cambay.[2] The carriage of goods was far cheaper from Rattalow because the distance was shorter, the roads were better and the duties were lower.[3] He told Duncan that he had made the acquaintance of the rajas of Wadhwan and Limri, the Kathies of Jusdan and the girasias of Dhandhuka.[4] In October he reported that 'a vast number' of merchants from the surrounding districts had applied to build at Rattalow.[5] His success could not fail to influence the Bombay government.

De Souza was in a uniquely strong position to direct the government's policy, for besides his personal influence with Duncan, and his commercial relations with other influential members of the settlement, he had close connexions with the gaikwar and with many of the petty rulers of Gujarat. In 1802 he was the chief negotiator between Duncan and the gaikwar, and in February 1803 Duncan commended his services to Wellesley when de Souza received a knighthood of the Order of Christ from the prince regent of Portugal. Duncan wrote of de Souza's service with him in Gujarat in 1802 'as thereafter with Major Walker the Resident at Baroda, his Agency with the Members of the Native Government &

---

[1] BSPP, range 381, XXXII, 2815: de Souza to Duncan, 3 June 1802.
[2] BPP, range 342, LVII, 3298–302: de Souza to Duncan, 29 September 1802.
[3] *Ibid.* 3502: de Souza to Duncan, 12 October 1802.
[4] *Ibid.* 3302: de Souza to Duncan, 29 September 1802.
[5] *Ibid.* 3509: de Souza to Duncan, 12 October 1802.

personal influence with the Raja Anund Rao himself proved of the greatest utility towards bringing that Mahratta Durbar into those connections of close confidence and habits of reliance on the British power in India...'[1] Alexander Walker expressed similar views and told Duncan in January 1803 that he was lost without de Souza's services.[2] The two men worked closely together throughout the negotiations with the gaikwar, and between them they directed Bombay's policy in Gujarat and Kathiawar for the next three years. Walker was a shrewd man and his integrity was beyond suspicion. At the time when, guided by de Souza, he was deciding on the expansion of British power in Gujarat he expressed no doubts about de Souza's advice or motives. The months which de Souza spent away from his business appeared to be used for the public good alone.

There would still be no grounds to doubt this, however strong the suspicion, were it not for the existence among Walker's papers of a letter which he wrote to Duncan in April 1806,[3] when, a sadly disillusioned man, he confessed that he had been blind about de Souza. De Souza, he told Duncan, had 'always had the character of a man of great duplicity and cunning', but Walker had put this down to prejudice when he first came to know de Souza well in Gujarat. Then Walker had been greatly impressed by de Souza's zeal for the Company's interest and he could not praise his services highly enough. But at some date which he does not mention, though it would appear to be after 1804, Walker learnt from Raoba, the gaikwar's minister, that de Souza's long and daily visits to Raoba's house were spent in the transaction of his private affairs. These included negotiations, amounting to blackmail, for a personal grant of land to de Souza and advantageous concessions in cotton. As soon as Walker knew of this he reported it to Duncan and denounced de Souza's actions to Raoba. But before this, Walker acknowledged, de Souza had availed himself by every means of the resources of Gujarat and had reaped great private commercial advantages from his position. Gujarat as well as Malabar had its Murdock Brown.

But in 1802 both Walker and Duncan were ignorant of de Souza's schemes, and not only were they convinced by him that the

[1] BSPP, range 381, LIII, 547–53: Duncan to Wellesley, 6 February 1803.
[2] WB 180, a.2, box 2: Walker to Duncan, 14 January 1803.
[3] *Ibid.* a.5: Walker to Duncan, Baroda, 4 April 1806.

Company should acquire Ranpur and Dhandhuka, but the governor sought his opinion on the policy which Bombay should pursue in Cutch. The province of Cutch was in a state of turmoil and civil strife in 1802. Two opposing parties fought each other for power: one was composed of the merchants and monied men, the banians, and the other of the landowners or girasias. Although the banians were the weaker party they held power because they were united and were able to benefit from the divisions of the girasias. The immediate cause of the civil war was the rebellion of a former dewan of the raja called Fateh Muhammad against his master and the new dewan, the banian Hunsraje.[1] The raja appealed to the governor-general for help and Wellesley wrote to Duncan in May 1802 asking for information on affairs in Cutch.[2] Up to that time Bombay's relations with Cutch had been almost purely commercial involving the purchase of cotton on a fairly small scale.[3] Few people had any knowledge of the country, and Duncan applied to de Souza for information. De Souza was able to give him most of the facts of the civil war, and added to his account,

The Country, I am told is very fine and fertile and has two or three very good Ports. The Revenue is about fourteen Lacs of Rupees a year. If we could replace the Prince, keep possession of the Forts, and get one half of the revenue, it would be a very desirable Object and the more so because the whole of the Country is in the Sea Coast.[4]

Duncan was not slow to take up the suggestion of intervening and de Souza had to counsel caution. He advised against action 'without first sending there some clever and disinterested People, who will bring to you an impartial report of the Port, Place, the Country and all other Circumstances you may find necessary'.[5]

As a result, it seems, of de Souza's advice, Duncan commissioned Captain David Seton to go to Cutch and to find out from the raja what inducement there was for the Company to intervene.[6] Duncan had in mind a plan for controlling Cutch in the same way as he now controlled the gaikwar, by establishing a resident with the raja and a subsidised military force of one battalion with

---

[1] BSPP, range 381, XXXVIII, 6765–70: Captain D. Seton to Bombay, 18 November 1802.
[2] *Ibid.* XXXII, 2828: Bengal to Bombay, 29 May 1802.
[3] BCP, range 414, LXVII, 64–6: Surat to Bombay, 18 January 1801.
[4] BSPP, range 381, XXXV, 4810–11: de Souza to Duncan, 21 August 1802.
[5] *Ibid.* 4968: de Souza to Duncan, 6 October 1802.
[6] *Ibid.* XXXVI, 5238–45: Duncan to Seton, 25 October 1802.

artillery.[1] Seton was also given one other important task, that of finding out all the information in his power about the northern pirates, particularly those of Beyt, as the government had concluded that the only way of stopping their depredations was to organise an expedition against them.[2] Seton gave most of his attention to this side of his mission as he told Duncan that the country was too poor to subsidise a permanent military force. He recommended Bombay's joining with the raja of Cutch to attack the piratical ports of Porbander, Junagar, Beyt and Navanagar.[3] But Bombay was not able to act on the proposals as events were moving rapidly towards the treaty of Bassein and the presidency could not spare a single soldier for Cutch.[4]

However, Seton continued at his post and on 28 November he forwarded new proposals from the dewan Hunsraje to Bombay. In return for military help Hunsraje offered to prevent other Europeans from establishing a factory in Cutch and proposed to lower the duties on the Company's imports and exports, which included piece-goods, cotton, and horses, from 14 to 5 per cent of their value. He also repeated his offer to attack the pirates of Beyt and Dwarka. Seton emphasised the value of these concessions. 'The Cotton here is a very superior quality and was there a demand the culture of it would encrease, the indulgence in point of Customs would always secure the Company the preference.' On the pirates of Okhamandal he wrote, 'The situation of the Province of Ocka, to the windward in the Northeast Monsoon, of every seaport on this side of India, gives the pirates a great advantage in taking Vessels, it besides commands the entrance of the Cutch and Persian Gulphs, and is also the Key to all the Northern parts of the Guzerat by land'.[5] He urged the government to seize the place and save the annual loss of several lacs of rupees to Bombay's trade.

Thus by the end of 1802 and shortly before the treaty of Bassein Bombay was extending its political influence and territorial power to the north. It was a policy which Bombay pushed through on its own initiative and almost independently of Bengal. Wellesley gave a belated approval of what was done but in no way can it be called his own policy. Duncan and his council justified the

[1] *Ibid.*   [2] *Ibid.* 5247.

[3] *Ibid.* xxxviii, 6765–70: Seton to Bombay, 18 November 1802.

[4] *Ibid.* 6770–74: Duncan to Seton, 3 December 1802.

[5] *Ibid.* range 381, xxxviii, 6782–5: Seton to Bombay, 28 November 1802.

treaties with the gaikwar to the Court of Directors by claiming that they

must tend powerfully to establish on the firmest foundation the pre-dominance of the Honble Company's influence in Guzerat, and to facilitate our directing all the material operations of its future Adminis-tration, as far as our National Prosperity or the Benefit of the Honble Company, in view either to general Policy or to objects of Commercial Advantage may hereafter render advisable...[1]

But there is no doubt that the objects and strategy of this terri-torial expansion and the force which carried it through came from the private-trading interest of the settlement. De Souza was the key figure in planning and negotiating the strategy of expansion, but it was his friends and associates in Bombay, Bruce and Fawcett, Adamson, Charles Forbes, and Rivett, who carried Duncan along with them and presented the governor-general and the Court of Directors with *faits accomplis*.

It was not only in Bombay's relations with the gaikwar that the private-trading interest triumphed. On 25 October 1802 the peshwa, Baji Rao, signed a preliminary treaty of alliance with the Company, and on the same day was defeated in battle by Holkar and fled from Poona.[2] Bombay took little part in the negotiations which preceded the peshwa's signing the preliminary treaty. They were conducted by the residents at Poona under Wellesley's direct instructions and with the object of bringing the policy of the Maratha confederacy under British control. The acquisition of territory was not one of the governor-general's first concerns.[3] As Arthur Wellesley put it in 1806: 'The cession of territory for subsidy was the best mode of avoiding the disputes and incon-venience which had invariably attended these subsidiary alliances in other instances',[4] and the peshwa preferred this means of paying for a subsidiary force.[5] In the preliminary treaty which he signed on 25 October he promised to cede territory worth 25 lacs of rupees in Gujarat and the Carnatic.[6] Close thereupon consulted the Bombay government on the cessions which they wanted from the peshwa in Gujarat. Arthur Wellesley was later to claim that

---

[1] Home Misc. DCXXII, 19–24: Bombay to the Court of Directors, 25 November 1802.
[2] *Poona Residency Correspondence* x, ed. Sinh, 32–4.   [3] See above, pp. 168–9.
[4] Owen (ed.), *The Despatches etc. of the Marquess Wellesley*, ci.
[5] See above, p. 168.   [6] *Poona Residency Correspondence* x, ed. Sinh, 32.

'the necessity of guarding against French influence was one of the principal causes of the treaty of Bassein',[1] and Castlereagh was sufficiently impressed by the argument of the French menace to say that 'The main advantage of the treaty of Bassein I take to be, the increased footing it gives us in the Guzerat...'[2] On these grounds the historian S. J. Owen concluded that the cessions in Gujarat were chosen as a means of strengthening the Company's position there 'where a French landing had been pronounced by General Stuart even more dangerous than at Fort William itself'.[3]

This conclusion seems justified from Duncan's dispatch to Wellesley, dated 21 December 1802 in which he declared

Under the option allowed us to Select the Districts for the Jaydaud it appears to me that we ought to choose those nearest to our principal stations, and to prefer such as lie along the Sea Coast; not only for the purposes of Commerce, but because Territory so situated can always admit on our part of being more effectually defended, as well as serve to the more certain exclusion of our Rivals...[4]

He justified each choice individually on political grounds.

Our having Pitlaad and Dundooka &ca will be of much Political convenience, the former adjoining to, and immediately connecting with Cambay and Dholka; which last Pergunnah stands already Stipulated to be delivered over to us for the Jaydaud assignable by the Guicowar Government; and the other, as including the two Ports of Dollera and Gogo; besides that, the whole of this Western Tract is otherwise valuable for its opening a ready and easy Entrance into the Peninsula of Guzerat, which is still and has always been in a State of doubtful dependance; the Revenue derivable from it beyond the limits of Dundooka &ca depending on Moolickguiry...Our obtaining the Chouth of Cambay is also of material Political consequence, as tending to strengthen our footing in a seaport which must constitute to us always the Surest and easiest Entrance into Guzerat.[5]

This piece of reasoning by Duncan throws an interesting light on his other communications to the governor-general and the authorities in England in which he justified his expansionist policy. Nothing was entered on the official records at the time, but in 1805 Miguel de Lima é Souza casually revealed that the governor

---

[1] Owen (ed.), *The Despatches etc. of the Marquess Wellesley*, 274.
[2] *Ibid.* 258: Castlereagh to Wellesley, 4 March 1804.   [3] *Ibid.* xxiii.
[4] BSPP, range 381, XL, 111–14: Duncan's memorandum, 21 December 1802.
[5] *Ibid.* 114–16.

had asked him at the time of the peshwa's flight from Poona to give a full account of the latter's possessions in Gujarat and to pick out those which he thought Bombay should annex. De Souza had urged in reply that the presidency should acquire Dhandhuka, Ranpur, Gogah, Napad and the chauth of Cambay.[1] He had given his reasons for wanting Dhandhuka and Ranpur before May 1802,[2] and since then his greater knowledge of that area had apparently convinced him that Gogha also was a desirable port to possess. The chauth of Cambay was valuable not so much because of the revenue it brought but because it admitted 'the Appointment of a joint Collector with the Nabob, with the exercise of a certain share of Authority...'[3] It was this authority which the English needed in order to develop the port's commercial advantages. If one substitutes the word 'commercial' for Duncan's 'political' in his account of the advantages of the cessions, it is obvious that the scheme was based on de Souza's plan for the commercial penetration of Gujarat. Duncan merely dressed it up in a political guise. In fact he submitted two different schemes of territory to the peshwa. Both contained de Souza's proposals and the demand for the peshwa's share of the Surat chauth. But in the first one Bombay asked for the peshwa's part of the Surat Attavisi, a district of 1,653 square miles, which he shared with the gaikwar, and which produced almost one-eighth of Gujarat's cotton crop.[4] The peshwa refused to make the concession and, as nothing would change his mind, Duncan and Close, the resident, submitted a second schedule.[5] This substituted Ahmadabad for the Attavisi and included the peshwa's districts of Dabhoi, Amod, and Jambusar, and the peshwa's share of the Kathiawar tribute.[6] It is impossible not to see de Souza's Kathiawar strategy behind the last demand while Amod and Jambusar produced 8,000 bales of cotton.[7] It was a matter of urgency to conclude the treaty[8] and on 31 December only the cessions of territory remained to be settled. Then at the last minute the peshwa insisted on rejecting the second

[1] BRP, range 366, II, 673–4: de Souza to Bombay, 13 September 1805.
[2] See above, p. 197.   [3] BRP, range 366, XLVI, 1223: A. Walker to Bombay.
[4] BSPP, range 382, VII, 2732: Major Walker to Bombay, 15 July 1805.
[5] *Poona Residency Correspondence* x, ed. Sinh, 68: Close to Bombay, 30 January 1803.
[6] BSPP, range 381, XL, 38–47: Close to Wellesley, 30 December 1802.
[7] *Ibid.* range 382, VII, 2732: Major Walker to Bombay, 15 July 1805.
[8] *Poona Residency Correspondence* x, ed. Sinh, 69: Close to Bombay, 30 January 1803.

scheme in favour of the first. Close was induced to agree and he concluded the treaty in the last minutes of 1802.[1] Despite the sudden change Bombay still secured its nicely calculated commercial advantages.

That Bombay wanted this territory for commercial and not political reasons appears further from the views expressed by Henry Fawcett, the cotton merchant and accountant-general. In March 1803 he delivered a minute on the further measures which were necessary to prevent the adulteration of the cotton. He reported that the cotton which the Bombay merchants had bought in 1800, particularly that from the peshwa's district of Amod which was usually of the best quality, was 'very much adulterated by the grower or first purchaser who residing in a Foreign Country could not be subjected to English Law'. The evil could not be remedied, Fawcett declared, 'unless the Honorable Company were in possession of the Ports at which it is Shipped and enabled to frame regulations to the extent even of forfeiture in cases of great notoriety and fines in lesser instances of adulteration...'[2] It is obvious that this was more than a passing idea of Fawcett's. In April 1810 he, with other cotton merchants from India, gave evidence before a parliamentary committee of enquiry, and Fawcett described the adulteration of the cotton and the attempts of the Bombay government, 'which was then in the habit of paying attention to the representations of Merchants', to remonstrate with the Maratha authorities. Since these efforts had proved vain, Fawcett continued,

When part of those districts...were ceded to the Company, the greatest and most reasonable hopes were entertained that, by the adoption of proper regulations, and the establishment of Courts of Justice, effectual measures would have been taken to prevent adulteration, and to improve the quality of this staple article; and an example set to the neighbouring countries remaining under the Native Princes, which might have been followed up by still greater benefits...[3]

Fawcett undoubtedly spoke for the whole of the Bombay community which had interests in the cotton trade.[4] The concern which

---

[1] *Ibid.* 70.

[2] BCP, range 414, LXXIV, 413–14: H. Fawcett to the Bombay government, 3 March 1803.

[3] Parliamentary Papers, 1812, VI, Appendix 47 (Private Trade), 192.

[4] On 12 December 1802 Charles Forbes wrote to Robert Rickards about Maratha affairs, 'altho I do not pretend to be much of a Politician, nor shall I

he showed in March 1803 does much to explain why Bombay continued to seize every opportunity of increasing its possessions in Gujarat. When the gaikwar's subsidy payments to the Company fell into arrears the government was quick to ask for the cession of a tract of country in their place. It was no haphazard choice which made them ask for the gaikwar's share of the Surat Attavisi and failing that, territory 'near to the Sea, and so as to connect as far as may be found practicable with the Peshwa's Pergunnah of Dundooka, and the Gaicowar's of Dholka', both of which were already ceded to the Company.[1]

The influence of the cotton merchants was certainly paramount in Bombay's policy towards the northern pirates. In February 1803 the same group of Bruce, Fawcett and Company, Forbes, Smith and Company and Alexander Adamson, made strong complaints of the number of vessels which the freebooters had captured. The activities of the pirates, they declared, made it 'exceedingly difficult to carry on the Trade between this Port and the Guzerat, Cutch and Scind, the losses already suffered being estimated between two and three Lacks...', mostly of boats carrying cotton.[2] The government acted immediately by sending a naval force to attack the pirates' bases, and on 15 February Duncan again told the governor-general that Bombay must annex the territory to put an end to the menace.[3] But a report which Captain Seton made on the whole coast of Gujarat from Bhaunagar to Okhamandal showed that an attack on the pirates of Beyt would involve the Company in the politics of the surrounding country.[4] Seton described how the raja of Navanagar had lent money to the pirates and reimbursed himself by collecting the Beyt customs. He reported that the banians of Cutch were afraid that the sacred temples of Beyt would fall into the hands of the Company and so they gave money to the pirates to strengthen their defences. Bombay had to

attempt to answer for the justice of my plan, except upon the principle of *Might* and *right* generally going hand in hand were I the most Noble, I would leave the Paishwa to his fate, after having so often refused our tenders of assistance, and hearken to Holkar's proposals of routing Scindeah and dividing the Loaves & Fishes—taking for our Share the Guzerat and all the Sea Coast ...'; IOL, European MSS D.100, f. 49–49v.

[1] BSPP, range 381, XLII, 1862–5: Bombay to Major Walker, 20 March 1803.
[2] *Ibid.* XLI, 1159–65: Bombay merchants to the government, 8 February 1803.
[3] *Ibid.* 1287–9: Bombay to Bengal, 15 February 1803.
[4] *Ibid.* XLIII, 2837–9: Seton to Bombay, 27 April 1803.

prepare for a large-scale intervention in Kathiawar if it wanted to rid its trade of the piratical menace.

Since this was the case it is not surprising that Miguel de Souza, who had so many commercial interests at stake, should put forward a scheme which opened the way for Bombay's intervention in the area.[1] He recommended that the government should accept the proposals of the raja of Joriabunder who wished to place himself under the protection of the Company and in particular wanted Bombay's aid against the raja of Navanagar. The Joria chiefs had once ruled in Navanagar, but they had been expelled by the man who was then at the head of the state and who was in alliance with the pirates. The raja of Joriabunder wanted the Company's help as he feared that he would lose the small territory which was left to him.[2] In return he promised to provide 1,000 cavalry and 1,000 infantry for service with the Company anywhere in Kathiawar, and in particular against the Beyt and Dwarka pirates. Furthermore he offered to allow the Company to transport goods through his country free from duties and suggested that if Bombay wished to extend its trade the government might appoint agents at any of his ports.[3] Whether de Souza had anything to do with suggesting these proposals is not known, but they certainly accorded with his interests. Major Walker advised that they should be accepted, and the government pledged its friendship to Joriabunder.[4]

The close connexion of the pirates with the country of Cutch had interested Bombay from the first in the domestic factions of that country. But in April 1803 events in Cutch took another turn. Sunderjee, who had been the dewan Hunsraje's agent in his negotiations with Bombay, broke away from his master and declared that he had the means and support to supplant him as dewan. He asked for Bombay's help. Duncan sent his proposals to Wellesley and pointed out that if the Company sent an expedition into Cutch they could at the same time extirpate the Beyt pirates. But Cutch itself was attracting more of Bombay's attention. In the season 1800–1 the merchants had imported 3 lacs-worth of Cutch cotton into Bombay as against 28 lacs-worth from Gujarat. But in 1802–3 8 lacs-worth came from Cutch and 36 from Gujarat. By

[1] *Ibid.* XLVI, 5022–3: Duncan to Major Walker, 29 April 1803.
[2] *Ibid.* 5025–36: Major Walker to Duncan, 3 July 1803.
[3] *Ibid.* 5041–3: the proposed agreement with the Company, 13 June 1803.
[4] *Ibid.*

1804–5 the proportion had risen to 12 lacs-worth from Cutch and 31 from Gujarat.[1] So important was this growth of the cotton trade that in 1806 the reporter-general of external commerce was to remark 'should this Description of Cotton continue to answer in the China Market, it might be deserving the attention of Government to offer their friendly Interposition to obviate the frequent Dissentions between the petty Chieftains of these Districts, which, not unfrequently throw the most serious obstructions in the way of Trade'.[2] But in May 1803 Duncan did not give a hint of these commercial interests in his letter to Wellesley. He adopted his customary tactics. The Company should intervene, he declared, lest Cutch should attract the attention of the rulers of Sind or Afghanistan, or, a more distant threat, 'the French may, after their expected re-establishment in India, be tempted to extend their views to that Country, as the only one on either Coast, that may now be considered as lying still unexceptionably open to their Ambition...'[3]

But the Bombay government was soon more interested in the prospect of territorial acquisitions which were closer at hand and more intimately concerned with the prosperity of the settlement. The port and territory of Broach had always supplied a great part of the cotton which Bombay exported to China, and its cession to Sindhia in 1783 was the keenest felt loss of the Maratha war. Charles Malet demanded its restitution,[4] and the rapacious monopoly of trade practised by Sindhia's agent roused the bitter enmity of the Bombay merchants.[5] It was therefore natural that the government should seize the opportunity of re-taking it. As soon as Duncan heard from Colonel Collins that war with Sindhia was considered inevitable after the signing of the treaty of Bassein he sent off a letter to Wellesley saying that his government was planning to capture Broach.[6] This was on 22 June 1803. Not until 9 July did Wellesley independently order Bombay to occupy Sindhia's sea-ports. Wellesley's first concern was to cut Sindhia's communications,[7] but even Arthur Wellesley was aware that

[1] Bombay Commercial Reports, range 419, XLII, par. 40: 1 September 1805.
[2] *Ibid.* XLIII, par. 52: 31 October 1806.
[3] BSPP, range 381, XLI, 2673–6: Bombay to Bengal, 2 May 1803.
[4] See above, pp. 136–7.   [5] See above, pp. 160–1.
[6] BSPP, range 381, XLV, 4143–5: Duncan to Wellesley, 22 June 1803.
[7] Owen (ed.), *The Despatches etc. of the Marquess Wellesley*, 358: Wellesley to the Court of Directors, 25 September 1803.

Bombay gained a revenue of ten lacs of rupees with Broach and 'a valuable Territory in a Commercial point of view'.[1]

In retaking Broach Bombay at last secured the three 'shackles of Gujarat' which Charles Malet had seen as crucial to his plans of commercial expansion. But in the interval between Malet's first urging his schemes on Cornwallis and the capture of Broach, Bombay had extended its network of commercial relations further afield into Kathiawar and Cutch. There the problems of expanding trade under hostile and oppressive governments remained unchanged since Malet had faced them in Gujarat twenty years before. They could only be tackled, as Miguel de Souza realised, by taking the ports and seeking to channel trade through them to Bombay. This strategy, which Charles Malet had first conceived after his long experience at Cambay, was one of expediency rather than deliberate choice.[2] For the merchant to trade as he wanted, the whole society of Gujarat, Kathiawar and Cutch had to be turned upside-down and remodelled. Not only was the Maratha system of government oppressive and corrupt but its weakness and inefficiency left great areas of Gujarat and Kathiawar in a state of almost permanent disorder and devastation.[3] It was not enough to try to control the system from the top. A treaty of cooperation with the gaikwar was useless when his authority barely existed in Kathiawar. In Malabar, by contrast, the rajas had succeeded in organising the whole society under their authority and had ruled it in the interests of their enrichment by trade. All that the British had to do to control the trade was to control or depose the rajas. In 1803 the Maratha power could be defeated but not destroyed. Nor had the Company the men or resources to administer the turbulent provinces which acknowledged the suzerainty of Poona and Baroda. The conditions which restricted trade had to be attacked in two ways. At the top patience, diplomacy and time were necessary to convince the Marathas that their system of government had to be reformed. But as markets and profits could not await such reformations the system had also to be attacked at the bottom. If the Company controlled the ports they could give the merchants and manufacturers, money-lenders and other key figures in the local

---

[1] BSPP, range 381, LIII, 315: A. Wellesley to the governor-general, 10 January 1804.
[2] See above, p. 138.
[3] *Bombay Selections* XXXIX, 379–80: Walker to Duncan, 15 May 1808.

economy, a refuge and protection, and they could use those ports as bases whence to extend the Company's authority into the surrounding countryside. This was the policy which Malet had urged and which de Souza had adopted at Rattalow. By 1803 the way was open for its application in Gujarat and Kathiawar at large.

The two chief figures in this part of Bombay's policy in the north were de Souza and Major Alexander Walker. Walker was still innocent of de Souza's real interests and relied on him for advice. But he was not completely de Souza's tool. He was as convinced as the private merchants of the need to increase Bombay's territory in Gujarat in the interests of its trade. As the commander of the force which defeated Malhar Rao's rebellion and then as the first British resident at the court of the gaikwar, he was able to carry out the policy which he had outlined to Duncan in 1800.[1] But there is no doubt that during his first crucial years in Gujarat he leaned heavily on de Souza's knowledge and mediation.

It is in the light of this knowledge that one must examine his policy. At Baroda he set himself the task of restoring the solvency and reforming the administration of the gaikwar's government. One of his first concerns was with Kathiawar. The gaikwar collected tribute from the petty chiefs of Kathiawar in an annual mulkgiri expedition which was not only costly to himself but created havoc and devastation in many of the areas it visited. Walker was determined to put an end to the system and to make agreements with the Kathiawar chiefs for the peaceful payment of their tribute. Furthermore Malhar Rao had renewed his rebellion, had made his base in Kathiawar and was collecting an army together.[2] If the gaikwar's state and revenues were to be preserved and reformed it was essential for the Company to intervene. But Walker's ideas went beyond a mere military expedition. In August 1803 he proposed that the Company should consider annexing parts of Kathiawar.[3] By November he had so far matured his plans that he urged the Bombay government to give some of the territory conquered from Sindhia in the east to the gaikwar in return for cessions in Kathiawar which were far more valuable to the Company. He proposed that Bombay should send an expedition with the gaikwar to suppress the tributary chiefs whose

---

[1] See above, pp. 178–9.
[2] BSPP, range 381, XLVII, 5568–84: Walker's memorandum, 6 August 1803.
[3] *Ibid.* XLVII, 5575.

incursions into Gujarat and daily robberies of the merchants demanded action. The Company would then be in a position to acquire 'such commercial and commanding points in Kattywar as would at once ensure the obedience of this part of the Peninsula, and put into our possession, or place at our disposal, all the sources of its wealth'.[1]

Walker had definite ideas on which 'commercial and commanding points' he wanted. In October the Company's agent at Dhandhuka had written to him complaining that the rajas of Bhaunagar and Limri were engaged in hostilities and were molesting the merchants of Dhandhuka. If they were not checked the Company stood to lose between Rs 10,000 and 12,000 in customs dues from the loss of trade.[2] Walker was quick to act on the information. On 12 November he told the Bombay government that he had decided to settle the Company's claims on the gaikwar by taking over the latter's rights to tribute from the rajas of Bhaunagar and Limri. From Bhaunagar a tribute of Rs 70,000 was due, and from Limri Rs 30,000. Walker justified his decision by pointing out that it was desirable to improve the Company's connexion with the two rajas as the territory of Bhaunagar bordered on Ranpur and Gogah, and that of Limri on Dhandhuka, and both were the scenes of disputes and disturbances. These would not end, he declared, until the Company controlled both rajas. Limri would form a good frontier against the marauding Kathies, while Bhaunagar was a fine port coming between the Company's ports of Rattalow and Gogah. As it commanded two of the best entrances into Kathiawar, Walker concluded that he had obtained one of the most valuable cessions that the Company was likely to win for a long time.[3]

In January 1804 Walker carried this policy further when he received offers of territory from several chiefs in Kathiawar who wanted the Company's protection. He confessed that his geographical information about 'Jetpore, Chitul, Chitepore and Candala' was limited but he placed them between the River Sauree and Junagar, and reported that each had chiefs and forts and paid tribute to the peshwa, the gaikwar and the nawab of Junagar. The chiefs wanted the Company's protection against the oppressions of

[1] *Ibid.* L, 8097–9: Walker to Bombay, 3 November 1803.
[2] BRP, range 366, xxxix, 956–7: letter to Walker, 20 October 1803.
[3] *Ibid.* 951–3: Walker to Bombay, 12 November 1803.

the rajas of Bhaunagar and Junagar, and Walker recommended that Bombay should accept their offers of territory as

it would be useful to improve these connections in view to any future enterprise that we may pursue in Kattywar...The acquisition of a Sea Port in Kattywar would restrain the Pirates who are so formidable to the trade of this Country, and we should soon be able to introduce a System of order and Security, instead of that anarchy and discord which now prevails...[1]

Three days later Walker wrote to the Bengal government to explain his policy and to report that the gaikwar had succeeded in defeating Malhar Rao in Kathiawar and had captured him. But such was the state of Kathiawar, he insisted, with its petty kingdoms continually warring against each other, and the strong oppressing the weak, that the country would never be at peace unless the Company intervened and made settlements there. By maintaining a force in the country the Company could put a stop to the aggression and robbery and restrain the piracy which injured Bombay's trade. The Company would acquire good ports and by possessing the coast they could extend their influence to the mouths of the Indus. By this means they would secure commercial advantages and political benefits which no other nation could enjoy.[2]

The methods which Duncan used to recommend Walker's policy to the supreme government confirm the impression that he used the French menace almost always as an argument for taking territory which Bombay wanted for commercial reasons. On 22 February 1804 he wrote to Arthur Wellesley and pointed out the possibility of obtaining possessions in Kathiawar. He repeated the argument of taking territory in order to restrain the pirates, but added that the Company could not expect to shut out the French from the coast which extended from Diu to Okhamandal, if they did not possess at least one harbour within reach of it.[3] Only four days after Duncan wrote to Wellesley Walker suggested that Bombay should annex one such port, Mangrol. But this was part of a larger scheme to attack the nawab of Junagar who had been robbing the Company's merchants. Walker proposed that Bombay should annex all his sea-coast and forts and give his overlord, the

[1] BSPP, range 381, LIV, 1337–42: Walker to Bombay, 23 January 1804.
[2] *Ibid.* LIII, 560–74: Walker to Bengal, 26 January 1804.
[3] *Ibid.* LIV, 1366–79: Duncan to Arthur Wellesley, 22 February 1804.

gaikwar, similar territory in the interior.[1] But neither trade nor Duncan's plea of the French menace could prevail on Arthur Wellesley to agree to an expedition into Kathiawar, and the war which shortly broke out with Holkar put an end to the project for the time being.[2]

The habit of crying wolf, though, had its disadvantages. In October 1803 a French vessel did sail up the coast of Cutch and it was reported that the French planned to establish factories at Porbander, in Cutch, and in Sind.[3] In November 1803 the Bombay government had sent Captain Seton back to Cutch with instructions to keep the negotiations with its ruler open. The raja and his dewan had almost lost the country to Fateh Muhammad and there was a danger that the Company's influence would be totally eclipsed. But the governor-general did not answer Bombay's pleas for instructions, and when it became clear that the raja would not cede the port of Mandvi to the Company in return for help[4] the Bombay government lost some of its eagerness to forestall any French interest in the area. The raja's offer of a subsidiary treaty, the council declared, was insufficient, and its inadequacy could not be counteracted by any design for excluding the French from Cutch, since no less than two battalions would be needed for that purpose. Such a project could not be thought of until the raja of Cutch could find sufficient security to cover the expense and until the governor-general should give his consent, or 'unless indeed the French were to land any force in that part of India'.[5] While there was the possibility of advantageous cessions of territory or revenue Bombay had seized on the mere possibility of French interest in an area to justify demands for intervention, but when these failed, and although a French vessel had actually visited Cutch, Bombay discovered that the French had to land in force before they were willing to act.

Although Bombay undermined its own carefully built up myth in this way the fabrication had done its work. Wellesley was not impressed by Bombay's references to the French menace and Duncan's letters to him were usually met with silence. But the argument served to convince the home authorities. Although

---

[1] *Ibid.* range 382, III, 588–601: Walker to Bombay, 26 February 1804.
[2] *Ibid.* 604: 6 March 1804.
[3] *Ibid.* range 381, LIII, 43–8: Seton to Bombay, 23 December 1803.
[4] *Ibid.* range 382, LIV, 1296–1301: Seton to Bombay, 28 December 1803.
[5] *Ibid.* 1328–37: minute of the Bombay council, 22 February 1804.

Castlereagh had initially expressed his doubts,[1] the Court of Directors accepted in 1804 that the acquisitions would serve to exclude the French from Gujarat,[2] and in 1811 Robert Dundas was still insisting that this was their primary purpose.[3] The myth passed into history, while the commercial interests behind Bombay's thrust to the north were buried.

[1] See above, p. 196.
[2] Despatches to Bombay xxiv, 577–605: 28 August 1804.
[3] Rylands English MSS, Melville Papers 692, 1958: Robert Dundas to Duncan, 25 January 1811.

CHAPTER 7

THE CONFLICT OF INTERESTS,
1803–06

By the end of the year 1803 Bombay had accomplished its plan of expansion to the northward, and the presidency had acquired territory which at last produced enough revenue to cover its ordinary expenditure.[1] Trade continued to flourish, and the annexations brought some rich cotton-producing lands and the chief ports of Gujarat under the Company's control. In 1805 Major Walker estimated that out of a crop of 86,500 bales of cotton which could be expected from the north in a good year, 10,000 came from the Surat Attavisi, which was divided between the Company and the gaikwar, and 15,000 from the Broach pargana which was entirely under the Company's authority. Of the rest, 8,000 came from the peshwa's districts of Jambusar and Amod, 13,500 from the gaikwar's territory round Baroda, and 40,000 from Kathiawar of which some was drawn from the Company's districts of Dhandhuka, Ranpur and Gogah.[2] But although only one-quarter of the total was grown in the Company's territory, Bombay's control of the chief ports of Gujarat and Kathiawar allowed the Company a commanding influence over the trade.

The Court of Directors had made efforts since 1784 to carry cotton on a large-scale to China for their own profit.[3] But they had not sufficient capital to invest at Bombay and had achieved little success, although the supercargoes did not cease to urge the Bombay government to engage in the trade on its own account.[4] In July 1803 Bombay reported to the Court of Directors that it was forced to let the Company's ships which were sailing from Bombay to China to the house of Forbes and Company as it could not provide a cargo on the Company's account. But the government added by way of appeasing the directors and justifying the Gujarat policy,

[1] Revenue Letters from Bombay, 1803–13: letter of August 1804.
[2] BSPP, range 382, VII, 2732: Major Walker to Bombay, 15 July 1805.
[3] See above, pp. 128–9.
[4] BCP, range 414, LXXI, 301–2: Canton to Bombay, 28 December 1801.

but that predicament may in future be easily avoided in consequence of the large possessions and paramount influence obtained by the Honble Company in Guzerat whence it will be readily within the power of your Government to secure as much of the best assortment of Cotton, either in payment of the revenue or otherwise as your wants can probably ever amount to...[1]

The government lost no time in using its new proprietorship to help its piece-good investment. In October 1803 the resident at Cambay reported that the merchants and weavers were demanding too much for their cloths and they would not be beaten down to the level of the Surat prices.[2] The government reacted by ordering the assistant resident, John Smith, to tour the weaving towns which the Company had newly acquired, including Kaira, Nadiad, Dholka and Moonda, and to report on the cloths which they could produce for the Company's investment.[3] But Smith found that they cost more than the Surat piece-goods,[4] and he concluded that the Company had used its authority with good effect to lower the prices. He recommended that the Company should take advantage of its new position at Cambay to introduce the direct contract system there. The Surat commercial resident was fully aware of the advantage of having the weavers under his control. He transferred one of his contracts for piece-goods from the peshwa's city of Dabhoi to the Company's new possession Broach, again so that he could contract directly with the weaver and procure the cloths at lower prices.[5]

The exertion of the Company's influence in this field could not affect the private merchants of Bombay, although the energy and quickness with which the government reacted to the new conditions might have been a warning to them. But on 31 October 1803 the government ordered Major Walker to secure for the Company's exclusive benefit all the cotton grown in the Broach pargana and in Bombay's other possessions in Gujarat. They asked him whether this could best be done by buying the cotton directly from the growers or by taking it instead of revenue, at a price which would not encourage them to dispose of it to private agents. The govern-

---

[1] BCP, range 414, LXXV, 859–60: Bombay to the Court of Directors, 3 July 1803.
[2] *Ibid.* range 415, I, 1251–2: Holford to Bombay, 12 October 1803.
[3] *Ibid.* 1252–5.
[4] *Ibid.* III, 23–30: J. Smith to Bombay, 29 December 1803.
[5] *Ibid.* 87–94: Surat to Bombay, 23 January 1804.

ment sent similar instructions to the collector of Surat about the cotton growing within the limits of his district.[1]

The reference to securing the cotton before it could be disposed of to private agents hinted at a rather radical change in the relationship between the government and the merchants. It certainly marked the end of the policy of uniting their commercial interests to defeat the monopolistic practices of the northern dealers. The private merchants could only view with alarm the government's new determination to compete in the cotton trade and to exploit all their advantages of territorial sovereignty. It was an alarm which they would not have felt twenty years earlier when Rawson Hart Boddam had been the governor and Andrew Ramsay one of his council, and both were partners in a cotton firm, as were the governors Hornby, Crommelin and Bourchier before them.[2] Nor had the private merchants felt any such alarm during the years of Bombay's administration of Malabar. They had been too strongly entrenched within the government and the Malabar commission to fear that the Company could successfully compete with their trade. Rivett and Wilkinson, Bruce and Fawcett, Rickards and Adamson, and a host of smaller men, had run the government and directed its policy in the interests of private trade. The close-knit concerns and *esprit de corps* of the Bombay establishment which Walter Ewer described to Dundas had from the first been too strong for Duncan, the Bengal outsider. Corruption was only brought to light and punished when the Bombay servants were divided among themselves and it was in the interest of one faction to dispose of their rivals as in the case of Stevens, Taylor and Agnew.[3] Even if Duncan had not possessed his peculiar weakness and inability to judge character, the merchants' financial control over the government in the absence of an adequate land revenue must have kept a reforming governor within their bonds. As it was, Duncan's dependence on Scott and his friends only made the bonds tighter.

But Bombay's success in acquiring territory altered the presidency's position in India. In September 1803 Duncan wrote jubilantly to Scott,

this Coast is to the northward become by our recent reduction of Broach

[1] BCP, range 415, I, 1264–6: Bombay to Major Walker, 31 October 1803.
[2] BPP, range 342, XI, 98: D. Scott & Co. to Bombay, 23 February 1789.
[3] See above, pp. 108–9.

and our acquisition under the treaties with the Gaekwar and the Peshwa of such great consequence that even Marquis Wellesley has changed his mind...and is desirous that an administration should continue in its present form, as I conclude it will. We have now full 50 lacks of revenue to collect and proportionate territories to manage all the way from Demaun to the Gulf of Cutch, a distance of at least 250 miles in which our unquestioned sovereignty, or as unquestioned ascendancy, predominates.[1]

Duncan's great fear that Wellesley would dissolve his presidency was at an end, and he was also more confident that Bombay's new status would require his continuing as its governor. Lord Cornwallis had indicated to him that the authorities in London wanted to appoint General Maitland to succeed him, but with a new self-confidence Duncan insisted that he must be offered a seat on the Bengal council and the succession to Barlow before he would leave Bombay.[2] This new assurance meant that Scott was less important to him as the means of influencing the Court of Directors and the Board of Control. Duncan did not write to him after 30 December 1803.[3] Indeed by the end of 1803 Scott had lost most of his influence with both bodies. The shipping interest gained control of the Court of Directors and began their campaign against Wellesley and his protagonist Scott, whom they feared and hated because of the governor-general's policy of expansion in India and support for the private-trading interest against the Company's monopoly. Scott, who was forced to resign as chairman in August 1801, could only continue to influence Indian policy through the Board of Control. He had succeeded with Dartmouth, but Castlereagh was not so tractable, and after some vacillation over Wellesley's Maratha policy, Castlereagh sided with the directors and Scott's influence was at an end.[4]

Duncan was fortunate throughout his career in having friends in the right places to give him support. These connexions explain why he was able to remain at Bombay for an unprecedented time when there were many who were eager to supplant him. When he was in Bengal his uncle John Michie, who was chairman of the Company in 1786 and 1788, and Michie's friends of the city interest, gave him their support. Cornwallis, who valued Duncan's

---

[1] Philips (ed.), *The Correspondence of David Scott* II, 429–30: Duncan to Scott, 7 September 1803.
[2] *Ibid.* II, 430: Duncan to Scott, 7 September 1803. [3] *Ibid.* 434–5.
[4] Philips, *The East India Company*, chapter v.

honesty and willingness to work, recommended him to Dundas, and Scott was prepared to give him every support while he fell in with the policy of the private traders at Bombay. But even as Duncan had claimed the friendship of John Macpherson while he was the protégé of Cornwallis, so did he rely on Charles Grant while he was the ally of David Scott.[1] When Scott fell from power Duncan could hope to safeguard his position at Bombay by relying on Grant and adopting a policy that would win him the favour of the shipping interest. In June 1803 the Court of Directors had ordered Bombay to buy cotton on the Company's account and sent £100,000 in dollars for this purpose.[2] Duncan knew that his future depended on expanding the Company's trade at the expense of the private merchants.

But it was not only the change of power and policy in London which affected the Bombay government. Changes were taking place within Bombay society itself. The old corps of private-trading civil servants who had directed the policy of the presidency on lines of commercial and territorial expansion was gradually losing its hold over the establishment. James Rivett died in 1802, and in March 1803 Henry Fawcett, the accountant-general, returned to Europe. With their going, the private-trading interest lost two of the most influential members of the government and no one of the same character or position succeeded them. Most of the men of their generation and outlook had died or returned to Europe before them. Without Rivett Duncan's council was a more tractable body. Robert Rickards was employed in Malabar under the government of Madras.[3] J. H. Cherry who took Rivett's place as a member of council had lost one fortune in private trade, and since the establishment of the Surat commercial board he had set out to repair his loss by the commission he earned on the Company's piece-good investment. His interest lay with the Company's and not the private trade. There had always been individuals who kept aloof from the dominant group of civil servants, and after 1803 the presidency could offer prospects of honourable employment with hopes of promotion to many young men in the administration of its new territory. The military had never had private trading interests to the same extent as the civil servants, and when one of

[1] Michie Papers, MSS 5881, file 2: Duncan to John Michie, 2 February 1798.
[2] BSPP, range 381, LVI, 2602–8: minute of J. Duncan, 25 May 1804.
[3] Despatches to Bombay XXVI, 541–6: 2 May 1806.

their number, Major Walker, became the resident at Baroda with influence over the whole of Gujarat it was difficult to introduce corruption in that province on any large scale. Furthermore, wartime conditions, which involved high insurance premiums and the danger of losses at sea, made it difficult for young men to build up private trading concerns, and they looked to the service of the government for their future instead. Sir James Mackintosh's arrival in Bombay in 1804 as the judge of the Recorder's Court, which had replaced the old Mayor's Court, was a symptom of the change.[1] The professional administrator was taking over from the merchant.

Nevertheless, as Sir James was to discover, the influence of the private traders died hard.[2] The Maratha war made severe demands on the Bombay treasury, and in 1803 the government faced a financial crisis. Duncan was forced to ask Forbes and Company, and Bruce, Fawcett and Company for heavy loans, which they continued to provide in 1804.[3] The extraordinary demands of war prolonged a relationship between the private traders and the government which in every other way was being undermined. There can be no doubt that the merchants saw their danger and were determined to use every method to maintain the old relationship. On 22 January 1804 Charles Forbes wrote to warn Duncan that the prices of cotton at Canton had fallen by almost 50 per cent below those of the previous year. The cotton trade, he told him, had become a mere lottery in which the merchants competed blindly, encouraged occasionally by a little success. But the tide had finally turned against them, and unless the Company again united its interests with the merchants to force down the price of cotton to the northward the trade would not only ruin the merchants but inflict heavy losses on the Company.[4]

In the following month Forbes and Company, Bruce, Fawcett and Company, and Alexander Adamson, followed up this prelimin-

---

[1] Mackintosh (ed.), *The Memoires of Sir James Mackintosh* I, 223.

[2] *Ibid.* 271: 'There was no liberal public opinion to support me, and no firm government to frown down indecent reflections on the administration of justice'. Mackintosh wrote this after he had tried Henshaw, the customs master, for receiving bribes. He pronounced him guilty, but a very favourable report was afterwards made by the accountant-general at Bombay upon the audit of his accounts and the government recommended him to the favourable consideration of the Court of Directors (Personal Records X, 163).

[3] Douglas, *Bombay and Western India* I, 254–68.

[4] BSPP, range 381, LVI, 2645–9: Charles Forbes to Duncan, 22 January 1804.

ary letter by proposing measures which were intended to limit the Company's exports of cotton to China. The firms repeated that prices had fallen at Canton because of the large exports of the previous year and the competition which Bombay was beginning to feel from the cotton of Bengal. In addition they pointed out the exorbitant prices which the northern dealers were demanding and the continued adulteration of the cotton. Nothing, the firms insisted, but a large reduction in these prices and the limiting of the exports offered the hope of obtaining even the smallest profit in China.[1] They were prepared to limit their own exports, they told the government, if the Company would cooperate and revive the copartnership of 1801. Alternatively they suggested that the government should withdraw completely from the market if the private merchants would hire the Company's ships. They acknowledged that the Company had acquired a new interest in the cotton trade since they had won territory in Gujarat, but they claimed that four-fifths of the cotton exported from Bombay came from areas not under the Company's control. Their policy would only deprive the brokers of their large profits and would not oppress the cultivators. Finally they argued that the prosperity of Bombay's cotton trade and merchant fleet was far more important to the Company and produced a greater revenue through customs dues than the comparatively small tracts of cotton land in Gujarat.[2]

The anxiety of the cotton firms at the Bombay government's new policy was apparent on every page of their letter. As Fawcett was to tell the parliamentary committee, while they were hoping that the government would use its new authority to lower prices and improve the quality of the cotton, they 'had the mortification to see the new Sovereign assume the shape of a formidable rival, and exclude them from purchasing all but the refuse produce of the newly acquired territory'.[3] The Company's competition, they knew, would raise the price of cotton, as the growers and dealers would not enter into contracts with the private merchants until they knew whether the Company intended to enter the market, and this was always uncertain. If the Company decided to buy twenty

---

[1] BCP, range 415, III, 127–30: Bombay merchants to the Bombay government, 10 February 1804.
[2] *Ibid.* 130–4.
[3] Parliamentary Papers, 1812, VI, Appendix 47 (Private Trade), 192.

of thirty thousand bales the price of the remainder of the crop rose to an exorbitant height, and the private merchant had to decide whether he should withdraw from the market or buy cotton at a price which meant losses for him at Canton.[1] But a deeper fear of the private merchants was that the Company would use its sovereign power to procure advantages in the trade over and above that of possessing a large capital. In Malabar the merchants had used that power for their own profit, but in 1804 they feared what Sir Charles Forbes was later to state, 'It is perfectly well known that when the Company announce that they require a certain quantity of cotton, the growers and dealers look upon themselves as bound to supply it'.[2] The Bombay government's use of the Surat adowlat was sufficient warning that the Company's administration of justice in their new territories would favour their commercial interests. The merchants and cultivators of Gujarat knew that

the judges of those courts are the servants of the Company, that they are appointed by the government, that they are dependent upon the local government for further advancement in the service, and that an appeal from those courts lies to the court of adowlut, the judges of which were, until very lately, the governor and the members of the council, the very men, in fact, who appointed the judges of the provincial court, from whose decision the appeal is made.[3]

Under this system neither the cultivators nor the merchants had much hope of resisting the Company's demands.

The merchants' proposals of 1804 were an attempt to ward off the developments which they feared. The fact that between 1803 and 1805 the houses of Forbes and Company, and Bruce, Fawcett and Company supplied the Bombay treasury with nearly two and a half million pounds sterling, without which Wellesley could not have financed his campaigns against Sindhia and Holkar,[4] was a more compelling argument than the merchants' commercial pleas. The result was that on 25 February 1804 Major Walker informed his assistants that the government had decided to withdraw from the market and to leave the cotton trade open to the speculations of the merchants. He instructed his officials to help the merchants in their cotton purchases and to see that the cotton

[1] Parliamentary Papers, 1831, v, 137: the evidence of Sir Charles Forbes.
[2] *Ibid.*
[3] *Ibid.* 161: evidence of John Stewart.
[4] *Ibid.* 138: evidence of Sir Charles Forbes.

was not adulterated.[1] The government was only concerned to see that the growers obtained a price high enough to prevent their giving up the cultivation of cotton.[2] On 31 March the revenue official at Broach sold the whole quantity of Broach cotton to Miguel de Lima é Souza, 'agent to the Bombay Cotton Committee'.[3] The private merchants were closing their ranks.

But the private merchants had not reckoned with a Court of Directors in which their friend David Scott had lost all his influence to the shipping interest. In April 1805 an irate Court censured the Bombay government for its arrangements with the merchants and particularly for the way in which it had allowed Charles Forbes to influence its decisions. The Court accused Forbes of giving false estimates of the profits which cotton could be expected to earn in China, 'calculated for the express purpose of altogether deterring our Government from taking any share in the Cotton Concern...'[4] They pointed to the fact that in January 1804 Forbes had declared that the Company could expect no profit from shipping cotton to China, but on 11 May 'Mr. Forbes having ascertained, in a way not very correct or official, the very low state of the Company's Treasury', proposed to Duncan that the government should hand over to the merchants the cotton which it had bought before withdrawing from the market, in return for treasure which Bruce, Fawcett and Company were expecting from China.[5] When Duncan agreed to the proposal, the Court continued, it was not apparent whether he had read Mr Henshaw's report that the prices in China were high and that the Bombay merchants actually had contracts with the Hong merchants to sell cotton at 14 tales a pecul, whereas Forbes had declared that it would not fetch more than 8 or 9 tales.[6] Neither did they know whether Duncan had 'thought it singular that Mr. Forbes, who had in January so decidedly stated to him the depressed state of the China Market, should be now so desirous of taking the Company's Cotton off their hands'. But as Forbes's partner McIntosh had obtained a contract to sell cotton to the Chinese at 13 tales a pecul before August 1803, and as McIntosh's ship had arrived back at

---

[1] BCP, range 415, III, 185–6: Major Walker to Messrs Diggle and Steadman, 25 February 1804.

[2] BRP, range 366, XLV, 132–5: A. Walker to W. Steadman, 18 March 1804.

[3] BCP, range 415, III, 336–9: W. Steadman to A. Walker, 2 April 1804.

[4] Home Misc. CCCLXXIV, 108–12: The Court to Bombay, 10 April 1805.

[5] *Ibid.* 115–22.   [6] *Ibid.*

Bombay with the news on 17 November 1803, Forbes must have known of this contract before he gave his advice to the governor in the following January. In its conclusions the Court absolved Duncan from the charge of collaboration with the merchants, but added

we feel it indispensably necessary from the source of the information connected with this transaction, to direct our Government of Bombay will hereafter receive with great caution, information from Persons (however generally respectable) whose private interests must necessarily place them, in the particular instance in direct opposition to that of the Company.[1]

The Court was the more angry because in August 1804 they had sent to the Bombay government a plan for engaging in the cotton trade to China on a large scale.[2] To further this scheme the directors had suggested that Bombay should negotiate a commercial treaty with the gaikwar in the hope that it might increase the sales of the Company's staples and help them in their purchase of cotton cargoes for China and of coloured piece-goods for the African market.[3] Although the Court's displeasure must have made Duncan fearful for his career and produced letters in defence of the government and of Charles Forbes,[4] while the war and its demands on the Bombay treasury continued Duncan could not adopt the policy which the Court commanded. In December 1804 the government again made over their revenue cotton and the Company's tonnage to the merchants in return for a loan of 50 lacs, 30 of which were provided by Forbes, and 20 by Bruce, Fawcett and Company.[5]

But by the beginning of 1805 Bombay's financial position had improved sufficiently for the government to act according to the Court's wishes, and Duncan ordered all the Broach cotton to be taken as revenue by the Company and retained for shipment on their own account to China. The blow had fallen on the private

[1] Despatches to Bombay xxv, 3451: Court to Bombay, 10 April 1805. The original version had been 'we...lament that our Government of Bombay seem to be so much under the influence of persons whose Interest in this instance appears so decidedly to have been in direct opposition to the Company's'.
[2] *Ibid.* xxiv, 547–50: 24 August 1804.
[3] *Ibid.* 605–7: 28 August 1804.
[4] BCP, range 414, ix, 1536–45: minute of Thomas Lechmere, 12 August 1805; and Letters Received from Bombay xx, political letter, 27 December 1805.
[5] BSPP, range 382, iii, 120–5: memorandum of Duncan, 8 December 1804.

merchants. But they did not intend to see their trade snatched from them. In March 1805 the collector of Broach reported that the patels had been rioting and had demanded freedom to sell their cotton as they wished. The collector reported his suspicion that the agents of the cotton merchants had inspired the riots.[1] There was little future in this sort of agitation, though, when all the power and influence of Forbes and Bruce, Fawcett and Company failed to control the government. The merchants had to look to other means to preserve their supremacy in the trade.

It is significant that at this time Miguel de Souza took upon himself in addition to his other responsibilities the farm of the pargana of Gogah. De Souza was responsible for the Company's annexing it in the first place because he considered Gogah to be one of the chief ports of Kathiawar.[2] It had been one of the most flourishing ports of western India but under Maratha rule had been eclipsed by the rise of Bhaunagar, and when the Company acquired it most of the produce of the surrounding country was exported through Bhaunagar.[3] De Souza was eager to revive its trade because he was already engaged in a contest with the raja of Bhaunagar for the supreme control of the commerce of Kathiawar. His success at Rattalow in attracting trade away from Bhaunagar had led the raja to claim the ownership of part of Dholera. Major Walker and his assistant thought the raja had good grounds for his claim, but Duncan supported de Souza's case against the raja.[4] The raja had tried to make up for his losses by forcing the merchants in his territory to use another port in the neighbourhood of Rattalow called Soonder Aly. His policy was successful and injured Rattalow's trade, so de Souza sent a party of horse to the village and stopped the merchants from trading there.[5] De Souza's policy of violent competition against the raja, did not meet with Walker's approval. The resident thought it desirable to come to a good understanding with the raja, as he was one of the most important chiefs of Kathiawar and was established in the midst of the Company's possessions. His territories separated Gogah from Dholera, and Walker thought that the best way of increasing the trade through these ports was not by alienating the raja but by

[1] BRP, range 366, XLVII, 2203: G. L. Prendergast to Duncan, 5 March 1805.
[2] See above, p. 204.
[3] BRP, range 366, XLVI, 958–62: A. Walker to de Souza, 22 October 1804.
[4] BSPP, range 381, LIX, 4679–90: Duncan's minute, 3 September 1804.
[5] *Ibid.* 4637: A. Walker to Bombay, 2 July 1804.

improving the Company's commercial relations with him and by agreeing on joint regulations to promote the prosperity of the country.[1]

Walker's ideas were undoubtedly more sensible but he looked at the situation with the eyes of a servant of the Company. It was his responsibility to settle the revenue and administration of the Company's new territory and he realised that this could be very difficult unless steps were taken to conciliate the raja of Bhaunagar. For the raja collected tribute from twenty-six villages in the pargana of Dhandhuka and from fifty-nine in the pargana of Gogah, and he also owned part of Ranpur.[2] But de Souza was too much personally involved in the trade of Rattalow and Gogah to treat the raja of Bhaunagar in a political light. Half of Bombay's exports of cotton came from Kathiawar,[3] and he intended that neither the Company nor the raja of Bhaunagar should control the trade. He had hoped to farm all three of the parganas which he had urged Duncan to annex, Dhandhuka, Ranpur and Gogah, but as he had been held in Bombay on business when the Company took them over Walker had farmed out the first two to a Brahmin, much to de Souza's chagrin.[4] By 1805 Dholera was sending 10,000 bales of cotton to Bombay,[5] and de Souza intended to attract more of Kathiawar's cotton to Gogah. By this control of the ports he could preserve the dominance of the private merchants over the cotton trade.

His appointment as the farmer of Gogah inevitably brought fresh conflicts with the raja of Bhaunagar. The town of Gogah was in a ruinous state. Its fort and stone walls had fallen and its population was mostly gone. Trade and agriculture barely existed and the place lay open to the aggression of Bhaunagar. De Souza saw that the first step towards rebuilding the port's prosperity was to 'open a communication between Goga, and all the inner Countries, so as to enable the Merchants to bring their Goods, and to carry their returns safe without any impediment in the roads'. If this were done, he promised Bombay, the natural superiority of the port would make it a depot for all the trade of Kathiawar, and the merchants under the Company's protection would be able to push their trade deep into the country. To make this possible, he asked

[1] BSPP, range 381, LIX, 4638–40: Walker to Bombay, 2 July 1804.
[2] *Bombay Selections* XXXIX, 122, 125, 126.   [3] See above, p. 215.
[4] BRP, range 366, IL, 674–88: de Souza to Bombay, 13 September 1805.
[5] *Ibid.* XLVI, 1438–41: de Souza to Bombay, 12 May 1805.

the Bombay government to send him a hundred troops and help to erect new buildings.[1] But the raja of Bhaunagar tried to stop his plans at the beginning by preventing all communication between Gogah and Bhaunagar and by forbidding the merchants of Kathiawar who had agents or shops at Bhaunagar to have any dealings with Rattalow or Gogah. Most seriously of all he forbade the Bhaunagar lascars to serve on any boat which traded with Rattalow or Gogah, and the influence of these with the lascars of Gogah itself, Cambay and Surat, and the other ports of Gujarat, almost stopped trade completely.[2]

But de Souza was not easily deterred. He ordered two cotton screws to be set up at Gogah and got his agent at Limri to send him 110 candies of cotton, which the raja of Bhaunagar promptly stopped and seized on the road.[3] De Souza attempted to negotiate with him but the raja tried to get his way by bribery. He offered to allow de Souza to export his own cotton through Bhaunagar free of duty on the condition that de Souza persuaded Bombay to farm out Gogah and Rattalow to the raja. But de Souza wanted nothing less than supremacy in the trade of Kathiawar and he urged Walker to employ force against the raja.[4] Walker reported the disputes to Bombay, but his optimistic conclusion was that when the raja saw that the Company was determined to re-open Gogah's commercial relations with Kathiawar he would give up his opposition, and he told de Souza to be more moderate in his dealings with the raja.[5]

Since de Souza could not get Walker to act as he wanted he relied on his own initiative. He made agreements with the principal girasias of several villages in the Dholka, Dhandhuka and Ranpur parganas by which they ceded their villages to the Company. In his opinion this was 'the only way of preventing Bownagur Limree and the Cusbaty of Dolka having any interference or influence in our Parganah'. It was also part of his plan to get the girasias to submit to the Company's laws and by this means to prevent them from plundering and oppressing the cultivators to the detriment of trade.[6] Furthermore he asked the Bombay

[1] BSPP, range 382, XV, 2011–63: de Souza to Bombay, 6 August 1805.
[2] BRP, range 366, II, 575–85: de Souza to Bombay, 12 September 1805.
[3] BSPP, range 382, XV, 1959–70: de Souza to Walker, 3 June 1805.
[4] *Ibid.* 1970. [5] *Ibid.* 1956–9: Walker to Bombay, 11 June 1805.
[6] BRP, range 366, II, 610–63: de Souza to Walker, 28 August 1805.

government to allow him to take over the farm of Ranpur and Dhandhuka on the grounds that the Brahmin who farmed them was under the influence of the raja of Bhaunagar.[1] He also adopted his own means of protecting the merchants against the depredations of the petty chiefs of Kathiawar. He hired one of the chiefs to act as protector of all the goods which were carried into the interior.[2]

In all this activity de Souza marched ahead of the policy of the Bombay government. Walker and Duncan and his council were much more cautious about acting in Kathiawar. They ordered de Souza not to interfere in villages where the rajas of Bhaunagar and Limri had claims, and declared that they had no intention of intervening 'with any view of extending thro such a suspicious Medium the British Influence in Kattywar'.[3] But Walker did not cease to urge the Bombay government that the Company could not expand its trade in Kathiawar unless the government intervened to put down the regime of plunder, rapine and piracy.[4] He pointed out that the nature of the country and its society made it impossible to distribute goods wholesale as there was not a sufficiently large market in any one place and the communications were bad. Instead the trade was carried on in a number of small vessels which were limited in size not only by their owners' lack of capital but by the shallowness of the creeks and rivers up which they traded. Walker thought that the Company's ports of Gogah, Dholera and Cambay could serve as depots for the trade which was carried on by water, as could Dholka, Dhandhuka, Baroda and Ahmadabad for the inland trade, if only peace and protection were established throughout Kathiawar. It was essential to destroy the pirates and to establish sufficient influence to give security to the merchants.[5] He pointed out that the acquisition of Gogah 'seems to offer the means of a material saving in the export of Cotton from Guzerat. The establishment of Cotton Screws at Goga might obviate the necessity and the consequent expence of the previous exportation to Bombay, and Ships might take in their Cargoes almost from the Warehouse door of the Cultivator...'[6]

Duncan acted on this advice so far as to urge the governor-

---

[1] BRP, range 366, II, 674–94: de Souza to Bombay, 13 September 1805.
[2] *Ibid.* 605–9: de Souza to Bombay, 12 September 1805.
[3] *Ibid.* 663–5: resolution of the Bombay council, 13 March 1806.
[4] BSPP, range 382, VII, 2688–94: Walker to Bombay, 15 July 1805.
[5] *Ibid.* 2694–700.
[6] *Ibid.* 2702: Walker to Bombay, 15 July 1805.

general to intervene in Kathiawar. He pointed out the necessity of destroying the pirates, ending the plundering regime of the chiefs and abolishing the gaikwar's mulkgiri expeditions. It was typical of Duncan that he should seek to convince the governor-general by claiming that the whole coast afforded an easy entrance to the Company's European enemies.[1] But he responded to de Souza's pressure so far as to order that the whole produce of Dhandhuka should be exported solely through Gogah and Dholera and not through any of the raja of Bhaunagar's ports.[2] However 1806 began and Walker was still pressing without results for measures in Kathiawar which either by mediation or conquest would give the Company control of the area.[3]

While de Souza was fighting for his and the Bombay merchants' private commercial empire in Kathiawar, the Bombay government under the new and strict control of the Court of Directors was building up its cotton trade with China. In January 1806 it told the Court that it was sending 12,000 bales of cotton, the produce of its own territories of Broach, Hansot and Occlaseer to China,[4] and the following month it agreed to build new wharfs at Broach to speed the loading of the cotton.[5] When the government was forced to seek a loan of 12 lacs from the merchants in March 1806 it refused to assign the Broach cotton or the Company's China tonnage in payment, a sign that the power of the merchants was indeed nearing its end.[6] In their commercial letter of 30 April, the directors warned Bombay that, although they intended to persevere with the trade, the cotton from upper India which was exported through Calcutta was challenging the Gujarat produce both in price and quality at Canton, and they ordered Bombay to use all proper means to reduce the cost of their cotton.[7] The Company's commercial grip on Gujarat was tightening. Robert Holford urged the government to assume political and judicial power in Cambay through the instrument of the Maratha chauth

[1] *Ibid.* 2546–7: Duncan to Wellesley, 25 July 1805.

[2] BRP, range 366, XLVII, 2143–6: 9 November 1805.

[3] BSPP, range 382, XVI, 2892–4: Walker's report on Kathiawar, 1 January 1806.

[4] Letters Received from Bombay XX, par. 3 of a letter to the secret committee, 28 January 1806.

[5] BCP, range 414, XII, 270–2: Surat commercial resident to Bombay, 5 February 1806.

[6] BSPP, range 382, XV, 1446–7: 7 March 1806.

[7] Home Misc. CCCLXXIV, 136: extract of a commercial letter to Bombay, 30 April 1806.

which they had obtained from the peshwa. Cambay, he asserted, could be made to rival Surat as a commercial residency and factory.[1]

By March 1806 the splitting of interests in Bombay society which had gone on since the end of 1803 had reached a culminating point. The once homogeneous society of civil servants governing in the interests of their own private trade had been gradually breaking up since the turn of the century, and the triumph of the shipping interest in the Court of Directors made absolute the divisions between those who wanted to serve the commercial interests of the directors and those who intended to serve their own. On 31 August 1804 the Court passed a decree which changed the whole nature of the Bombay establishment. They demanded that all their civil servants at Bombay should give up their private commercial pursuits or resign from the Company's service.[2] This meant the end of the politics of the old Bombay presidency. Faced with the alternative Alexander Adamson resigned his office, and Messrs Crawford, Law, Inglis and Kinlock followed him.[3] There remained, however, de Souza. The necessity of his resigning his positions at Gogah and Rattalow or giving up his private trade was not pressed too heavily throughout 1805[4] and Duncan appears to have avoided the subject.[5] But he could not continue to avoid it, and in March 1806 de Souza was called upon to make his choice. He protested that he was acting in Kathiawar for the Company's commercial interests and not his own, and declared

unless I am allowed to Trade, I shall not be able to do anything either at Dollerah or Goga these are both Mercantile places and if I or somebody else in my room do not undertake to encourage Trade by setting Example, and running risk of bringing Commerce to them, neither one or the other place will become of that Consequence or importance which they are Capable of being Made, and the Company will derive no Advantage from my Agency.

As to giving up his own commercial interests, de Souza declared it was impossible as he had traded since 1775 and had too many

---

[1] BSPP, range 382, XXVIII, 2965–7: Holford to Bombay, 31 July 1805; and Factory Records, Cambay I, 86–9: Holford to Bombay, 11 May 1806.
[2] Despatches to Bombay XXVI, 548–55: 2 May 1806.   [3] *Ibid.*
[4] BRP, range 366, L, 744: de Souza to H. Diggle, 26 October 1805.
[5] *Ibid.* 748–9: de Souza to H. Diggle, 16 December 1805, 1 March 1806; and 756: 1 March 1806.

concerns to settle.[1] He therefore resigned his position at Gogah and Dholera and asked to be reimbursed for his expenditure on cotton screws and buildings. He continued his private commercial enterprises in Gujarat and in May 1806 he was acting as an agent for the Bombay merchants in buying cotton.[2]

It was the end of the private traders' domination of the Bombay government. It was not however the end of the private trade. The big firms continued to flourish side by side with the Company's commerce, and Walker saw that de Souza's commercial strategy in Kathiawar was not neglected. He continued to press for the Company's direct intervention in the peninsula.[3] In May 1806 it seemed as though much of de Souza's work at Dholera and Rattalow would be undone when girasias in the neighbourhood attacked and burned the settlements, inspired, it seemed, by the raja of Bhaunagar.[4] Walker pointed out to the Bombay government that the Company could not hope to pacify Kathiawar by making concessions to the girasias. The curse of Kathiawar, he said, was the vast number of petty independent states, and until these disappeared and one system of justice was established property and order could not be secured.[5] But it was not until 31 December 1806 that the supreme government gave permission for Walker to lead an expedition into Kathiawar to make terms with the principal chiefs.[6] The expedition crossed into the province in May 1807. In June Walker obtained in final settlement of the Company's jaidad the gaikwar's tribute from the raja of Bhaunagar. This had the advantage of excluding the gaikwar's mulkgiri army from the neighbourhood of the Company's possessions, and Walker declared 'by the influence which this cession affords over these Districts we acquire the full Commercial controul of the most trading part of the Guzerat, and it will also enable us to improve these advantages to the utmost practicable extent'.[7] Backed by his force of Company and gaikwari troops, and sometimes after military action, Walker concluded agreements with the major chiefs of Kathiawar including Bhaunagar and Porbander. The

[1] BRP, range 366, II, 699–702: de Souza to Bombay, 12 March 1806.
[2] *Ibid.* LI, 1543: de Souza to H. Diggle, 21 May 1806.
[3] BSPP, range 382, XVIII, 4114–22: Bombay to Bengal, 15 May 1806.
[4] *Ibid.* XIX, 4883–4907: B. Rowles to R. Holford, 22 May 1806.
[5] BRP, range 366, LII, 1964–80: Walker's report, 20 July 1806.
[6] BSPP, range 382, XXV, 319: Bengal to Bombay, 31 December 1806.
[7] *Ibid.* XXXI, 4692–700: Walker to Bombay, 19 June 1807.

chiefs agreed to pay set sums of revenue to the gaikwar and to keep the peace in Kathiawar.[1] Porbander ceded half of its port to the Company.[2] Walker planned to attack the Okhamandal pirates and to annex their territory, but Bombay received instructions from the Court of Directors which forbade them to take this course on the grounds of general policy.[3] Walker had to be content with negotiations and he exacted a pledge from the tribes of Okhamandal to give up piracy.[4] He also forced the Kathi tribes to give security against their plundering for a period of ten years.[5] The way was open for a further expansion of Bombay's trade and the work which had been planned by de Souza was completed.

The year 1806 marks a turning point in the development of the Bombay presidency. Although it did not see the end of Bombay's intervention in Kathiawar and Cutch or the final expansion of the presidency, it was symbolic of the transformation of the British empire of the eighteenth century into that of the nineteenth. After 1806, the division between the private merchants on the one part and the soldiers and administrators on the other became harder, and the rulers began to develop into a caste. The social life of Bombay, which Walter Ewer criticised in the 1790s when a governor and members of his council publicly kept Maratha women became something of the past. Ewer's creed that 'were it not for the veneration in which the European Character is held in this Country, it would be very difficult to Govern so extensive an Empire & so many millions of subjects', and his insistence that the easy society he described 'debases that dignity of Character, undermines the Authority of Government, and loosens the Bonds which attach the people to the prince',[6] replaced the easy relations which came from partnerships in trade.

Furthermore the whole status of the Bombay presidency was changed. In 1808 the government reported with pride to the directors that the Court's order for the provision of three extra cargoes of cotton above their usual investment could be more than

[1] *Bombay Selections* XXXVII, 242.
[2] *Ibid.* 273.
[3] BSPP, range 382, XXXV, 8288: Walker to Bombay, 12 December 1807.
[4] *Bombay Selections* XXXVII, 261.
[5] *Ibid.* XXXIX, 360.
[6] Home Misc. CDXXXVIII, 13–23: W. Ewer to Henry Dundas, 30 November 1796.

met by their own resources without drawing on Bengal.[1] Revenue matters were occupying greater attention and the old trades on which Bombay had built her greatness were either dying away or had ceased to expand. By 1806 the trade in pepper from the Malabar coast to Europe had declined beyond all hope of recovery,[2] and the same year marks the final slump after the boom of the early war years in the export of Indian textiles to Europe. The Berlin decrees and the competition of English machine-made cloth meant the end of the export of Surat piece-goods to London. In 1798 the Company had sold £3,000,000 of Indian textiles, but in 1807 the sales had slumped to £433,000.[3]

There remained the cotton trade from India to China in which Bombay's supremacy continued. Although Bengal sent 11,65,809 tales worth of cotton in the season 1810–11 to Canton, Bombay exported 37,23,684 tales worth, of which only 3,20,984 tales was the property of the Company.[4] But the importance of the cotton trade to the Company's tea investment was fast diminishing as the opium trade carried all before it. By 1809 opium had definitely superseded cotton as the most lucrative branch of commerce at Canton.[5] In 1807–8 Bombay exported the largest amount of cotton in its history, Rs 90,25,238 worth, but after this peak the trade slumped and only Rs 23,39,896 worth was exported in 1812–13. The exports did not reach the level of 1807–8 again until 1817–18.[6] The pressure of an expanding trade on a society which was not adapted to fulfil the demand diminished: suddenly in the case of the pepper and piece-good trade, and more gradually in raw cotton. Both the commercial and social conditions of the Bombay settlement which had combined to direct it on a course of territorial expansion were passing away.

But the Company continued to send its cargoes of raw cotton to China and to monopolise the produce of the Broach pargana. This policy led to a final conflict with the merchants. In 1808 Robert Rickards, who was again a member of the Bombay council, delivered

---

[1] Letters Received from Bombay XXII, par. 3 of a letter of the financial department, 20 February 1808.
[2] Bastin, *The Early South-East Asian Pepper Trade*, 48.
[3] Philips, *The East India Company*, 155.
[4] J. Macgregor, *Commercial Statistics* IV–V, 737–40.
[5] W. E. Cheong, 'Some Aspects of British Trade and Finance in Canton... 1784–1834', an unpublished Ph.D. thesis (London, 1962), 24.
[6] Macgregor, *Commercial Statistics* IV–V, 737–40.

a minute in which he criticised the government's method of taking cotton in payment of the Broach revenues.[1] The minute was the beginning of a storm. The directors refused to accept his criticisms,[2] and in October 1810 they censured his opinions in strong terms. They also condemned him for supporting the demand of Bruce, Fawcett and Company and Forbes and Company that the Company should withdraw from the Bombay cotton trade and be content with an annual supply of 4,000 bales from the private firms.[3] The Court dismissed Rickards from the Council. From that point the battle between the Company and the Bombay private merchants came into the open. Rickards returned to England and formed the Indian agency house of Rickards, Mackintosh and Company, which was connected with the China trading firm of Thomas Dent and Company.[4] In print and before the parliamentary committees of enquiry he attacked the whole system of the Company's Indian trade and revenue. He told the parliamentary committee of 1812–13 that the Company exercised a cotton monopoly 'to the positive exclusion of all private buyers from the Company's districts' and that this monopoly had the effect of 'nearly doubling the price of cotton in Guzerat'. The price which the Company paid for their own cotton he claimed was fixed by 'the judge, the collector, and the commercial resident who exercise the whole civil authority of the district...over a slavish, patient, and forbearing people'. This price was 10 or 12 per cent lower than that which the cultivators received in the Maratha districts. It meant that the private merchants had to pay far more for their own cotton, and in 1809 when the price reached Rs 175 a candy there was no profit to be made on it at Canton.[5] In a pamphlet which he published in 1813 Rickards attacked the whole system by which the Company combined commerce with political power and he accused the Company of holding back the expansion of British trade in India.[6] As a result of this pressure the Board of Control forced the directors to abolish the system by which the

[1] Letters Received from Bombay XXIII, par. 68 of the letter in the commercial department, 14 October 1808.
[2] Home Misc. CCCLXXIV, 197–9: the Court to Bombay, 5 January 1810.
[3] *Ibid.* 248–53: the Court to Bombay, 22 February 1811.
[4] Parliamentary Papers, 1830, V, 269.
[5] Parliamentary Papers, 1812–13, X, 181–7.
[6] *The Present System of Our East India Government and Commerce Considered* (1813), 23, 34, 36.

Bombay government took revenue in cotton or exercised any form of compulsion over the cultivators.[1] In 1831 Rickards again played a prominent part in bringing the case against the Company, and Sir Charles Forbes and John Stewart, another Bombay merchant, supported his evidence.[2] The conflicts ended with a victory for the private trade, and the final separation of political and commercial power in the government of British India. The power of the East Indian private-trading interest had asserted itself to the last in the direction of imperial policy and even after 1834 its influence was not at an end.

[1] Home Misc. CCCLXXIV, 691–705, 761.
[2] Parliamentary Papers, 1831, v, 148, 159, 244.

CHAPTER 8

CONCLUSIONS

This study of the Bombay presidency has attempted to explain the expansion of British territory in western India during the age of Cornwallis and Wellesley, and the relation of this movement with British imperial policy as a whole. The first conclusion which emerges from it relates to the interpretation of British imperial policy in the second half of the eighteenth century. Instead of seeing territorial expansion in India in this period as an exception to a general policy of developing trade and avoiding political commitments,[1] one is led to conclude that one cannot without qualification define the imperial policy of these years in this way. Even if it were true that the industrial revolution had gone far enough in Britain by 1770 or even 1800 to enable British textiles to force Indian hand-woven fabrics out of Asian markets, which the evidence would disprove, the history of British trade in the nineteenth century shows clearly enough that the cheapness or superiority of goods was by itself not enough to command markets. It has been shown that, even at the height of the free-trading policy when British technical and commercial superiority was assured, it was necessary to exert political and military power in some areas to promote and safeguard trade.[2]

If this was the case in the nineteenth century it must have been more true of an earlier period, especially when one examines the nature of British economic expansion in the second half of the eighteenth century. The thrust of trade to the east which distinguished it was not carried by the export of British goods. It was the product not of an industrial but a commercial revolution based on the capture of the inter-Asian and European–Asian trade. Insofar as this process owed anything to developments in Britain it was the work, not of manufacturers, but of the statesmen who drafted and passed the Commutation Act, which quickly brought the tea trade from China to Europe into British hands and enormously

[1] Cf. Harlow, *The Founding of the Second British Empire, 1763–93*, I.
[2] J. Gallagher and R. Robinson, 'The Imperialism of Free Trade', *The Economic History Review*, 2nd series, VI (August 1953).

increased the demand for tea. This demand caused the inter-Asian or 'country trade' to expand in response to the greatly increased opportunities of trade at Canton. But if the Commutation Act created these opportunities, it was the private trader and 'country captain' who ensured that they were seized for British profit. Professor Furber has shown how this 'obscure and unsung soldier of fortune' outdistanced his Asiatic and European rivals to dominate the Asian trade and how 'he became more and more the essential part of the system whereby British power drew the great regions of a continent more closely together'.[1] The other aspect of the corruption and laxity which pervaded the East India Company's affairs in the eighteenth century was the freedom which it allowed to the enterprising private trader to acquire capital and build ships and to navigate them at will in eastern waters. This, compared with the 'centralisation of control and inadequate initiative in the hands of the men on the spot' which had been the characteristic of the Dutch company,[2] brought the Asian trade into British hands and knit it to the British economy.

Since this economic expansion was based on commercial and not industrial superiority it relied more heavily on the cooperation of the local communities and on favourable conditions for trade. It is easier to sell cheap and attractive goods in disturbed social or economic conditions than it is to organise a community to grow, clean, pack and transport enormous quantities of cotton or pepper, or to make piece-goods with all the delicate financial and commercial transactions involved in the enterprise. A study of the East Indian archipelago in the same period has shown that the organisation of local society did not permit any expansion of British trade without the intervention of British power,[3] and it is this fact which stands out in the history of the west coast of India.

It was not the competition of the French and other European traders which primarily troubled the Bombay merchants, although it could be a severe irritant as in the case of the Portuguese at Surat and the Mahé traders. This could be defeated by paying higher prices and by developing a more efficient organisation, and if the Court of Directors was not willing to do this the private

[1] Furber, *John Company at Work*, chapter v.
[2] Tapan Raychaudhuri *Jan Company in Coromandel, 1605–90* ('Sgravenhage 1962), 210–11.
[3] H. R. C. Wright, *East Indian Economic Problems of the Age of Cornwallis and Raffles* (1961), 293–4.

merchants were ready to seize the Company's trade. More difficult to deal with were obstructions like the embargo imposed on British trade by Tipu Sultan. But this was superficial and temporary when compared with the entrenched barriers within society itself. Tipu Sultan could be forced to lift his embargo by diplomatic pressure or military action, but no external pressure could force a society to organise itself for the benefit of foreign trade when its structure and interests made it unwilling or incapable of doing so. In Malabar, after the expulsion of Tipu Sultan's troops, political authority broke down, and the highly organised commercial system on which the European merchants depended threatened to dissolve in the wave of communal violence between the Hindus and Moplahs. It was this fact which determined the British to take over the government of the province and the responsibility for law and order. But once in possession of power they found the temptation to enforce a monopoly of foreign trade too great and pursued the policy which the Portuguese and Dutch had tried before them. In the course of their attempts to increase their share of the trade they found it necessary to change the structure of the government and to take power from the hands of the Malabar princes.

In Gujarat the situation was more difficult still. The Maratha powers and petty Muslim princes were either hostile or at the most were indifferent to the progress of foreign trade, and when not actually restricting exports they did nothing to improve the conditions of trade. As the Chinese market expanded the Bombay merchants demanded a greater production of cotton, a steady price, good quality and dependable supplies, safely and easily transported to Bombay for the short shipping season to Canton. But the cotton districts which were directly administered by the Marathas suffered from the rapacity which was characteristic of their administration, and monopolies such as that exercised by Sindhia's agent in Broach discouraged greater production. The weakness and corruption of the government made it unable or unwilling to control the price-raising tactics of the cotton-dealers and the widespread practice of adulterating the cotton.

The situation could only be amended if the cotton-producing territories were brought under British control, or if new areas could be opened for cultivation. The latter strategy was not an easy one, as outside Broach and the well-established cotton areas political authority barely existed. The Marathas collected chauth and claimed overlordship of most of Gujarat and Kathiawar, but the merchants were faced with a largely unexplored coast which was infested with pirates, preyed on by bands of robbers, subject to petty warring chiefs, where cultivation could only be carried on at subsistence level, and where property and life were in constant danger. Even if the immediate problems of peace and security could be overcome the territory had to be developed economically and opened to trade. Settlements of cultivators had to be organised, roads built, ports opened, capital invested and a whole agricultural and commercial community built from a waste land. This scheme, as much as the assumption of power in the Maratha cotton districts, demanded British military force and administration. This is the theme of British territorial expansion in Gujarat and beyond. Both in the north and in Malabar merchants found it necessary to exert political power in order to safeguard and extend their trading interests.

This was not a new situation in European contact with Asia. Albuquerque and Jan Pieterszoon Coen had attempted to capture the Asian trade for the Portuguese and Dutch by seizing strategic points on the trade routes, but neither power had avoided the necessity of taking territory. Although this was partly because of the monopolistic policy which they like their British successors pursued towards the spice trade, it was also because of the social and economic conditions of the country which in the seventeenth as in the eighteenth century limited the expansion of trade. One conclusion of a recent study of the Dutch trade on the Coromandel coast is that

the experiences of the Dutch Company on the coast were in many ways typical of European commercial activity in 17th century Asia. Initially their chief obstacle was an unfavourable institutional framework—unfavourable not merely to the trade of foreign companies, but to all economic activities which could possibly expand production or raise the producers' standards of consumption...Rapacity of transferable local officials or revenue farmers who had no care for the economic future of the people or the region under them, was part of the administrative system of the period and this fact affected adversely all concerned.[1]

Wherever the commercial pressure was great enough and the military weakness of the local community allowed it, the European

[1] Raychaudhuri, *Jan Company*, 210.

powers took territory for trade. When the British achieved naval and military supremacy in the East the demand was for piece-goods for the European market. This attracted them to Bengal and the Coromandel coast, and it was in these areas where political and military power was weakest that they made their first acquisitions of territory. Later with the growth of the country trade and the relative decline in the value of the piece-good trade Bengal's commercial importance diminished for a time while that of Bombay grew. But territorial power creates problems of defence and administration which lead to the further expansion of power beyond the original area of economic development,[1] and Bengal and Madras had reached this stage when conditions were bringing about the first expansion of British power on the west coast. This was not a defensive movement to protect Bengal from the French, but the result of new commercial demands on the local society and the weakening of its military power. Whereas the Mysorean and Maratha armies had kept the English in check earlier in the century, by 1790 Tipu Sultan's hold on the west coast was undermined by the years of rebellion in Malabar, and internal political strife and administrative weakness was breaking up the Maratha power at the same time. The number of pleas for intervention which local chiefs and merchants made to the Bombay government showed where the opportunity lay.

This explanation of British territorial expansion in India, in terms of commercial pressure on unsatisfactory economic and social conditions, links the extension of territory on the west coast with that in Bengal, and the whole not only with British policy elsewhere but with the main stream of European policy in the East. What gave this particular period its distinctive feature was the prominent part played in the process of expansion by the private merchant and the demands of the country trade. It was the merchants who faced the practical problems of increasing their exports and whose profits were so closely bound up with the solution, and it was they who had the detailed knowledge of the land and society. The information and pressure of David Scott, George Smith, Charles Malet and Scott's associates in Bombay, convinced Henry Dundas of the necessity to preserve and expand the Bombay presidency. The close association of David Scott with Dundas and the period of their power in the government and the

---

[1] Gallagher and Robinson, *Ec.H.R.* VI, 6.

Court of Directors was of enormous use to the Bombay private traders. But it was not long before the men on the spot were outstripping even these two advocates of expansion. Scott had left Bombay before the cotton trade from Gujarat had fully developed and so he had no first-hand experience of the abuses and difficulties that arose to hinder it. Moreover, aware of opposition from the shipping interest and other reactionary forces in the Court of Directors he sometimes tried to restrain the expansionist views of his associates.[1] But such was the structure of Bombay society and the merchants' power over the government, partly a matter of finance and partly of personalities and interests, that they were able to direct the policy of the Bombay government and, because of Lord Wellesley's acquiescence or indifference, to take the decisions on territorial expansion.

In Malabar the private-trading interest gained complete control of the administration with disastrous results for the country. Malabar in the 1790s shared all the miseries which overtook Bengal and Madras after Clive's victories. The corruption and self-interested policies of the Company's servants and their determination to exploit power for their own commercial advantage did much to bring about the social upheavals and economic decline which were its fate for much of the nineteenth century. In Gujarat and Kathiawar on the other hand one sees the imperialism of the private traders in a more constructive form. Miguel de Souza's activities on behalf of his own and his friends' commercial interests had as their object the opening of a wild and oppressed area to trade, cultivation and prosperity, and provide evidence of his skill, knowledge, resourcefulness and courage.

Although the private-trading interest undoubtedly dominated the Bombay government up to about 1804 and directed its expansionist policy, often under the cloak of defence against the French menace, two other men, not private traders, were outstanding for the part they played in the process. Charles Malet and Alexander Walker saw in Gujarat, Kathiawar and Cutch the possibility of extending British power in a commercially profitable but also in an honourable and beneficial way. Walker is an example of the new type of administrator, trained in the army, who was becoming more prominent in the Madras and Bengal presidencies with the gradual reform of the civil service. But Malet's policy was the

---

[1] Philips (ed.), *The Correspondence of David Scott* I, 75.

result of his lonely years at Cambay where he was able to observe the decadence of Moghul and Maratha rule and the opportunities for British expansion. Both are significant because they saw the national economic interest behind the expansion of private trade, and because they evolved a concept of British imperialism which although based on commercial and territorial aggrandisement yet embraced generous principles of justice, peace and prosperity for the subjects of the empire.

The pressure for territorial expansion came from India, but events in Europe were not without some influence. Henry Dundas's policy was influenced by his Indian correspondents but his support was necessary for the continued supremacy of the private trade. The fall of Pitt's government and the failure of the private-trading interests to capture Castlereagh's support led to the defeat of David Scott and an attack by the shipping interest in the Court of Directors on the power of the Bombay merchants. The determination with which the directors, once freed from the influence of Scott, set out to wrest a share in the cotton trade from the private merchants suggests that the failure of the Court to profit by changing commercial prospects was not entirely due to inefficiency or conservative business methods. David Scott must have known a great deal about the exploitation of Malabar, the interests of his friend Murdock Brown, and his other Bombay associates, and at the least turned a blind eye to their activities, while he was personally responsible for ensuring that when the province was taken over by Madras, Bombay retained the commercial establishments on the coast. Whether the order forbidding the Bombay civil servants to trade would have been given had he retained his influence over the Court and the Board is a debatable point. But when the directors dispatched that order there is no doubt that it was the end of an epoch in the politics and trade of Bombay.

This might suggest that the expansionist policy in western India was after all a retarded movement, the result of social conditions in the Bombay presidency which elsewhere had been purged by Cornwallis's reforms. This is to argue that the expansion on the west coast was not in the mainstream of imperial policy and that when the civil service was reformed the presidency was absorbed in the policy of promoting military and political interests which it is said distinguished the Indian policy of the period.[1] This is a key

[1] Harlow, *The Founding of the Second British Empire* I, 370.

question because if, as it has been argued, the policy of territorial expansion was pursued in response to the economic and social conditions of the coast and the commercial demands made on it, it is important to know why that policy was halted.

It is clear that social conditions in Bombay were not the major factor. This study shows that the men who were directing the main lines of imperial policy held views of British interests which involved the expansion of the inter-Asian trade and the taking of territory in the East to promote that end. Henry Dundas saw India as an integral part of the British empire which existed for the growth of British trade. The Court of Directors too played no small part in the assumption of power in Surat, a measure which they believed would forward their piece-good trade, while they had no hesitation in using political power in Malabar and Gujarat to expand their spice and cotton trade. The reason why the private traders and Duncan, their pawn, sought to use the French menace as an argument for expansion was that they were intent on expanding only their own trade, not the Company's. The evidence suggests that the change which came over the politics of the Bombay presidency about 1806 was due as much to changed economic as social conditions. The decline of the spice and piece-good trade removed some commercial pressures from the scene, and the competition of Bengal cotton, and above all opium, meant a slackening of the Chinese market for Bombay produce and the easing of commercial pressure on the north-west coast. Moreover the territorial acquisitions which had been made, the taking of ports and parts of the hinterland in Gujarat and Kathiawar, the establishment of political control over the gaikwar's country, and the treaties which Walker made and enforced with troops in Kathiawar, had done a great deal to improve the conditions in which trade was carried on. The spectacle of the Company's using its territorial power to establish a command over trade was not one which encouraged the private merchants to urge the further expansion of the Company's influence, and the more enterprising of them turned to attack the whole basis of the Company's trade with India.

The expansion of the Bombay presidency shows both eighteenth- and nineteenth-century imperial techniques at work. If 'willing- ness to limit the use of paramount power to establishing security for trade' is the distinctive feature of the British imperialism of free trade, in contrast with the mercantilist use of power to obtain commercial monopolies through political possession,[1] then Bombay shows the period of transition between them. In Malabar neither the private merchants nor the Company could resist the temptation to establish a monopoly of the spice trade once they had assumed the political power which they had sought to safeguard their trade, and the directors followed the same monopolistic principles in their policy towards Surat and the cotton-producing areas of Gujarat. But at the same time Charles Malet, Alexander Walker, Miguel de Souza and other private merchants were planning and executing schemes which, while taking coastal territory and commanding points, were ready to let them serve as centres drawing by competitive and not monopolistic power the commerce of the surrounding country into English hands. But the continuity of technique was but one aspect of the wider continuity of policy which in the eighteenth, as in the nineteenth, century was a 'combination of commercial penetration and political influence' designed 'to command those economies which could be made to fit best'[2] into Britain's own. For twenty years or so Bombay and the west coast of India fitted perfectly into Britain's economy and bred men like Scott and Rickards who did much to influence the development of British imperial policy in the nineteenth century.

[1] Gallagher and Robinson, *Ec.H.R.* VI, 6.
[2] Gallagher and Robinson, *Ec.H.R.* VI, 11.

BIBLIOGRAPHY

MANUSCRIPTS

INDIA OFFICE LIBRARY

Bombay Secret and Political Proceedings
   Range D, vols. 71–5
   Range E, vols. 4–11
   Range 380, vols. 65–75
   Range 381, vols. 1–59
   Range 382, vols. 1–35

Bombay Commercial Proceedings
   Range 414, vols. 47–75
   Range 415, vols. 1–12

Bombay Reports on External Commerce
   Range 414, vols. 39–43

Bombay Revenue Proceedings
   Range 366, vols. 12–57

Bombay Public Consultations
   Range 342, vols. 2, 11–14, 34

Bombay Mayor's Court Proceedings
   Range 417, vols. 57–58
   Range 418, vols. 2–3, 11–14, 16, 18, 21, 29

Surat Factory Records
   Vols. 76, 79, 80

Cambay Factory Records
   Vol. 1

Letters Received from Bombay
   Vols. 8–23

Revenue Letters Received from Bombay
   Vol. 1

Despatches to Bombay
   Vols. 7–28

245

Letters from the Board of Control to the Court of Directors
Vols. 1–3

Letters from the Court to the Board
Vols. 1–3

Letter-Books of the Board of Control
Vols. 1–2

Minutes of the Board of Control
Vols. 1–2

Personal Records
Vols. 1–20

The Home Miscellaneous Series

Vols. 60, 65, 81, 84, 85, 86, 107, 108, 115–18, 120–3, 125, 132–4, 138–46, 149, 153, 154, 156–60, 163, 165, 166, 167, 183, 188, 210, 211, 241, 242, 260, 333, 334, 340, 374, 377, 387, 392, 405, 406, 432–4, 436, 438, 439, 445, 456 a, b, c, e, 457–79, 481, 492, 493, 503, 504, 505, 539, 567, 585, 591, 605–610, 612, 614, 615, 616, 618, 620, 622, 627, 640

Miscellaneous Letters Received
Vol. 85

Charters and Treaties
Charters vol. 11

European Manuscripts
D.100   The correspondence of Charles Forbes
E.216   Private letters from Sir Arthur Wellesley

Additional European Manuscripts
D.534, 588–9   Letters and memoranda of David Scott

European Photostats
Vol. 12   The letters of George Barnes, 1789–1823

Microfilmed material

(a) Reels 647–50: the Melville papers in Harvard University Library. Reel 647 includes correspondence between Jonathan Duncan and Robert Dundas, 1808–11, and an index to some of Henry Dundas's correspondence; reel 648 includes letters from John Shore, General Stuart and Sir John Macpherson to Henry Dundas; reel 649 includes the correspondence of Jonathan Duncan with Henry Dundas; reel 650 includes the enclosures in Duncan's letters to Henry Dundas, and Sir Robert Abercromby's letters to Henry Dundas.

(b) Reels 606–7: the Melville papers in the Ames Library of South Asia, Minnesota.

PUBLIC RECORD OFFICE

The Cornwallis Papers
   PRO 30/11/7–58, 111–32, 134–48, 150–60, 162–3, 165, 168, 171–5, 177–9, 182–8, 193–4, 199

The Chatham Papers
   PRO 30/8/157, 176, 179, 188, 354, 358, 361, 362

The Dacres–Adams Papers
   PRO 30/58/1–6, 10

Colonial Office Records
   CO 77/25, 26, 55, 57, 58

Privy Council Records
   PC 1/65/B33; PC 1/66/B39

Board of Trade Papers
   BT 1/1–100; BT 3/1–13; BT 6/42–3, 140, 227, 246

Chancery Masters' Exhibits
   C 110/168, Hovey v. Blakeman: Correspondence and accounts, Bombay, 1769–98. The bundle includes letters from John Forbes (*see below*).

BRITISH MUSEUM

The Wellesley Papers
   Add. MSS 12,580, 12,582, 13,693–702, 13,456–464

GUILDHALL LIBRARY MUNIMENT ROOM, LONDON

The Michie Papers
   MSS 5881–2

JOHN RYLANDS LIBRARY, MANCHESTER

The Melville Papers
   Boxes 523, 670–99, 926–7

The Pitt Papers
   Boxes 907–8, 928–35

The Phillipps MSS (the papers of Richard Johnson)
   Boxes 173–95

NATIONAL LIBRARY OF SCOTLAND

The Melville Papers

MSS 20, 21–57, 1060, 1064, 1069, 1072–4, 2956, 3385–7, 3594, 3834–5, 3844–9

The Walker of Bowland Papers (see the preface, p. x above)

PRIVATE MSS: THE FORBES PAPERS

This is a scattered collection, mostly in private hands, not sorted or catalogued. I was able to trace the papers over a period of several months with the help of Sir John Forbes of Newe, Aberdeen, the Hon. Robin Campbell of Forbes, Campbell and Co., Eastcheap, and Mr E. J. Bunbury. The papers relate to the Forbes family and the agency house founded at Bombay in 1767 by John Forbes and carried on by his nephew Charles. The firm is one of the oldest in India and still carries on business at Bombay as Forbes, Campbell and Company. The papers do not throw much light on the politics of Bombay in the period covered by this book but they give much information on commercial affairs and are an interesting source for social history.

The main parts of the collection are as follows:

1. At the India Office Library: European MSS D.100, containing a large part of Charles Forbes's correspondence.
2. The contents of a black tin trunk in the offices of Forbes, Campbell and Company, 51 Eastcheap, London.

This is a very miscellaneous collection of letters, memoranda, photographs, newspaper cuttings and an unfinished typescript history of the firm by E. J. Bunbury. Some of the letters are from or to Charles Forbes, but the collection also covers the whole of the nineteenth century.

3. The papers at Castle Newe, Aberdeen.

Miss Bettine Forbes wrote a history of the Forbes family and transcribed many of the family letters in a typescript volume bound in red leather and entitled 'Forbes of Newe' which is in the possession of Sir John Forbes. In this she lists all the family papers which were kept at Newe but have since apparently disappeared. Among the letters she transcribes are many written by Charles Forbes to ships' captains, merchants and Company servants at Bombay, on the west coast, and at Canton.

BEDFORDSHIRE RECORD OFFICE

The Pym Papers

PM 2749

LINCOLNSHIRE ARCHIVES OFFICE, THE CASTLE, LINCOLN

Jarvis V/B/1 (A journal kept by Lieutenant G. R. P. Jarvis on a journey from Columbo to Calicut, 1794–5)

Bibliography

The Ancaster Papers
   3 Ancaster 9/21/1

The Monson MSS
   Vols. 53, 98

PRINTED SOURCES

OFFICIAL PUBLICATIONS

Parliamentary Papers

Report from the Committee on the Account between the Public and the East India Company. Sess. 1805 (197) vol. 6.

First Report from the Select Committee on the Affairs of the Company. Sess. 1808 (261) vol. 3.

Second Report from the Select Committee on the Affairs of the Company. Sess. 1810 (363) vol. 5.

Third Report from the Select Committee on the Affairs of the Company. Sess. 1810–11 (250) vol. 7.

Fourth Report from the Select Committee on the Affairs of the Company. Sess. 1812 (148) vol. 6.

Supplement to the Fourth Report of the Committee. Sess. 1812 (151 and 182) vol. 6.

Report from the Committee of Correspondence to the Court of Directors on the subject of the Trade with the East Indies and China. Sess. 1812–13 (78) vol. 8.

First Report from the Select Committee on the Affairs of the East India Company. Sess. 1830 (644 comprising 99, 155, 236, 246, 396, 514) vol. 5.

Second Report from the same Committee. Sess. 1830 (655) vol. 5.

Report from the Select Committee of the House of Lords on the present state of the Affairs of the East India Company. Sess. 1830 (646) vol. 6.

Report from the Select Committee on the present state of the Affairs of the East India Company; and on the state of the Trade between Great Britain, the East Indies, and China. Session 1831 (65) vol. 5.

Selections from the records of the Bombay presidency (New Series) Nos. 15, 16, 37, 39 (Bombay, 1855–6).

English Records of Maratha History: The Poona Residency Correspondence, ed. Sir Jadunath Sarkar.

   Vol. I *Mahadaji Sindhia and North Indian Affairs, 1785–94* (ed. Sir Jadunath Sarkar) Bombay, 1936.

   Vol. II *Poona Affairs, 1786–97* (ed. G. S. Sardesai) Bombay, 1936.

   Vol. III *The Allies' War with Tipu Sultan* (ed. N. B. Ray) Bombay, 1937.

   Vol. VI *Poona Affairs, 1797–1801* (ed. G. S. Sardesai) Bombay, 1940.

   Vol. VII *Poona Affairs, 1801–10* (ed. G. S. Sardesai) Bombay, 1940.

   Vol. X *The Treaty of Bassein and the Anglo-Maratha War in the Deccan, 1802–4* (ed. R. Sinh) Bombay, 1951.

   Extra volume: *Selections from Sir C. W. Malet's letter book, 1780–4* (ed. R. Sinh) Bombay, 1940.

Trade and Empire in Western India, 1784–1806

Malabar Report: Reports of a joint commission from Bengal and Bombay
. . . on the province of Malabar in the years 1792 and 1793 (Madras, 1862).

Logan W. (ed.), *A Collection of Treaties, Engagements and Other Papers of Importance Relating to British Affairs in Malabar* (Madras, 1891 and 1951).

The Bombay Directory, 1792.

Dodwell, E. and Miles, J. (eds.), *Alphabetical List of the Honourable East India Company's Bombay Civil Servants, 1798–1839* (1839).

CONTEMPORARY PAMPHLETS

Fullarton, W., *A view of the English Interests in India, an account of the military operations in the Southern Parts of the Peninsula 1782–84* (1788).

Rickards, R., *The Present System of Our East India Government and Commerce Considered* (1813).

Smith, N., *Observations on the Present State of the East India Company* (1771).

CONTEMPORARY BOOKS

Bruce, J., *Historical View of Plans for the Government of British India, etc.* (1793).

Buchanan, F. H., *Journey from Madras, through the Countries of Mysore, Canara, and Malabar, 1800–1* (1811).

Dalrymple, A., *Oriental Repertory* (1791–1808).

Elmore, H. M., *The British Mariner's Directory and Guide to the Trade and Navigation of the India and China Seas* (1802).

Elwood, A. K., *Narrative of a Journey Overland from England to India.* 2 vols (1830).

Forbes, J., *Oriental Memoires.* 4 vols (1814).

Graham, M., *Journal of a Residence in India* (1813).

Hamilton, W., *The East Indian Gazetteer* (1815).

Macpherson, D., *Annals of Commerce.* 4 vols (1805).

—— *The History of the European Commerce with India* (1812).

Milburn, W., *Oriental Commerce*, 2 vols (1813).

Rickards, R., *India*, 2 vols (1829–32).

Taylor, J., *Letters on India* (1803).

Wales, J., *Bombay Views* (1800).

Wilks, M., *Historical Sketches of the South of India* (1810–14).

MEMOIRS AND CORRESPONDENCE

Furber, H. (ed.), *The Private Record of an Indian Governor-Generalship, being the Correspondence of Sir John Shore* (1933).

Historical Manuscripts Commission: *Report on the Manuscripts of the late Reginald Rawdon Hastings*, F. Bickley (ed.) (1928).

——*Report on the Palk Manuscripts in the possession of Mrs Bannatyne*, H. D. Love (ed.) (1922).

Mackintosh, R. J. (ed.), *The Memoires of Sir James Mackintosh*, 2 vols (1836).

Martin, M. (ed.), *The Despatches of Marquis Wellesley*, 5 vols (1837).

Owen, S. J. (ed.), *A Selection from the Despatches, Treaties, and other Papers of the Marquess Wellesley during his Government of India* (1877).

Philips, C. H. (ed.), *The Correspondence of David Scott*, 2 vols (1951).

Ross, C. (ed.), *The Correspondence of Charles, first Marquis Cornwallis*, 3 vols (1859).

Spencer, A. (ed.), *The Memoires of William Hickey*, 4 vols (1913–25).

SECONDARY WORKS

Anstey, V., *The Trade of the Indian Ocean* (1929).

——, *The Economic Development of India* (1931).

Banaji, D. R., *Bombay and the Sidis* (1932).

Bastin, J., *The Native Policies of Sir Stamford Raffles in Java and Sumatra: an economic interpretation* (1957).

——, *The Changing Balance of the Early South-East Asian Pepper Trade.* Papers on South-East Asian Subjects, No. 1, University of Malaya in Kuala Lumpur (1960).

Bearce, G. D., *British Attitudes towards India* (1961).

Choksey, R D., *A History of British Diplomacy at the Court of the Peshwas, 1786–1818* (1951).

Coates, W. H., *The Old 'Country Trade' of the East Indies* (1911).

Das Gupta, A., *Malabar in Asian Trade, 1740–1800* (1967).

Dodwell, H. H. (ed.), *British India, 1497–1858.* The Cambridge History of India, Vol. v (1929).

Douglas, J., *Bombay and Western India*, 2 vols (1893).

Edwardes, S. M., *The Rise of Bombay* (1902).

Embree, A. T., *Charles Grant and British Rule in India* (1962).

Furber, H., *Henry Dundas, first Viscount Melville, 1742–1811* (1931).

——, *John Company at Work* (1948).

——, *Bombay Presidency in the mid-18th Century* (1965).

Gallagher, J. and Robinson, R., 'The Imperialism of Free Trade'. *The Economic History Review*, second series, vi, August 1953.

Greenberg, M., *British Trade and the Opening of China, 1800–42* (1951).

Gupta, P. C., *Baji Rao and the East India Company, 1796–1818* (1939).

Hamilton, C. J., *The Trade Relations between England and India, 1600–1896* (1919).

Harlow, V. T., *The Founding of the Second British Empire*, Vol. i, 1763–93 (1952); Vol. ii (1964).

Hatalkar, V. T., *Relations between the French and the Marathas, 1668–1815* (1958).

Huttenback, R. A., 'The French Threat to India and British Relations with Sind, 1799–1809', *The English Historical Review* LXXVI, October 1961.

Imperial Gazetteer, The (1908).

Logan, W., *Malabar*, 3 vols (1889, 2nd ed. 1951).

Macgregor, J., *Commercial Statistics*. Vols IV and V (1848).

Mayer, A. C., *Land and Society in Malabar* (1952).

Mill, J., *The History of British India*, 9 vols (1848).

Misra, B. B., *The Central Administration of the East India Company* (1959).

Narain, V. A., *Jonathan Duncan in Varanasi* (1959).

Panikkar, K. M., *A History of Kerala* (1960).

Pares, R., A review of V. T. Harlow's 'The Founding of the Second British Empire', in *The English Historical Review* LXVIII, April 1953, 282.

Parkinson, C. N., *Trade in the Eastern Seas, 1793–1813* (1937).

——, *War in the Eastern Seas, 1793–1815* (1954).

—— (ed.), *The Trade Winds* (1948).

Philips, C. H., *The East India Company, 1784–1834* (1940).

Pritchard, E. H., *The Crucial Years of Early Anglo-Chinese Relations, 1750–1800*. Research Studies of the State College of Washington, IV (1936).

Raychaudhuri, T., *Jan Company in Coromandel, 1605–90* (1962).

Redford, A., *Manchester Merchants and Foreign Trade, 1794–1858* (1934).

Roberts, P. E., *India under Wellesley* (1929).

——, *History of British India under the Company and Crown* (3rd ed., 1952).

Robinson, F. P., *The Trade of the East India Company* (1912).

Rushbrook Williams, L. F., *The Black Hills—Kutch in History and Legend* (1958).

Sen, S. N., *Anglo-Maratha Relations during the Administration of Warren Hastings, 1772–1785* (1961).

Stokes, E., *The English Utilitarians and India* (1959).

Sutherland, L., *The East India Company in Eighteenth Century Politics* (1952).

Tripathi, A., *Trade and Finance in the Bengal Presidency, 1793–1833* (1956)

Weitzman, S., *Warren Hastings and Philip Francis* (1929).

Wright, H. R. C., *East Indian Economic Problems of the Age of Cornwallis and Raffles* (1961).

UNPUBLISHED THESES

Cheong, Weng Eang, 'Some Aspects of British Trade and Finance in Canton, with special reference to the role of Anglo-Spanish trade in the eastern seas, 1784–1834', Ph.D. London (1962).

Dé, Barun, 'Henry Dundas and the Government of India, 1773–1801', D.Phil. Oxford (1961).

Sheik Ali, B., 'English Relations with Haidar Ali, 1760–82', Ph.D. London (1960).

INDEX

Index

Mackintosh, Sir James, 97, 220
McIntosh, Captain, 223
Mackonochie, Alexander, 100–1
Macpherson, John, 39, 42, 43, 52, 94–5, 130, 131, 219
Madras, 10, 12, 13, 27–8, 46, 124, 128, 139, 164, 240, 241
  capture by the French, 4
  commissioners, 36
  government of, 5, 6, 8, 15, 44, 102–3, 124, 126, 180, 219, 242
  merchants of, 18
  Mysorean threat to, 13, 16
  reform of, 24
  trade of, 21, 82
Mahé, 33, 55, 59, 62, 66, 71, 72, 105, 108, 109, 116–18, 124, 126, 237
  commercial resident of, 111, 113
  control of pepper supplies, 60–1, 64, 66, 67, 69, 76 and n., 77, 78, 79, 82, 83, 84, 85, 87, 88, 89, 91, 92
  proposed annexations nearby, 70, 81
Mahi River, 30, 136, 137, 138, 147
Maitland, General Sir Thomas, 218
Malabar
  Coast, 13, 32, 37, 38, 52, 233
  commercial residents of, 98, 124, 181
  conquest of by Haidar Ali, 13, 16, 33
  customs dues of, 90, 98, 121
  debasement of coinage in, 98–100
  English commercial privileges in, 36–7
  exploitation of the timber in, 100–1
  kingdoms of, 33
  merchants of, 14, 33, 83–4, 105, 184
  mint, 90
  peace plans for, 57–72, 143
  pepper monopoly in, 86–91
  Portuguese trade with, 26
  proposed annexation of, 68–9
  rebellion of 1803, 126
  revenue settlement of, 70
  society of, 33
  supervisor of, 90, 108–15
  trade of, 21, 33, 45, 64, 233
  violence in, 67–9, 238
  see also pepper and Mahé
Malabar commission (1st), 26, 71, 102, 217
  abolition of the pepper monopoly by, 91, 93, 104

appointment of Duncan and Boddam, 88–9
appointment of Farmer and Dow, 70, 73
changed policy of, 83–8
criticism of E.I. Company's government in India, 75–6
influence of Murdock Brown on, 76–83
new plans for revenues, 92
objections to the governor-general's policy, 74
opposition to the pepper monopoly, 76–81
proposal for direct rule, 89
Malabar commission (2nd)
  abolition of, 126
  appointment of, 113
  dispute with Duncan, 119–21, 122
  membership of, 113–14, 177, 178
  policy of, 115–23
Malabar rajas, 33, 37, 40, 46–7, 61, 62, 64, 69, 71, 81, 86, 121
  concessions to, 107
  E.I. Company exercises power over, 87, 238
  new position of, 92, 106–7, 120
  pepper policy of, 74–5, 83–4, 105–12, 116
  powers of, 76, 80, 84, 126, 209
  rebellion against Tipu, 40, 240
  threat to deprive them of power, 87–9, 117, 119
Malacca straits, 51
Malay archipelago, 53
Malet, Charles, 51, 179, 240–1, 244
  on Gujarat, 136–40, 148, 158–9, 208–9, 210
  on Malabar, 44–5, 49, 57–8, 70–1, 73
  on Maratha government, 31, 132
  on Surat, 135–6, 142–3, 146, 174
  resident at Cambay, 28–9, 30
  resident at Poona, 15, 160
Malhar Rao, 193, 194, 196, 197, 210, 212
Malwan, raja of, 27, 32, 159, 168, 172, 184
  pirates of, 168, 184
Manaji Gaikwar, 146
Mandvi, 188, 213
Mangalore, 36, 38, 65, 82
  treaty of, 13, 14, 37, 40

Index

Index

Ships' captains, 9, 15, 16, 19, 20, 21, 223
Ship owners, 9, 21, 22, 23, 25, 26, 54
Shore, Sir John, 1st Baron Teigmouth, 90, 95, 104, 112, 123, 146, 147, 148, 160, 162
Sibbald, James, 55, 66
Sind, 30, 124, 141, 158, 165, 166, 206, 208, 213
Sindhia, 16, 30, 129, 130, 131, 133, 144, 145, 146, 160, 161, 162, 163, 168, 185, 189, 206, 208, 210, 222, 238
  Mahadji, 146
  Dowlat Rao, 146
Siraj-ud-daula, 5
Smee, J., 102
Smith, George, 240
  friendship with D. Scott, 55
  letters to H. Dundas, 37–43, 51
  plan for exporting Indian products to Canton, 51–2, 53, 128–9
Smith, James, 25
Snare, John, 134
Soonder Ali, 225
Sounda, 63
Souza, Miguel de Lima é, 134, 174, 179, 207, 223, 241, 244
  conflicts with the raja of Bhaunagar, 225–9
  early history of, 171, 184
  proposes annexations in Gujarat, 191–3, 196–9, 202–4, 210
  proposes annexations in Kathiawar, 207
  resignation from E.I. Company's service, 230–1
Spaniards, 3
Specie, export of, 7, 38, 52, 56, 65, 136
Spencer, J., 102
Spices, 3, 24, 33, 58, 60, 61, 65, 69, 103, 243, 244; see also cardamoms, cloves, nutmegs and pepper
Stevens, James, 25, 90, 108, 109, 110, 113, 114 and n., 115, 116, 217
  pepper policy of, 110–11
Stewart, John, 235
Stewart, Robert, Viscount Castlereagh and 2nd Marquis of Londonderry, 180, 196, 203, 214, 218, 242
Stuart, General James, 117, 121, 163, 176–7, 179, 203
Sugar, 21

Sulivan, John, 45
Sulivan, Laurence 19–20, 21, 24
Sumatra, 122n., 125
Sunderjee, 207
Supercargo, 56, 160, 188, 215; see also Canton
Surat, 1, 12–13, 28, 30, 32, 46, 73–4, 124, 138, 140, 167, 191, 198, 230, 237
  adowlat, 132, 155–6, 161, 170, 173, 222
  annexation of, 164–5, 168, 170–4, 184–5, 188, 191, 243
  bakshi of, 185
  bankers of, 171
  capital of, 17
  chauth of, 132, 135, 139, 141, 146, 148, 154, 156–7, 162–3, 170–1, 185, 187, 190, 194
  chauthea of, 132, 135, 136, 142, 145, 153, 154, 156, 161, 162, 171
  chief of, 73, 108, 131, 132, 133, 135, 141, 142, 143, 145, 149, 153, 162, 184, 185
  collector of, 217
  commercial value of, 49–50, 147
  contractors, 150, 151, 152, 153, 156, 161, 170, 173
  Cornwallis's enquiry into, 47
  corrupt government of, 27, 171
  cotton trade of, 29, 129, 134, 152, 157, 162, 175, 217
  decline of, 30–1
  E.I. Company's regulations in, 172
  English desire for increased power in, 136–7, 142–3, 162, 164, 175, 196
  kooskie, 132, 153, 164
  latty, 153–4
  Maratha disturbances in, 131, 135, 154, 156–7
  monopolies in, 31
  naib of, 142
  nawab of, 27, 30, 132, 135, 141, 142, 143, 146, 150, 151n., 152, 153, 154, 155, 156, 157, 161, 162, 163, 164, 165, 169, 175, 185
  need for reform in, 141–2, 153, 161–2, 171, 174
  piece-good trade of, 15, 31, 128, 129, 133, 144–5, 149, 150–5, 160, 161–2, 166, 170, 171–4, 175, 195, 216, 233

Index

Index